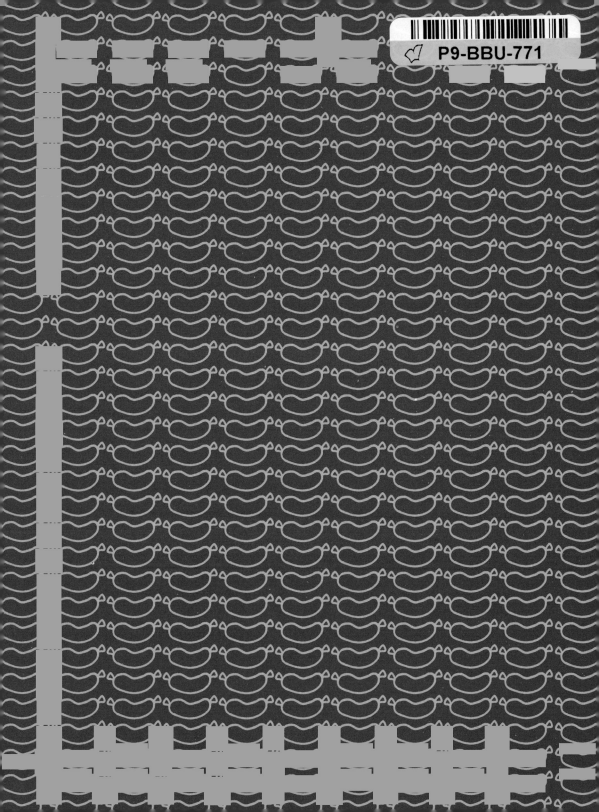

THE WURST OF LUCKY PEACH

A treasury of encased meat

CHRIS YING
and the editors of Lucky Peach

ILLUSTRATIONS BY TIM LAHAN

CLARKSON POTTER/
PUBLISHERS
New York

Selected material originally appeared in *Lucky
Peach Issue 10: The Street Food Issue* (2014).

Library of Congress Cataloging-in-Publication Data
is available upon request.

ISBN 978-0-8041-8777-0
Ebook ISBN 978-0-8041-8778-7

Printed in China

Design by Walter Green
Photographs on pages 36, 43–44, 46–47, 49–52,
54–55, 57, 90, 92–93, 95–100, and 191 by Chris
Ying; page 58 by Magnus Nilsson; pages 61–62 by
David Quist; page 144 by John Cullen; and pages
147–148, 150–151, and 153 by Adam Gollner

10 9 8 7 6 5 4 3 2 1

First Edition

FOR JAMI AND HUCK,
SAUSAGE LOVERS BOTH

Sausage Rest

The Wurst

Chris Ying

Every now and then in this food-writing business you have to cover something that you just don't care about. *The city's best tuna tartare. What's new with tea.* This is not one of those instances. I love sausage. I might be at the world's greatest lobster restaurant, but if there's sausage on the menu, I would get the sausage.

Sausages accomplish everything that the practice of meat cookery strives for. Rather than seasoning, marinating, rubbing, or injecting meat with flavor, why not just grind salt, spices, and herbs directly into the meat? Why not make meat and flavor one?

Chefs pay top dollar for ideally marbleized animal flesh. With sausage, you can add as much fat as you want and distribute it as you see fit. It's like playing God—God of a universe that can be piped into an animal intestine, anyway.

Sausage makes use of offal and tough cuts of meat better than any other form of preparation. They're stuffed in an intestine, for crying out loud.

Do you like chicken or beef or fish but wish it tasted a little bit more like pork? Sausage can do that. What about a meat product that tastes best when cooked well done—interested? Done.

All of these facts and others conspire to secure sausage's place high atop our lists of most favorite things (right above raindrops on roses and just below whiskers on kittens). So when it came time to elect a lead title in our new series of single-subject cookbooks, I volunteered a book about sausages called *The Wurst of Lucky Peach*. My fellow editor Peter Meehan—a devotee of tubesteaks and puns—was immediately on board.

Peter and I and a small handful of other staff members at *Lucky Peach* are old enough—the rest are baby geniuses—to be familiar with book series like *Time-Life*'s *The Good Cook* and *Foods of the World*. Our parents bought us sets of encyclopedias from which we wrote school essays. We love books that are obsessively narrow in scope, single-minded in their exploration of a topic, thorough in their investigation, rigorous in their completeness. The River Cottage handbooks come to mind, as do the Canal House Cooking books. James Peterson. Michael Ruhlman. *Chez Panisse Fruit*. *Chez Panisse Vegetables*.

This is not any of those. *The Wurst of Lucky Peach* is packed tight with sausage intel, but it is not all-encompassing. It is not the last word on sausage. It's a book about the sausages we find fascinating, whether because of how they taste, how they're made, or how they're eaten. It's a book that's meant to be as entertaining as it is useful to cook from. When we conceived this series, we imagined books that you could read in the bathroom just as easily as in the kitchen.

With that bit of casing out of the way, let's get down to the meat of the matter. First, a little bit of history.

SAUSAGE HISTORY

Like all culinary inventions that preceded Soylent, sausage was born of necessity. It's designed to make the most out of meat—not only of the off-cuts and strange bits, but the leftovers you just can't eat right away.

While cynics may see more sinister motives in chopping up an animal and stuffing it inside of its own intestines, sausage making is really about extending the life of meat. The word *sausage* comes from the Latin *salsus,* meaning "salted." To be sure, salt plays a major role in the purpose and flavor of sausage. The salt in sausages represses microbes that might otherwise spoil meat. As Harold McGee explains, it also dissolves and redistributes myosin, a protein in muscle fiber that acts as a binding agent.

Sausages have been documented at least as far back as ancient Greece and evidence points to their existence in ancient Egypt and Asia. From there, they proliferated wherever colonialism and trade took them, and flourished in places that dig on swine.

The multitude of sausage varieties is vast but can be broken down very, very broadly into two categories: the fresh and the fermented. There's more than a little overlap and myriad subcategories.

HOW THIS BOOK IS ORGANIZED

For the sake of only opening one can of worms at a time, this book tries to keep it fresh. We more or less stick to uncured, raw, perishable sausages. We avoid salumi and charcuterie—that is, sausages that have been hardened against rot through salting, smoking, and fermentation. Of course, being compulsive sausage eaters, we let a few cured sausages slip in, especially those that fall under the category of summer sausage: semi-dry, less salty, predominantly smoked specimens.

The bulk of this book's exploration comes in the form of a curated atlas we call the Sausage Quest. It's divided into six geographic regions from which we selected a group of sausages with no rhyme or reason other than they tickled our fancy. The Quest is sprinkled with in-depth contributions from our writerly friends from around the globe who have firsthand knowledge of their local offerings.

Then there are the Tubesteak Crusades: expansive travelogues documenting the encased meats of five locales, as experienced by me and our sausage Knights Templar: Gideon Lewis-Kraus, Lisa Abend, Amelia Gray, and Adam Leith Gollner.

When you get to bringing your own wieners into the world, you'll find the recipes in this book broken down into sections: Let Your Sausage Loose (uncased sausage), Detective Sausage on the Case (cased), Play with Your Wiener (dressed-up hot dogs), and the International Sausage Café (sausage-based dishes), plus a section on the best sausage-cooking practices.

Finally, there are rants: op-eds addressing American sausage culture. For instance, why beans have no place on hot dogs.

Hey, why do they call them hot dogs, *anyway?* you're asking. In the late 1800s, speculation about what was really being stuffed into sausages led to jokes about ground-up dogs—thus, hot dogs. The jokes don't hold up, but speaking of jokes . . .

SAUSAGE-BASED HUMOR

We tried halfheartedly to limit the number of dirty jokes in this book but failed often and with gusto. Sausage's phallic nature never ceases to make me giggle, and although *The Wurst of Lucky Peach* is rife with references to this fact, there could have been more. Please feel free to jot down your own additions in the margins, or ask me in person about my affinity for wiener humor.

HOW THE SAUSAGE GOT MADE

Some of this book is drawn from the best wurst content we've published in our magazine. The majority, however, is brand new—ground and cased especially for you. Our team dug deep into our libraries and address books to pull together as much accurate sausage reconnaissance as possible. But sausages—especially those eaten on the street—are an ever-evolving food. If you've got something to add or amend, we want to know! Email sausageboss@lky.ph.

As for the recipes in this book, they come from all over the place—both our own kitchens and the kitchens of chefs who make exemplary versions of our most beloved sausages and sausage dishes. There's tangy chorizo from Rick Bayless and fatty duck crépinettes from Suzanne Goin. The sausage I make every year for Thanksgiving is in here, as are recipes for breakfast sausage and fluffy pancakes in which to wrap them. Now they're yours to stuff yourself with. Enjoy.

Wherever there is meat, there is sausage. For most of history, mankind has made sausage as a means to stretch off cuts, organs, and leftovers into further deliciousness. Some places in particular— Germany, Thailand, the United Kingdom, and the United States—have refined the practice into high art. But wherever you are in the world, chances are good that you can find meat in tube form.

Sausage Quest is a survey of sausages and sausage dishes from around the globe. It's not comprehensive— completists should look elsewhere—but rather an arbitrary selection of our favorite specimens. For each entry, you'll find the following stat sheet:

WHERE: region, country, or city of origin (as specific as we can be)
MEAT: pork, beef, fish, fowl, or otherwise, or, in the case of sausage-based dishes, which sausage is the main ingredient
PREPARED: how it's heated to appropriate eating temperature
SERVED: instructions for not looking like a fool when you eat this, including appropriate accompaniments; special occasions when it's served; etc.

The Quest is divided by geographic region. The sausages appear in alphabetical order, with the occasional exception of longer entries written by *Lucky Peach*'s motley cast of lovable contributors. For the sake of letting their sausages breathe, we allowed them to slip a bit out of order.

Our adventures begin in Europe, home to the world's most diverse population of indigenous sausages. Not all sausages originated here, but you can trace a great deal of the Western world's wieners back to central Europe. Germany and Austria wrote the codex from which the American hot dog was created. Chorizo spread—and evolved— from Spain to the Spanish-speaking world. From Europe, we follow the sausage east(ish) to Africa, then on to Asia and across the Pacific to Australia, before finally landing in the Americas.

EUROPE

If sausages were an alien race, Europe would be the mothership. From classical beauties (boudin blanc, käsekrainer, kielbasa) to modern monstrosities (currywurst, tunnbrodsrulle), the whole sausage canon is on display here.

Alheira

During the fraught centuries of the Portuguese Inquisition, one way in which Jews were identified was by the fact that they didn't have sausages hanging in the local smokehouses. In order to blend in, they created *alheira*—a garlicky sausage made with poultry or game, visually indistinguishable from pork-filled ones. Since then, alheira has been absorbed into the broader Portuguese sausage canon. Many varieties now contain pork—in fact, geographically protected alheiras require specific local breeds of pig—and are enjoyed around the country, boiled or pan-fried, with rice or fries and a runny egg.

WHERE: Portugal
MEAT: traditionally anything but pork; now, pork
PREPARATION: boiled or pan-fried
SERVED: with rice or fries and a runny egg

Andouillette

Call it earthy, call it musky, but let's be real—*andouillette* tastes like shit (fans will append "in a good way" to that description, but we dare not be so bold as to assume your preferences for animal butt). Warnings not to confuse this with Cajun smoked Andouille (page 109) are probably moot. Makers of this French-heartland sausage mix pork stomach with intestines and a whole mess of tripey things—including the mesentery and the omentum (don't ask)—then shred everything into fettuccine-like ribbons and stuff it all into a pig's colon.

Andouillette comes hot or cold. Hot, it'll likely be pan-roasted, chopped up, and blanketed under a sharp mustard-wine sauce. Just be prepared to put up a fight when ordering: Waiters will do their best to discourage tourists from ordering andouillette. But don't let their warnings scare you off—it has plenty of fans. If you're particularly picky about your andouillette, scan bistro and brasserie menus for an "AAAAA" or "5A" label—the official thumbs-up of the Association Amicale des Amateurs d'Andouillette Authentique, a jury of critics and journalists devoted to the stuff.

WHERE: France
MEAT: a mélange of pork offal
PREPARATION: poached, grilled, or pan-roasted
SERVED: cold, or warm with mustard sauce

Bangers and Mash

Bangers = sausages. Mash = mashed potatoes. Bangers and mash = pan-fried pork sausages lodged in a hillside of buttery mashed potatoes, maybe wetted down with a splash of onion gravy. It's quintessential pub grub and can be made with whichever sausage you like, although peppery, coarse-grained Cumberland (page 21) sausages are particularly popular in alehouses and home kitchens throughout England.

WHERE: UK
MEAT: pork
PREPARATION: pan-fried
SERVED: with mash(ed potatoes)

Black Pudding

Attention UK blood sausage marketing team: You were on the right track in swapping *blood* for *black,* but you missed the mark in designating your national *boudin noir* as a "pudding." Why not black "cake," seeing as a pan-fried slice of this classic breakfast side looks like nothing so much as a perfect round of moist chocolate cake? Nobody wants to dip their spoon into cold jiggly blood *pudding* . . . . But seriously, folks, both the words *boudin* and *pudding* derive from the Latin *botellus,* meaning "sausage." Black pudding is a dense blend of oatmeal, spices, pork fat, and blood (usually reconstituted from dried powder form these days). Some makers still add the traditional and very British-sounding pennyroyal, an astringent mint-like herb, but otherwise, that's it. The texture ranges from spongy to crumbly, and the flavor is decidedly milder and less ferrous than one might expect. The best, gentlest introduction to the sausage might be at breakfast, where it very often appears as part of the classic fry-up (see Full English Breakfast, page 24). Black pudding is most appreciated in the Midlands and northern England, with Bury in Lancashire granted unofficial black-pudding-capital status. At the World Black Pudding Throwing Championships, held the second week of September in Ramsbottom, England, people come from all over the countryside to try knocking Yorkshire puddings off a twenty-foot scaffold by underhand tossing black puddings (it has something to do with a historical beef between Yorkshire and Lancashire—probably best not to ask). One pound sterling gets you three tries.

WHERE: UK
MEAT: pork blood and fat
PREPARATION: baked or boiled, then sliced and pan-fried
SERVED: as part of a full English breakfast

Botifarra

Chorizo might be the most well known member of the Spanish sausage canon, but in Catalonia, *botifarra* is king. Botifarra encompasses a motley crew of meats. Fresh botifarra is a thick sausage made from coarsely ground, very lean pork and seasoned simply with sea salt and black pepper. What sets it apart from most sausages in Spain is that it contains no pimentón (smoked paprika). *Botifarra negra* is Catalonian blood sausage. *Botifarra de perol* is filled with offal, and *botifarra blanca* is a lean sausage enriched with egg. There's even a dessert version, *botifarra dolça,* cured with sugar and seasoned with cinnamon and lemon.

WHERE: Catalonia, Spain
MEAT: pork
PREPARATION: poached, grilled, pan-fried, stewed
SERVED: as is, with white beans, or in myriad dishes

Boudin Blanc de Rethel

Tucked into the hills of the Champagne-Ardenne region of France is Rethel, a blink-and-you'll-miss-it sort of town with one very good reason not to blink. In 1626, a former Louis XIII courtier named Chamarande opened a charcuterie here and his white sausage has been sought after ever since. There are many white sausages and puddings to be found around Europe, but this one enjoys protected geographical indication from the EU. Diehards favor *boudin blanc de Rethel* for its exceptional richness, thanks to eggs and milk and the absence of any bready fillers as in other boudins blancs. There are variations, however. The grandfather of the current owner of Charcuterie Demoizet in the heart of Rethel bought the shop in 1939 from a direct descendant of Chamarande. Besides the original style, Demoizet offers sausages studded with truffles, foie gras, and wild mushrooms. The classic accompaniments to boudin blanc de Rethel—once it's been poached and browned in butter—are stewed apples and some bubbles from a neighboring vineyard. But if you really want the full white-out experience, save your visit for the end of April, when the Brotherhood of the Boudin Blanc de Rethel hosts an all-day fair and competition: Trophies are awarded for the tastiest entries, and past festivities have included a pig-squealing contest and open-air concert featuring runners-up from *The Voice: France.*

WHERE: Rethel, France
MEAT: pork
PREPARATION: poached, then browned in butter
SERVED: with stewed apples and Champagne

Boudin Noir

In the beginning, there was *boudin.* Before sausage was sausage, cooks mixed blood from a freshly killed pig with onions and fat, stuffed it into intestines, and boiled it, because what else are you going to do with all that blood and intestines? Add some cereal (rice or oatmeal) to the mix, and you had cheap, filling, delicious sustenance. Boudin (later known as *boudin noir,* or black pudding, or blood sausage to distinguish it from blood-free versions) remains popular and abundant throughout Europe but probably reaches its pinnacle in France, where cooks enhance their boudin noir (as is their wont) with a healthy addition of cream and butter.

WHERE: France
MEAT: pork blood
PREPARATION: poached, grilled, or sliced and pan-fried
SERVED: as is, or in innumerable configurations

Boutefas

This smoked pork-and-bacon-filled sausage from the French-Swiss region of Vaud in western Switzerland looks like a loaf of challah, because it's stuffed inside a pig stomach. It can be sliced and eaten cold or boiled first, in which case you'll often find it atop *papet vaudois,* a creamy mishmash of leeks and potatoes cooked in cream.

WHERE: Switzerland
MEAT: pork and bacon
PREPARATION: smoked
SERVED: cold; or boiled and sliced, atop a papet vaudois

Ćevapi

WHERE: Queens (via southeastern Europe)
MEAT: lamb, beef, and pork
PREPARATION: grilled
SERVED: with pita-like bread, pepper paste, and a sour cream–like product

Skinless sausages are the orphans of the sausage world. Unless frozen, they must be cooked soon after being made, and are always in danger of falling apart during handling or grilling. In an affront to their basic identity, they're sometimes mistaken for oddly shaped meatballs. Such is the case with *ćevapi*, the delectable skinless sausages of the former Yugoslavia and nearby countries. The Time-Life book *The Cooking of Vienna's Empire* (1968) misidentifies them as "meat balls made of lamb and beef and grilled on skewers." The author's enthusiasm for these little meat bombs is evident, but he's simply failed to comprehend the essential sausage-ness of ćevapi. And I've never seen ćevapi cooked on a skewer.

Ćevapi are eaten in Austria, Bosnia, Bulgaria, Croatia, the Czech Republic, Macedonia, Montenegro, Romania, Serbia, Slovakia, Slovenia, and the United States (where Queens, the Bronx, and Milwaukee are hotbeds). Each of the countries of southeastern Europe has its own take, and the formula varies further within countries, regions, and religious groups. One advantage of the skinless ćevapi is that their lack of a nonporous barrier on the outside allows them to absorb more smoke, hence the preferred method of cooking is over charcoal. A disadvantage is that they are prone to drying out if overcooked. A perfectly grilled ćevapi is superior to most skin-on sausages in terms of richness of smoky flavor.

The irreducible elements of the recipe involve coarsely chopping one or more meats from a list that includes lamb, beef, and pork, kneading them into a paste, then forming them into solid cylinders that usually fall between two and three

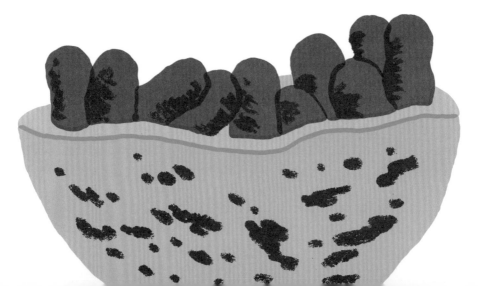

inches in length. The girth of these sausages also varies, with admirers more often praising ćevapi for circumference than for length. "That's some nice fat ćevapi," you might hear someone say, waiting by the grill, fork at the ready.

Sometimes finely minced onions or garlic (or both) are added to the paste; sometimes the meat is further bound with egg white, giving the ćevapi a rubbery consistency. Sometimes the meat is extruded through a funnel. Normally, ćevapi is served with condiments. Of course the condiments fluctuate, too. Common choices include *ajvar* (a bright red pepper paste that can be mild or fiery), *kajmak* (a thick clabbered milk product), mustard and onions mixed together, plain yogurt, or sour cream. A small loaf of pita-like bread called *somun* or *lepinje* is occasionally offered with the ćevapi to create makeshift sandwiches.

Where did ćevapi come from? Most would trace the origin to the Ottoman Empire, which encompassed the Balkans from the fourteenth century until the second decade of the twentieth century. The Turks ate longer ground-meat cylinders called kufta kebabs that were cooked on skewers, and sometimes laced them with onions and red peppers to make adana kebabs. The word *ćevapi* is likely derived from "kebab."

But kufta and adana are only two among dozens of kebabs in Turkish cuisine, whereas in the Balkans, ćevapi has attained a singular status and a cultlike following wherever it's found. I went to a Serbian backyard picnic in Glendale, Queens, at which the proud host barbecued huge heaping platters of grilled pork loin, shrimp, and chicken wings and legs. But not until the ćevapi were brought out did oohs and aahs issue forth from the assembled guests, who were mostly Serbian or Romanian. Ćevapi exercised a magnetic hold on them.

When I want ćevapi, I go to a tiny shack underneath the N tracks in Ridgewood, Queens, and get them grilled by a Serbian former nurse who worked in a clinic in Bosnia before emigrating. She puts her ćevapi in a lepinje sandwich with ajvar and yogurt, then adds lettuce, tomato, and onion. One paradox of American ćevapi is that they are rarely homemade and almost invariably bought from butcher shops. Fortunately, the Balkan butcher from which my Serbian nurse procures her meat is a ćevapi specialist.

For whatever reason, there are few references to ćevapi in food books. Perhaps this is because they are so taken for granted in their native countries as to be almost invisible. But so strong is the yearning for the sausages that it has affected the form of their name. Ćevapi are more often spoken of by an affectionately diminutive form, *ćevapcici,* which means "little ćevapi," as though you might talk sweetly to them as they sizzle on the charcoal grill or flat-top griddle, "C'mon, my darling ćevapcici, cook to golden brownness so that I may gobble every one of you!"

—ROBERT SIETSEMA

Burenwurst

These spicy pork-and-ham sausages are found at *Würstelstände* (sausage stands) throughout Austria, where they're poached in hot water—grilling or frying would burst their skins. The wealth of German dialects and subdialects means this standby goes by many names: *Burenwurst, Buanwuascht, Burenhäutl, Burenhaut, Burenheidl, Klobasse,* or *Haße*.

WHERE: Austria
MEAT: pork
PREPARATION: poached in hot water
SERVED: with sweet or spicy mustard on a crusty roll

Cervelat

In 2008, a ban on the import of animal parts from Brazil sent waves of panic through meat eaters in Switzerland. Had well-to-do Swiss diners developed a taste for tamarin? No, as it turns out, makers of cervelat (a.k.a. cervelas), Switzerland's favorite sausage, had grown dependent upon the imported intestines of a species of humped cattle called the zebu to produce large amounts of consistently sized cervelat, and supplies were running out. The ban—invoked over fears of Mad Cow—forced butchers to experiment with other casings, at which they universally scoffed. Zebu intestine, they said, has an ideal curve and color, bursts and blossoms at the ends when grilled to perfection, and peels easily once cold. During the panic, one national butchery association estimated that the zebu ban would deprive Swiss eaters to the tune of twenty-five stubby smoked sausages each year. Cervelat has been vital to the Swiss culinary fabric since the late nineteenth century. Its name derives from cerebellum, because the sausage originally contained pig's brain; but modern recipes call for beef, pork, bacon, ice water, spice, onion, and, of course, zebu casings. Thankfully, in 2012, after careful risk assessment, the ban on zebu casings was lifted, and joy returned to the people of Switzerland.

WHERE: Switzerland
MEAT: beef and pork
PREPARATION: grilled
SERVED: as is, in sandwiches, or sliced cold in salads

Chipolata

Christmastime in the UK means a whole lotta chipolata: Britons gobble up about a thousand miles of these skinny, herb-infused pork sausages over Christmas (and more yet, cold, on Boxing Day). A significant number of those chipolatas will take the form of "pigs in a blanket," though not the same frozen-food-aisle party apps found Stateside. In England, they double down on the pork, replacing the pancake "blanket" with a shawl of streaky bacon. The love for these links goes all the way to the top: HRH Prince Charles sells a rosemary-honey version (through his decades-old charitable organic food company, Duchy Originals, and a partnership with Waitrose markets) made from free-range pigs.

WHERE: England
MEAT: pork
PREPARATION: pan-roasted or grilled
SERVED: at Christmas, wrapped in streaky bacon

Choucroute Garnie

WHERE: Strasbourg, France
MEAT: usually pork (sausages and other cured, salted cuts), but also sometimes duck
PREPARATION: braised with sauerkraut and Riesling
SERVED: with Alsatian Riesling

Strasbourg is the European city of your dreams, the embodiment of charming. The Ill River weaves under and around its cobblestone streets and half-timbered buildings that look like they're made of pastry. Our Lady of Strasbourg is really the only imposing structure in the city, and it's a beautiful cathedral. (One of the city's other big architectural draws is the local weir, the Barrage Vauban. Do you know what a weir is? I didn't either, but it's very pretty.)

Strasbourg is the capital of Alsace, France's easternmost region. If Europe were a soft-serve machine, Alsace would be like getting a swirl of French and German, and it would taste like sausage and sauerkraut. More specifically, it would taste like choucroute garnie.

The dish essentially takes pot-au-feu—that most emblematic of rustic French stews—and subjects it to the German reverence for sausages and sauerkraut. Choucroute garnie translates to "topped sauerkraut." What exactly it's topped with is variable, but only as far as there is variability between one cut of pork and the next. (Although, if you're lucky, you can also stumble into versions of choucroute made with duck instead of pork, like the one at Au Coin des Pucelles—a cramped, weathered, and perfect little hole-in-the-wall in Strasbourg; see their Choucroute Garnie recipe, page 222.) A mixed assembly of fresh, smoked, and salted meats, along with a bevy of sausages and whole potatoes, are simmered in dry Alsatian Riesling, stock, and sauerkraut spiced with juniper berries, garlic, and cloves. The process tames the cabbage's pungency, but the potatoes benefit the most, soaking up smoke and salt and juices while they cook.

You can find choucroute all over town, at bistros that range from tourist traps to local dives. Sausagewise, usually you'll encounter a few varieties in the heap: finely grained beef/pork *knackwurst* (Strasbourg's official sausage; the local butcher shop, Porcus, stocks a supply of the annual winner of the Knack d'Or, a.k.a. Golden Knack competition), frankfurters, and smoked Montbéliard sausage. It's a dish built for winter: over-the-top meaty, belly-warming stuff that suffuses everything within the same four walls in meaty perfume. **–CHRIS YING**

Churchkhela

With apologies to our friends in Tbilisi, the only entry in the Sausage Quest from Georgia is not exactly a sausage at all. Though it's shaped and hung like a salami, *churchkhela* is a trompe l'oeil. It's candy—long strings of nuts (usually walnuts) are dipped repeatedly in flour-thickened *badagi* (concentrated grape juice) before being hung to air-dry. The finished candies can sometimes develop a thin layer of powdery sugar that looks uncannily like the white mold on the casing of a salami.

WHERE: Georgia and nearby countries, where it's commonly known as walnut or grape *sucuk* (or *sujuk*)
MEAT: none
PREPARATION: strung, dipped, and dried
SERVED: as is

Coburger Bratwurst

This entry comes in the form of a letter from one of our readers and loyal sausage acolytes.

Hi,
My first job as an engineer was at the Montreal office of a German screw-compressor manufacturer. When I visited the headquarters in the Bavarian town of Coburg, about two and a half hours from Frankfurt, I was introduced to a truly unique street sausage. Cooked over burning pinecones by street vendors in little, often portable shacks, the Coburger Bratwurst is a thin, slender, ten-inch-long sausage served in a spherical bun the size of a lemon. Delicately charred, with the lingering fragrance of the pinecone smoke, it is simply garnished with mustard. At the time of my visit they only cost 1 euro. The disproportionately small bun not only allows you to grip the sausage tight enough in one hand to prevent it from slipping out as you take bites, but lets you inhale the aromas emanating from the sizzling sausage. You can eat it in one hand, the same way you would drink from a wineglass: inhaling and tasting at the same time. Not only is the Coburger Bratwurst delicious, but the shape is admittedly sexual. So like many other great German creations, the Coburger Bratwurst mixes practicality with a subtle touch of *erotisch*.
I really enjoy your magazine, thanks.
Rohan Rosario

WHERE: Coburg, Germany
MEAT: pork
PREPARED: delicately charred on a grill over pinecones
SERVED: in a lemon-size bun with a tasteful slather of yellow mustard

Cotechino (and Zampone)

An annual presence on holiday tables in north-central Italy is a slow-simmered cotechino, either as part of a bubbling pot of *bollito misto* or on its own, served over a heap of lentils. Carved into thick slices, the filling is firm and sticky with lip-coating collagen. Cotechino is made from pork shoulder, fat, and gelatin-rich skin, flavored with warm spices (clove, cinnamon, nutmeg) and a good glug of wine, stuffed tight into extra-large natural casings to produce a sausage as thick as a baby's leg. In the case of *zampone*, cotechino's direct descendant, the casing is literally a leg—a deboned pig's trotter. Both products originate in Modena; zampone was invented during a siege of the city in the early 1500s, when limited supplies forced some creative thinking.

WHERE: north-central Italy
MEAT: pork
PREPARATION: boiled
SERVED: in the wintertime, with stewed lentils or in bollito misto

Crépinette

A loose patty of ground pork and spices (and truffle, if you're fancy) enveloped in a cobwebby square of *crépine,* or caul, the fatty membrane surrounding the stomach and intestines of pigs and sheep and cows. When cooked, the crépine melts away, basting the sausage. In Provence, the local crépinette is known as a *gayette* and includes pork liver and bacon in the farce. In the Gironde, crépinettes are served as the turf to oysters surf. And in England, they're made with offal and breadcrumbs and known as "faggots."

WHERE: France, England (as "faggots")
MEAT: pork and pork offal
PREPARATION: grilled, baked, or fried
SERVED: traditionally with mashed potatoes

Cumberland

The Cumberland sausage was born in the eighteenth century in the northwest English county of Cumbria. It was traditionally made from a breed of now-extinct (as of the 1960s) pig, and spiced with a relatively exotic (for its time) mix of white and black pepper, thyme, sage, nutmeg, mace, and cayenne that came by way of the Cumbrian town of Whitehaven—once the third largest port in the country. Cumberlands come in a distinctive shape, a thick pinwheel of meat—coarsely ground belly and shoulder, along with rusk (hard, dried bread) crumbs and ice water—that's been cased but not twisted into links.

WHERE: Cumbria, Great Britain
MEAT: pork
PREPARATION: pan-roasted
SERVED: with mash; as part of a Full English Breakfast (page 24); or in Toad in the Hole (page 33)

Drei im Weggla (Nuremberg Bratwurst)

Nuremberg won a European Union Protected Geographical Indication for the *Nürnberger Rostbratwurst* in 2003. Throughout the city's storied, turbulent history, the little sausage has stood firm. For the past seven centuries, breweries and street vendors have been selling these finger-size (regulations specify 7 to 9 centimeters in length) links—ten or twelve or fifty to a plate, with heaping sides of sauerkraut and fresh horseradish. However, the *Drei im Weggla*—literally, "three in a bun"—is the local way to take your brats: a crusty, bulbous bun is filled with a trio of marjoram, mace, and onion-infused sausages (crunchy from grilling; that's the *rost* part of rostbratwurst) and slathered with sharp yellow mustard.

WHERE: Nuremberg, Germany
MEAT: pork
PREPARATION: grilled
SERVED: three sausages in a circular bun slathered with mustard

Currywurst

WHERE: Berlin and Hamburg
MEAT: pork
PREPARATION: roasted or deep-fried, depending
SERVED: sliced and drenched with a ketchup–curry powder sauce, fries to the side

One would be hard put to come up with a city whose signature dish is as unappealing as Berlin's, though it ultimately makes some sense that a city as endlessly preoccupied with its own low-rent self-image would offer up to its visitors something as disgusting as currywurst. The only important, lingering question about currywurst is whether it ought to be avoided because it's boring or because it's gross. Partisans of boredom argue that currywurst ought never to be eaten on definitional grounds: Currywurst is cut-up hot dog, smothered in ketchup, then dusted with paprika. Surely Berlin's most famous contribution to world food culture has to be more complicated than that?

Partisans of currywurst's grossness would argue that there is, in fact, something more to it. There's the option to have it *mit* (with) *oder* (or) *ohne* (without) *Darm* (Darm). Darm means guts. You can have your smothered, paprika-dusted cut-up hot dog either with sausage casing, or you can have it without sausage casing, in which case your cut-up hot dog looks even more like cross sections of limp, wrinkly dick. Either way, where English allows you to forget what sausage casing is made of, the Germans throw it in your face every time you forget that you should never, under any circumstances, eat currywurst by asking if you want it with or without guts. The reason that Berliners began eating it "without guts" is that there was once a guts shortage, and even after the guts shortage came to a reassuring end, there were Germans who thought, You know what? This disgusting cut-up hot dog we inexplicably like to eat? Well, we like it even better and even less explicably when it's not cased in guts! Thus the gutless, wrinkled-dick option endures to this day.

So, we return to the original question: What's the best reason not to eat currywurst? Is it because it's so uninspired, or because it's so revolting? If currywurst continues to exist, future generations will be forced to keep up a pointless, ineffectual debate over this unanswerable question. My advice? Make sure never to run for mayor of Berlin. If you do, they not only make you eat it, they also take your picture.

—GIDEON LEWIS-KRAUS

Frikandel

WHERE: Benelux
MEAT: chicken, pork, beef, horse
PREPARATION: boiled, then deep-fried
SERVED: as is or with condiments

The English translation for "sausage" in Dutch is the autologically unfortunate word *worst*, which may or may not be a coincidence. There is much speculation about what goes into a *frikandel*, the street sausage of Holland. The consensus seems to be that it's an unholy trinity of pig, chicken, and cow offal, but also sometimes horse. I was under the impression that horsemeat had been phased out in the Netherlands after a horsemeat study made headlines in Holland in 2006, but I was wrong! While most of the big meat-snack manufacturers like FEBO and Beckers stopped using it, there are others like Mora that still do. Mora says that horse gives their snacks "a distinctive taste that is appreciated."

The Frankenmeat frikandel takes the form of a long, dark brown, symmetrical cylinder. It is a skinless sausage, so there is an argument that it is not sausage at all. The frikandel are boiled to keep them from falling apart, then deep-fried when they are to be eaten.

The most popular way to order a frikandel is with mayonnaise, curry ketchup, and minced onion. This is what is known as a *frikandel speciaal*. It is also affectionately known as an *open ruggetje,* which means "spina bifida." (I know that's terrible. And I don't really know how it came about. My best guess is that the Dutch term for spina bifida literally translates to "open little back" and the frikandel speciaal reminded someone of a baby's spine.)

And yet the frikandel is something of a point of national pride for the Dutch, who eagerly consume the sausages late at night, post–pub crawl, alongside tourists and stoners. They are served at the ubiquitous snackbars or through one of dozens of walk-up food automats dotting the country. The most popular chain in Holland is FEBO, which also sells croquettes, hamburgers, fried cheese puffs, and assorted other drunk food. This is known as *uit de muur eten,* "eating out of the wall," and simply involves tossing 1.60€ into, well, a wall, and retrieving your unhealthy snack by way of one of dozens of small glass doors. Getting hot food at three a.m. in such a retrofittedly futuristic manner is easily the coolest part of the experience. **–LUCAS PETERSON**

Frankfurter Würstchen

A thin, finely textured pork sausage smoked at low temperatures over beechwood, a proper frankfurter has a nice snap to it and lots of smokiness. Though it lacks the formal legal status of a Protected Geographical Indication, a local German law has restricted the manufacture of *Frankfurter Würstchen* to the area around Frankfurt am Main since 1860, meaning imitators from other German regions must qualify their labels to read "in the Frankfurter style." Doesn't seem to deter the numerous beef franks and frankfurters that populate American grocery shelves, though. (And in actuality, our ballpark franks bear closer resemblance to *Frankfurter Rindswurst*, a pure beef sausage, than to the traditional Frankfurter.)

WHERE: Frankfurt, Germany
MEAT: pork
PREPARATION: smoked, then poached
SERVED: on rye bread with mustard and/or horseradish, with a side of sauerkraut or potato salad

Full English Breakfast

In the totalitarian Britain of 3030, every man, woman, and child will be required by law to consume this breakfast every morning to fuel their work in the vibranium mines of New Old York. For now, it remains optional but relatively standardized nonetheless: a full English Breakfast (a.k.a. fry-up) will almost always include back bacon, fried eggs, roasted tomatoes, toast or fried bread, mushrooms, baked beans, and at least one sausage. A bottle of HP Sauce, a relative of A.1. Steak Sauce, always accompanies the fry-up, ready to be poured liberally over the lot of it. What fills the sausage slot depends on where you are, and could be black pudding, white pudding, red pudding, haggis, lornes, Cumberlands, Lincolnshires, chipolatas, Oxfords, Manchesters, Glamorgans, Marylebones, and on and on. Fry-ups are served virtually everywhere in the UK, but if you'd rather not chance a mediocre meal that will knock you down for the better part of a day, you could get recommendations from the English Breakfast Society, where they take their fry-ups very seriously: The chairman is currently petitioning Parliament to turn the first Sunday in April into National English Breakfast Day.

WHERE: UK
MEAT: pork, usually
PREPARATION: pan-fried
SERVED: with back bacon, eggs, tomatoes, toast, mushrooms, and baked beans

Haggis

The exaggerated punch line in every tired joke about Scottish cuisine, haggis, for the record, is: sheep's pluck (heart, liver, lungs) chopped up and mixed with oatmeal and suet (fat from around the kidneys), packed into the animal's stomach (or an artificial casing) and boiled. It's almost always served with neeps and tatties (boiled turnips and mashed potatoes), except when it's served in one of the many defiantly proud haggis dishes in Scotland: Chippies (fish-and-chip shops) swap it in for cod; Indian restaurants sell haggis pakora fritters; any place that serves breakfast will invariably include it in their take on the Scottish fry-up. There are also haggis burgers, haggis pizza, haggis nachos at the Arcade Haggis & Whisky House in Edinburgh. The pinnacle of haggis-eating, though, must be the Burns Supper ceremony, celebrated each January in honor of Scotland's most treasured poet. After the haggis is solemnly presented to the bleating of bagpipes, an honored guest gives a booming recitation of Robert Burns's "Address to a Haggis," honoring that "great chieftain o' the puddin-race." Get your fill, as you won't be able to smuggle any haggis back with you (sheep lungs have been a US import no-no since 1971).

WHERE: Scotland
MEAT: sheep pluck
PREPARATION: stuffed in a stomach and boiled
SERVED: with neeps and tatties; and in various other novelty guises

Käsekrainer

The standard-bearer for cheese sausages the world over, *Käsekrainer* have Emmentaler mixed right into the smoked pork mince, so every bite releases little reservoirs of oozy cheese. This national treasure figures on the menus of *Würstelstände* (sausage stands) throughout Austria, and the busiest and perhaps best is Bitzinger, in Vienna. Lines get long around ten p.m., when a steady stream of society-set types pours out of the city's glittering opera house just across the street. They all seem to order the same thing: Käsekrainer in a crusty roll with mustard and—

crucially—a coupe of champagne, which Bitzinger sells by the glass.

WHERE: Austria and Germany
MEAT: pork
PREPARATION: griddled
SERVED: on a roll with mustard

Kielbasa

Kielbasa is simply the Polish word for "sausage," and at any given time a butcher shop in Warsaw could be selling dozens of different types of kielbasa. The term first shows up in the eighteenth century in reference to long, thick, dark ropes of sausage, but eventually came to refer to any type of sausage in Poland, from pork-based ones, to others made with wild boar, rabbit, and deer. The problem is, if everything is kielbasa, then nothing is kielbasa. Some distinctions: Kielbasa with marjoram is common in western Poland. Smoked kielbasa is sometimes called *podwawelska*. There's kielbasa *jalowcowa* (juniper flavored), *czosnkowa* (garlic), and *kminkowa* (caraway). There are kielbasa named for their region: *Krakowska, lisiecka, ślaska*. There's *myśliwska*, which is meant to be taken on fishing and hunting trips. The sausage brought to us by the Polonia (Polish diaspora), known to us as plain old kielbasa, would best be described as *Polska kielbasa wedzona* (Polish smoked sausage). It's celebrated especially in Chicago, home of the Maxwell Street Polish (page 121).

WHERE: Poland
MEAT: usually pork
PREPARATION: hot- or cold-smoked
SERVED: cold, grilled, stewed, etc.

Kiszka

Kiszka means "guts" in Polish, which is apropos, as liver, heart, kidneys, and pancreas could all be contained within this sausage. The offal is rounded out with skin, fat, and blood, and flavored with less visceral stuff like onions and marjoram; like most blood-filled sausages, kiszka also usually contains a grain like buckwheat or barley. International variations on kiszka can be found around Eastern Europe, including beef ones and *kishke*—an Ashkenazi Jewish version filled with flour or matzo meal and schmaltz, usually served drenched in gravy—but classical kiszka (or *kaszanka,* same thing) is a full-on celebration of pig. You'll spot it on homey-restaurant menus throughout Poland (usually in the company of rye bread, horseradish, and dill pickles).

WHERE: Poland (and other parts of Eastern Europe)
MEAT: pork, usually, but also beef and sometimes just chicken fat and flour
PREPARATION: poached, grilled, pan-fried, or unleashed from its casing and cooked with onions
SERVED: as is; or with rye bread, horseradish, and pickles

Lecsókolbász

Lecsókolbász is a bespoke sausage tailored specifically to outfit *lecsó,* a classic Hungarian stew made with peppers, paprika, and tomatoes. Lecsókolbász (*kolbász* means "sausage") is made of coarsely chopped pork and pork fat, seasoned heavily with paprika. The mixture is stuffed into natural casings, either in long coils or twelve-inch lengths, cured overnight, then cold-smoked for three to five days over beechwood. The sausage is spicy and smoky—flavors it happily donates to lecsó—but where lecsókolbász is a one-stew kind of sausage, lecsó isn't so into monogamy. The stew takes on a variety of different sausage suitors, depending on the mood of the cook.

WHERE: Hungary
MEAT: pork
PREPARATION: smoked
SERVED: in lecsó, a Hungarian stew

Linguiça do Baixo Alentejo

The term *linguiça* covers a wide swath of smoked pork sausages originating in Portugal and proliferating with colonists and expats to various corners of the planet. This version, from the historical province of Baixo Alentejo, must be made in that area and from the Alentejano breed of pigs raised in areas with oak groves. The sausages are seasoned with salt, pepper, dried garlic, white wine, paprika, and red pepper, and appear as a ten-inch horseshoe-shaped link. The flavor is slightly spicy and smoky, but mild overall. It can be served sliced on a platter or in *cozido,* a rich stew that hosts various types of meat as well as cabbage, carrots, turnips, and collard greens.

WHERE: Portugal
MEAT: pork
PREPARATION: smoked
SERVED: sliced or in stew

Lorne

Equal parts pork and beef mixed with rusk (hard, dried bread) crumbs and baked in a square mold. Patties of this Scottish mainstay (also known by the self-evident moniker "square sausage") pop up at breakfasttime in fry-ups, and at other times of the day drenched with sweet-tart HP Sauce and stuffed into a split roll. No one's sure anymore where the name came from, but one theory has it named for early-twentieth-century Glaswegian comedian Tommy Lorne, who used to say the catchphrase "Sausage are the boys!" Okay . . .

WHERE: Scotland
MEAT: beef and pork
PREPARATION: baked in a square mold
SERVED: as part of a Full English Breakfast (page 24), or in a roll

Loukaniko

Apicius, the legendary Roman cookbook of the fifth century, describes a smoked sausage called *lucanica*—the culinary and etymological forefather of *linguiça, longaniza,* and Greek *loukaniko.* Most of the time, when people are talking about loukaniko, they're talking about a pork or lamb sausage scented with orange zest and fennel, but like its relatives, loukaniko doesn't necessarily refer to one single sausage. In northern Greece, loukaniko is often made with leeks. In Cyprus, the sausages contain red wine and whole black peppercorns. Loukaniko can be cured, smoked, or fresh, but in most instances it's served char-grilled.

WHERE: Greece
MEAT: pork, lamb, or a combination
PREPARATION: grilled
SERVED: sliced, with a squeeze of lemon

Mititei

Legend has it that *mititei,* also known as *mici,* was created in the town of Bucharest in 1900 when a chef famous for his sausages ran out of casings. Not wanting to disappoint patrons, he rolled the meat—seasoned with garlic, cumin, and coriander—into rough sausage shapes and grilled them. The result was a tube-shaped hamburger of sorts that has become a staple in Romania.

WHERE: Romania
MEAT: beef
PREPARATION: grilled
SERVED: with mustard and bread

Mortadella

Mortadella making begins in a badass machine called a *sterminio* (the "exterminator") that grinds and churns cured pork into an emulsified purée. Cubes of fat (specifically from the pig's throat) are folded in next, along with whole peppercorns and pistachios, wine or almond liqueur, and spices like coriander, aniseed, and myrtle berries. The mixture is forced into natural or synthetic casings and poached. A cross section of mortadella looks like the surface of an untouched pint of rocky road—a mosaic of white fat, emerald nuts, and little black peppercorns against a light rose background. *Trattorie* and *osterie* throughout the Boot offer mortadella in limitless guises: as an antipasto in irregular cubes; seared black-brown and drizzled with balsamic vinegar; pureed and mixed with veal to fill tortellini; sliced Kleenex-thin and piled atop focaccia (or whipped into an airy mousse and presented with a cube of focaccia as a dish called "memory of a mortadella sandwich" at Massimo Bottura's Osteria Francescana in Modena). It can be profitably added to the meat mix of a Bolognese sauce: substitute up to one-quarter of the recommended meat by weight with mortadella that has been chopped or ground. Though its geographically protected name, Mortadella Bologna, implies that it's always from the city in Emilia-Romagna (and explains why we know it as "bologna"), mortadella can also come from Piedmont, Lombardy, Veneto, Trento, Marche, Lazio, and Tuscany and still be considered mortadella. Of course, we also know fine specimens of unofficial stuff that originate from as far afield as the good ol' US of A and São Paulo, where it's shaved thin and piled high with melty cheese on the Brazilian city's signature sandwich (see recipe page 169).

WHERE: Emilia-Romagna first, but also around the world as bologna
MEAT: pork
PREPARATION: emulsified and poached
SERVED: in innumerable ways

Porilainen

The term *porilainen* is both the demonym for residents of Pori and the name of this local university-student-created dish. A fat pork-and-onion sausage (usually sold under the brand name Metsästäjä—"The Hunter") is sliced into a half-inch round. then slid between two pieces of white bread and panini-pressed, creating a hamburger made of hot dog meat. Of course, who else but sleep-deprived students on the hunt for something hot and quick would grill cheap sausage and stuff it between even cheaper white bread? Typical toppings include gherkin relish, raw onions, ketchup, and mustard.

WHERE: Finland
MEAT: pork
PREPARATION: grilled
SERVED: sliced, stuffed between two pieces of white bread

Sausage Rolls

A thick log of seasoned loose pork sausage bundled in puff pastry, vented with a few decorative slits, and washed in egg or milk before being baked to a flaky golden brown, sausage rolls can be found all over England and the Commonwealth countries—a cheap, portable snack. At its best, the sausage roll is the perfect delivery system for salty, herbaceous sausage, drippy with fat and juices to be soaked up by tender pastry. At worst, the sausage shrivels and shrinks away from a tough pastry shell, leaving hollow pockets of pork-scented air to be filled with consumer disappointment.

WHERE: UK and Commonwealth
MEAT: pork
PREPARATION: wrapped in puff pastry and baked
SERVED: on its own

Pølsevogn

WHERE: Copenhagen
MEAT: pork
PREPARATION: boiled
SERVED: simmered and stuffed in a split bun or hollowed-out bread sleeve, with mustard and ketchup on the side

Street eats are a rarity here in Copenhagen; maybe because it's just too damn cold five months of the year and people don't want to go outside.

Hot dog stands—which in Danish are called *pølsevogn,* meaning "sausage wagon"—have been part of the landscape for some ninety years now. You can still find very good ones around town. Two notable stands are John's Hotdog Deli and DØP. The sausages on offer are pink and long—much longer than the buns that hold them. They're cheap snack foods, and people from all generations, from time to time, visit the pølsevogn.

I have to be honest, though: Hot dogs are not really my thing. But occasionally visiting friends will crave them, and I'll succumb to the power of a pink farce in an intestine. **—RENÉ REDZEPI**

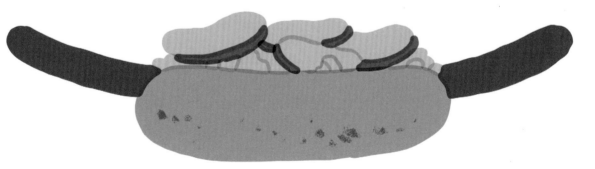

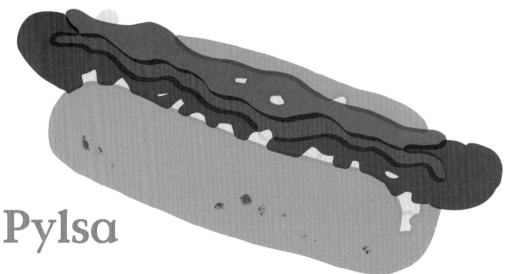

Pylsa

WHERE: all over Iceland
MEAT: lamb, pork, beef
PREPARATION: boiled
SERVED: on a steamed bun with ketchup, Icelandic mustard, a mayo-based rémoulade,
   raw chopped onions, and fried onion bits

Icelandic hot dogs are called *pylsa* (plural: *pylsur*), and they're made from lamb
mixed with pork and/or beef fat, which, as one vendor put it, "Helps 'em float." Pylsur
are longer and slimmer than most American hot dogs, and the meat is crammed into
an artificial casing so snappy that it pops when you bite it. They're beloved across
Iceland, eaten day and night (which, during the summer and winter in Iceland, are
basically one and the same) at kiosks, stands, gas stations, and convenience stores,
by locals and tourists alike. Bill Clinton stopped by one of Reykjavík's most famous
stands, Bæjarins Beztu Pylsur ("The Best Hot Dogs in Town"), a few weeks before his
bypass surgery. The owners named a with-mustard-only tubesteak after him.

Smooth and slightly funky, pylsur are perfectly enjoyable plain on a fluffy
steamed bun, but true glory is only found with the addition of toppings. *Eina
með öllu* means "one with the works," which includes ketchup; a brown, sweetish
mustard called *pylsusinnep;* a mayo-based sauce mixed with relish called *remúlaði;*
and two types of chopped onions: raw, and fried to crunchy, salty oblivion. (Tubs
of fried-onion bits are sold under the name Cronions. They will put French's out of
business during green-bean casserole season, should they ever make it to America.)
Some stands offer extra toppings like chili sauce or creamy shrimp salad, but
purists don't stray from the classics, and neither should you.

Perhaps part of the reason that pylsur are so appealing is their price: a pylsa
can be had for pocket change, no small feat in a country where the price of a beer
hovers around ten dollars. **–JAMIE FELDMAR**

Salsiccia di Bra

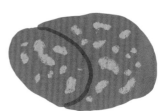

WHERE: Bra, Italy
MEAT: veal
PREPARATION: cased raw
SERVED: five or six to a plate, with an aperitivo

The smallish Piedmontese town of Bra is notable for more than just its punch-line name; it is also the birthplace of both Slow Food and a sausage-world oddity. In Italian culture, where almost every town in every region has a proud take on preserved pig parts, the *salsiccia di Bra*—made with veal and almost always eaten raw—is a total anomaly.

Where elsewhere in Italy, when the daily *aperitivo* begins and snacks of olives and focaccia shellacked with an old crust of desiccated tomato paste might be a standard accompaniment to a Negroni or a glass of Dolcetto, in Bra it is an arrangement of five or six pale pink pillows of unadulterated raw sausage. And almost without fail, the bite-size, sweet, delicately flavored sausage seems to win over even the most hysterical about and prejudiced against eating raw meat.

Before the Bra, sausages made of anything other than pork were banned in Italy. Some suggest it was due to hygiene hysteria, while others bet that the prohibition was yet another way to torment the local Jewish community. However in 1847 a decree by Carlo Alberto of Savoy announced that a single beef sausage would indeed be permitted in what was to become Italy (then part of the Austrian Empire), but that it was only to be made by the butchers of Bra.

Originally consisting solely of chopped and pounded (not minced) lean veal, spiced vaguely with cinnamon, mace, and fennel seeds, and tubed into ram's or goat's gut, the recipe has altered slightly since. To avoid spoilage, a percentage of pork fat was introduced and the meat is now some-times augmented with mature Robiola or toma della Langhe cheese and a splash of Arneis. Yet the fundamentals and the Savoy-era rules around provenance remain. To call it salsiccia di Bra, the butcher must be in business in the town, the basic composition respected, and the meat must come from the local Fassone Piemontese breed. **—DAVID PRIOR**

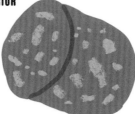

31

Saveloy

Bright, unearthly red hot dogs, factory processed with such mouthwatering ingredients as tetrasodium diphosphate, potassium nitrate, and iron oxide (responsible for that bright red tint). Spices vary by brand but are usually plentiful, and might include mace, cardamom, sage, ginger, and paprika. You'll find them at chip shops in the UK and parts of Australia, served boiled or batter-fried ("battered savs"), accompanied by fries and your choice of corn syrup–based sauce.

WHERE: UK and Commonwealth
MEAT: pork
PREPARATION: boiled or battered and fried
SERVED: with chips

Sheftalia

A Cypriot *crépinette, sheftalia* is made with fatty cuts of minimally spiced pork and/or lamb, ground and shaped into small éclairs and enveloped in a web of caul fat—the membrane that surrounds the organs of a pig (or sheep or cow). Grilled over an open flame, the caul fat sticks around long enough to help the sheftalia keep its shape, before it melts away, basting the sausage on its way down to the fire below. Once charred and juicy, the sausages are bundled in *pide* bread with tomato and onion.

WHERE: Cyprus
MEAT: pork, lamb, or a mixture
PREPARATION: charcoal-grilled
SERVED: with pide, tomato, and onion

Sucuk

For a super satisfying, low-on-liras dinner in Istanbul, just follow your nose down Kadırgalar Caddesi. That heady meat-over-flame perfume will carry you all the way to Maçka Park, where a fleet of little stalls all sell the same thing: grilled *sucuk,* an air-dried beef sausage zingy with cumin, sumac, and red pepper. Go stand in whichever line is the longest; you'll be rewarded for the wait with a few plump sausages tucked into unleavened *lavaş* bread, usually filled out with a fajita-like mix of griddled onions and peppers. A confidently uttered *"acili olsun"* (ah-jee-lee ohl-soon, "let it be spicy") will get you a schmear of fiery red pepper paste. If you prefer your sausage in the morning, look for a plate of *sucuklu yumurta,* one of the country's most popular breakfasts and a simple two-ingredient hangover killer: sucuk heated in a dry pan, with a couple eggs gently fried in the sausage's rendered fat.

WHERE: Turkey
MEAT: beef
PREPARATION: air-dried, then grilled or fried
SERVED: in lavaş bread or with eggs as breakfast

Thüringer Rostbratwurst

Along with the Nürnberger (see Drei im Weggla, page 21), this is one of two German bratwursts with protected geographical indication. (The oldest known recipe, dating back to 1613, is held in the Weimar State Archives, along with the earliest documented reference to it in 1404.) In order to be called *Thüringer Rostbratwurst,* a sausage must, as commemorated by the EU, be fifteen to twenty centimeters long, filled with medium-fine "coarsely trimmed pig-meat" and "possibly also trimmed veal or beef," spiced with salt, pepper, caraway, marjoram, and garlic. And they must come from the state of Thuringia. The *rost* part of the name refers to the grate above a charcoal flame, which the grill-meister traditionally rubs with bacon fat before throwing on the brats. He'll then baste them with beer throughout the grilling process, for flavor but also to cool the natural-casing skins and pre-vent charring. You can ask for mustard with your sausages, but do so at your own risk: In some parts of the region the condiment is considered *verboten,* and you may get a sneer. If you like your sausage with a side of camp, don't miss *Hans Wurst and the Love Sausage* at the German Bratwurst Museum in Holzhausen, a farcical, musical retelling of the Thüringer rostbratwurst's early-fifteenth-century origins.

WHERE: Thüringia (and throughout Germany)
MEAT: pork and sometimes veal or beef
PREPARATION: Grilled over an open flame
SERVED: as is or on a bun

Toad in the Hole

Sausage links baked in popover-like Yorkshire pudding batter (then some-times doused with onion gravy). When toad in the hole first appeared in English cookbooks in the eighteenth century, indiscriminate recipes called for meat scraps or leftovers with the spoiled bits removed. Today, any (unspoiled) pork sausage will do; the exact specimen varies by region (see our recipe, page 219). As with most things, you can find it in big cities, but the best toad in the hole still resides outside the capital, in low-lit pubs at the end of country lanes.

WHERE: UK
MEAT: pork
PREPARATION: baked in Yorkshire pudding batter
SERVED: with onion gravy

Tunnbrödsrulle

The *tunnbrödsrulle* is excessive in a way you might not associate with Nordic food. This late-night Swedish monster wraps a piece of lavash around a long, skinny hot dog (or two), mayonnaise, shrimp salad, mashed potatoes, and heavy squiggles of mustard and ketchup. They're almost exclusively served at stands whose hours coincide with those of homeward-bound clubgoers—perhaps the only people in the world who might have need or desire for such a concoction.

WHERE: Sweden
MEAT: pork and shrimp
PREPARATION: griddled
SERVED: wrapped, with mashed potatoes, onions, peppers, shrimp salad

Verivorstid

Verivorstid is blood sausage from
Estonia, the northernmost of the Baltic
nations. Alongside *seapraad* (roast
pork), *hapukapsas* (sauerkraut), and
piparkoogid (gingerbread cookies), it is
the centerpiece of Estonian Christmas.
Each winter, families elbow-deep in a
tub of pork, onions, marjoram, blood,
and pearl barley funnel the mixture into
casings by hand. The horseshoe-shaped
links are boiled until firm and saved for
Christmas Eve. When it's time to serve
them, they're roasted until the skin
darkens and blisters.

WHERE: Estonia
MEAT: pork and pork blood
PREPARATION: boiled and then roasted
SERVED: as the main attraction of a proper
   Estonian Christmas

White Pudding

White pudding is the exsanguinated
cousin of Black Pudding (page 14),
substituting coarsely ground pork shoulder for pork blood. They are otherwise
similar: An oatmeal base is blended with
fat and meat and accented with ginger,
mace, and nutmeg. (The same basic
relationship exists between *boudin blanc*
and *boudin noir* in France, *morcilla* and
morcilla blanca in Spain, and *Blutwurst*
and *Leberwurst* in Germany.) Sliced
thick and pan-fried, white pudding is the
yin to black pudding's yang in full breakfasts throughout the United Kingdom.
In Scotland, you can also find white
pudding battered and fried (but really,
what *can't* you find battered and fried
in Scotland?) and served with fries and
malt vinegar—a mealie (as in "oatmeal")
pudding supper, as it's locally known.

WHERE: UK
MEAT: pork shoulder and suet
PREPARATION: baked or boiled, then sliced
   and pan-fried
SERVED: as part of a Full English Breakfast
   (page 24)

RANT

MUSTARD

Peter Meehan

Ketchup is an acceptable condiment on hot dogs, but only for children and degenerates. And not for my children.

—My Dad and All the Dads of the Greater Chicagoland Area

Coming into consciousness in the Middle West of America, one is raised knowing that to put ketchup on a hot dog is like wearing diapers to middle school—some people are going to do it, but you don't want to be one of them unless absolutely, medically necessary.

I could say that this belief stems from tradition, but that would be skirting the truth, which is this: Mustard is the king of condiments. It is alpha and omega, sun and moon; kimchi and ketchup wash its feet and anoint its shoulders with liniments when it is sore from the weight of the crown.

It is GLORIOUS and RESPLEN-DENT when it is school-bus yellow and tastes of turmeric and the national anthem. Yellow mustard is the condi-ment that makes hot dogs hot dogs, and the rest of the garbage that people put on them is either for fun—hot dog cosplay, let's call it, which we will not malign in the sex-positive pages of this tubesteak missive—or folly, as in what happens to hot dogs EVERY DAY on the streets of New York as the careless robotic populace toddles by, an outrage being perpetrated on every midtown corner.

Though I was originally suspicious of Dijon mustard, which I first saw being passed between two lonely old queens who were being squired about the countryside in his-and-her Silver Shadows, we have welcomed it into our lives, our refrigerators, and our ambigu-ously Euro-leaning sausage conquests— for me, it mitigates the lambiness of a merguez like nothing else.

Weißwurst would be a pointlessly tumescent ghost penis of a joke sausage were it not for the faint domination of sweetness in the Bavarian mustard that is its natural partner, its raison d'être. To walk into a Polish delicatessen and breathe in the variety of kielbasas and mustards—This one is spicy enough to light your nose hairs on fire! This one comes in a cute collectible glass beer stein!—is to be like an exhibitionist on his first nude beach, inhaling the salt air of the sea and the liberation of endless possibility.

The uncapturable and irreducible scope of mustard profusion matched, caringly, with the right specimens from the ever-uncoiling universe of sausage-dom makes for the most infinite, and one of the most deeply satisfying, adven-tures in human eating.

And you were going to put *what* on that hot dog?

35

Germany

Gideon Lewis-Kraus

Every great or average German meal comes at the courtesy of two people or institutions: the one that made the beer and the one that made the sausage. (Sauerkraut is something either might competently make in his or her spare time.) As those responsible for Germany's two greatest complementary products (the complement of philosophy and poetry coming in a distant second), the two culturogastronomic producers work in harmony and good fellowship. But their relationship remains at base a rivalry, and one of the outstanding debates of German culture is their quarrel over which of the two has the right to claim the longest history of obeying the rules.

Bavarian beer brewers are proud to have been following the rules since 1487, when Albert IV, Duke of Bavaria, established the foundations of the first *Reinheitsgebot*, or "purity order," of 1516, which specified that beer could legally contain only water, barley, and hops; by the following century the law had been widely taken up throughout the Holy Roman Empire. The Reinheitsgebot is often esteemed as one of the oldest food-purity laws on the books, though there are records of the leaders of antiquity imposing fines or punishments on purveyors of unsafe comestibles. When Bismarck united Germany in 1871, Bavaria would only agree to the union if the statute was made the law of the nation, so Germans consider the decree to represent a fundamental tenet of the German state.

The making of sausage had also long been a regulated industry, but for centuries the sausage makers had to concede that, though they followed the rules with unimpeachable discipline and enthusiasm, they had not been following the rules for quite as long as the brewers next door. So it was some cause for celebration when, in 2000, an amateur historian discovered, in the Weimar city archives, a worn handwritten document from 1432, which stipulated that *Thüringer Rostbratwurst,* among the most famous of German sausages, could be made only from "pure, fresh pork." The law disallowed parasites, beef, and offal. "See!" the sausage makers crowed. "Everything in our house has been in order longer than it has in yours." In the ongoing German Following the Rules Championship, the sausage makers had come out ahead. They could boast of being the most consistently obedient.

Needless to say this is a preposterous competition, but conversations about these laws, and their history, is a higher-stakes affair than it might initially seem. There are some cultures that are at once committed to the way they do things and happy to acknowledge that they do things that way because that's simply the way things have always been done. This is often true of, say, Japanese culture. What tends to be different about German culture is that the way things are done has behind it not merely the force of tradition but the force of good sense. The implication is: For the few hundred medieval years in which we were running the European show, we developed a set of best practices, and we've chosen to stick with them. Over the last five hundred years, we haven't simply been Following the Rules for their own sake, but because those rules represent merely a formalized expression of the best way to do things. Their authority isn't arbitrary, it's natural.

The reason that this feeling is so important is that it conceals, behind the psychic protection of choice, a reality that's a lot messier. Not that this is a bad thing. It's what culture is. Culture is the invention of compelling stories for why and how we have come to *want* to do something that we probably *had* to do anyway.

There is an argument to be made that sausages, and particularly sausages in Germany, are one of world history's great examples of this general principle of a kind of evolutionary bad faith; after all, the most famous thing that Chancellor Bismarck never said was that "if you like laws and sausages, you should never watch either one being made." This was only attributed to Bismarck in the 1930s, and has been traced back more accurately to an 1869 comment by an American lawyer called John Godfrey Saxe, who said that "laws, like sausages, cease to inspire respect in proportion as we know how they are made." This transformation seems revealing. As attributed to Bismarck, it communicates a level of disgust: If we knew how gross the ingredients were, we'd no longer find the sausage palatable. The key emotion is *revulsion*. But the original quotation makes the point not in terms of revulsion but in terms of respect.

The idea, then, behind the original food-purity laws is that they defend a product that we wouldn't mind seeing produced—a product that would seem neither revolting nor dishonest. At the end of an exhibition on the history of the *Nürnberger Bratwurst*, a video monitor showed contemporary footage from a nearby production facility, where a clean man in a clean white apron put his scrubbed hand into a never-before-used stainless steel cart to mix the white salt with the green marjoram and the brown mace, which an invented-that-day robot then poured from the stainless steel cart into a thick curtain of ground pork falling in slow heavy ribbons onto a state-of-the-art conveyor belt. Everything in the video gave the appearance that the entire production facility had been built to specification that morning, used for exactly one production line, and would be disassembled overnight and reconceived anew the next day.

This was a literal, and oddly hypnotic, picture of how our more respectable sausages are made; but the overall effect, when taken as part of a broader perspective on Germanic sausages, was that the whole thing was something of the *haus* of sausage's Potemkin village. The very reason that the original food-purity laws had to be enacted was that the whole point of sausage in the first place was a repository for offal. Historically, there really are only two reasons to make a sausage. One is to create meat that keeps longer: A cured sausage is salted and/or smoked to produce a protein supply with a shelf life longer than a day or two. The other is to figure out something to do with the parts of the animal you might otherwise feel a little sheepish about serving somebody. Cured meats cure best in dry climates, which is why classic ultramontane sausage—and in particular those made in the high-*Mitteleuropaïsche* belt running from, say, Alsace to Vienna—is the fresh sausage. And the ur-example of the fresh sausage is the blood sausage.

In a real sense, then, all sausages are really blood sausages at heart. The logic goes something like this: The ultimate leftover is the blood, and whether you're a starving peasant or a rapaciously efficient butcher-capitalist, you want to do *something* with it. After all, animals have just pints and pints of the stuff. Spleen, lungs, all the other assorted bits of unlovely inside can be chopped up and spiced and otherwise disguised and served as something legit and classy. But unless you're going to give your guest a pint of blood, you have to get creative with it. The first thing you need is a vessel. The blood sausage was properly born when somebody looked over at his or her pile of animal remainders and realized that he or she could simply pour the blood from the runoff bucket into the intestine and tie off both ends. As somebody must've realized, though, these primitive blood balloons were prone to splatter, an event from which even the most casual dinner party might have trouble recovering. So then they got to thinking that if they mixed the blood inside the intestine with crumbs and croutons of the stale bread they had lying around, the whole thing could then be cooked and presented in solid, sliceable form. Thus was the sausage—an original and ingenious case of refuse repackaged as value—the offspring of simple, absolute necessity.

The food-purity laws, in turn, function as part of the alchemy of desire. It's not as though Weimar's 1432 anti-offal decree made everybody cheer that they no longer had to come home to plates of encased blood; they'd gotten used to their encased blood, had come to cherish it. They just now had an opportunity to say, "This isn't something we're eating because we *have* to—after all, now we can afford pure, parasite-free pork—it's something we're eating because we *want* to."

One might hazard the assessment that most things have pretty unglamorous and utilitarian origins, and that culture operates as a kind of burnishing force, the post hoc stories we tell about how we've gotten here. Narrative tradition forms a complement to legal quasi-fictions like food-purity laws. If that exhibition in Nuremberg closed with a video about how sausage was made—a video, for what it's worth, one would likely never see in the States—the whole exhibit leading up to it was dedicated to showing how the very *idea* of sausage had been made.

Nuremberg sausages are famously small, much shorter than the wurst of the north and west, and of less girth than those of the south and east. The city has a bit of a complex about it, though the consistent message is that what they lack in size they make up for in quantity; local menus offer six, eight, ten, sometimes fifty to a plate, and on the street they're served three in a bun. Embroidered explanations abound. One legend refers to the fact that Nuremberg, a city of great strategic and political significance to the Holy Roman emperors, was heavily fortified with thick defense walls. The city was locked at curfew, and the local story says that the Nürnberger was made deliberately small so that latecomers might still be fed through the keyholes in the city gates. Another story relates the fate of local patrician judge Hans Stromer, locked up for life for insolvency, gossip, and possible treason. He had enough friends in the city administration that they agreed to one final correctional wish: that he be fed two Nürnbergers a day. These, too, were passed by the bailiff through the key-

hole, and legend has it that he ate some 28,000 sausages over the next thirty-eight years of his life.

Everybody more or less seems to know that the real reason for the size of the Nürnberger—now canonized at seven to nine centimeters in length and no more than twenty-five grams in weight—was simply a matter of a rise in late-medieval pork prices; the local council decided that for reasons of marketing and cost they would present their specialty as a higher-quality product.

The concealment of utilitarian or economic origins, or origins in simple survival, can thus be achieved by legal doctrine, on the one hand, or anecdotal mythology, on the other; but the real work of culture-as-obfuscation or culture-as-burnishment goes on in the day-to-day practices that make up our food rituals. If Weimar's Thüringer rostbratwurst reveals the legal scheme and the Nürnberger rostbratwurst the anecdotal one, it's in upper Bavaria that practical tradition is paramount.

The reigning sausage of Munich is the *Weißwurst,* or white sausage. Nowhere are Germans so strict about sausage consumption as they are about the weißwurst. Most importantly, they are only to be eaten in the morning; as the saying goes, *Die Weißwürste sollen das Mittagsläuten nicht mehr hören,* or, "Weißwurst must never hear the noon church bells." They're usually served in a little basin of warm water, and the casing is never eaten; real connoisseurs consume by *zuzeln,* or by taking the sausage in the hand and sucking the meat out of the casing. *Lucky Peach* first learned this from the Wikipedia article about the weißwurst that our intern sent along to prepare us (myself and *LP*'s Chris Ying and Walter Green) for a crusade through the sausage holy lands—France, Germany, Austria. As your correspondents sat midmorning at a Bavarian butcher counter sucking the green-flecked white from their soggy condom wrapper, they looked around and realized they were the only customers so compromised— though they were not the only customers accompanying their breakfast with wheat beers—and they worried their intern, left behind at home to man the fort, had diabolically changed the Wikipedia entry to humiliate them. As it turns out, zuzeln is a time-honored tradition, even if one of your correspondents couldn't think of a more unpleasant way to eat a sausage. (There are YouTube instructional videos for those who can't get the hang of it on their own.)

Both of these traditions—of eating them before their noon expiration hour, and serving them in warm water—are supposed to prevent the local breakfast from making its consumer sick. As Chris put it, "That cause might have been helped by simply heating it more." But the weißwurst, though this doesn't help its popularity, is constitutionally lukewarm. As the story has it, an innkeeper on Munich's main square, on the celebratory Sunday before Mardi Gras in February 1857, realized that he'd somehow run out of the sheep's casing that's used for the Bratwurst. His customers were waiting and he became frantic. He sent his assistant out to find more casings, but the assistant could only find pig casings. In haste, the innkeeper stuffed the casings, but feared that the sausages would explode in the heat of the grill or in water at a roiling boil; he steamed them, instead, and served them the way Bavarians have come to love them: tepid. Ordinarily the highest praise you can bestow upon a German sausage is *knackig*, a thoroughly off-putting word whose meaning lies somewhere between "crunchy" and "tumescent"—"crunchingly tumescent" really captures the lack of appeal—but the weißwurst is perhaps the only fresh sausage that's praised for remaining limp and tepid. The only problem with the limp, tepid sausages, of course, is that, post-church bells, they might kill you. But the scenery of those church bells, and the presence of a new rule for everybody to follow, only added to their ultimate appeal.

That original beer-purity law, the Reinheitsgebot, which in hindsight has come to represent the administration of science and cleanliness to the brewing process, also ultimately represented a political calculation: Beer could only be made with barley to ensure that rye and other grains remained available and reasonably priced on the food market. When Bavaria insisted upon the national adoption of the law as the precondition of their joining Bismarck's unified Germany, it was a matter of protectionist economics: Bavarian brewers used it to wipe out the competition from the other German states. (It worked. A price of unification was that many local brewing traditions died out across the Germanic lands.) The law had gone from being a tool of political strategy to one of market monopoly, all under cover of health and safety.

But it's not always the case that culture is elaborated to cover up the cunning of history, to make excuses for why what's come before ought to keep coming after; sometimes culture allows for novelty and expansiveness. Toward the end of the sausage swath they mowed through Mitteleuropa, your correspondents reached the boundary of the German world: the border with Hungary, in Burgenland, the easternmost sliver of Austria. The local pig had long been the Mangalitsa, a mid-nineteenth-century crossbreed of Austro-Hungarian wild boar and Serbian hog that was mostly lard, and thus prized along the Balkan periphery of the dual monarchy for tallow. With the rise of the Iron Curtain, the area, once so central, grew isolated and poor, and the fat, round Mangalitsa was given up in favor of animals with greater meat content; lard had become less important than protein.

With the end of the Cold War and the increasing porousness of national borders, the local butchers have once more found a use for the Mangalitsa. Your correspondents met with one local butcher who'd gone on vacation over the mountains to Italy and realized that he could make prosciutto with his own pigs just as well as the Italians could; he went home to begin production, and eighteen months later he was trucking his cured hams up to farmers' markets in Vienna. Like his father before him, he'd always been a blood sausage maker—it's what the region is known for—but he'd come to understand that in the new Europe he'd only survive if he diversified his product. Of course, it meant teaching his neighbors new tastes and new consumption habits, but that was all part of his trade. It wasn't, after all, that hard of a sell: All he had to do was reach back four or five generations to say that what he was doing now, even if it looked totally different, was a continuation of what everybody's great-great-grandparents were doing back then. Maybe it wasn't quite prosciutto, but it was the same animal, and the same cultural history and craftsmanship brought to bear.

That bit about just going on vacation, though, and figuring you could do something just as well as the Italians could, and needing to go to market with a more diverse product line—well, that wasn't quite going to do for a proper origin story of the future famous cured Mangalitsa of Burgenland. There wasn't enough intrigue or comedy. But the butcher's son was his apprentice, watching his father carefully out of the corner of his eye, and someday he'd have to come up with tales to tell his children. He'd surely edit and embellish and embroider, and the coincidences and necessities of his father would become the traditions and legends and desires of his grandchildren.

For more from Gideon's adventures in Mitteleuropa, see the accompanying photos (with additional thoughts from Chris Ying and Walter Green). ⟶

EURO TRIP

DAY ONE, FRANKFURT

CHRIS YING: Walter Green—art director of *Lucky Peach,* irresistible charmer, vernal spirit, and member of our expedition party—and I arrived in Frankfurt about fifteen hours before our writerly companion, Gideon Lewis-Kraus. We figured we'd hit the ground running—our directive being to sample all the sausage we could find on a roughly east-west-oriented fishhook-shaped trail from western Germany to the Austro-Hungarian border. Pictured here is a plate of currywurst, the street-food staple of sliced sausage soaked in ketchup and dusted with curry powder, that Walter and I walked clear across Frankfurt to eat, on what turned out to be some bad intel. It was terrible. Currywurst is terrible.

GIDEON LEWIS-KRAUS: Chris had sent me a proposed itinerary, with a very long justification for why he believed that this fishhook trail represented the most efficient way to take in the major sausages of Mitteleuropa; if I remember correctly, he included an Excel file, a PowerPoint deck, and a whole sheaf of yellowing newspaper clippings that described a rich, prewar culture of pan-European sausage enthusiasm. I didn't read the spreadsheet or click through the deck, but I did glance at a map, and mostly I was just very happy that we weren't going to Berlin, where I knew Ying and Walter would want to sample the currywurst. Just a short time earlier, I'd written a small item for *Lucky Peach* explicitly warning people off of currywurst—I believe, in a fit of pique, that I described

it as "a limp, wrinkly dick"—and when I subsequently discovered that their first stop would be currywurst, in Frankfurt, I tried to back out of the trip. I agreed to come in the end, but only after they had eaten their currywurst. This is how it came to be that all of us began our trip in a foul temper—for my part, because they had ignored my warnings; and, for theirs, because they had eaten currywurst.

CY: That same night, Walter and I went on a crawl through Frankfurt's *Apfelweinwirtschaften*—beer halls pouring very dry, lukewarm, almost savory apple ciders to accompany an array of very heavy, very meaty dishes. We went hog wild with our sausage ordering: *Rindswurst* (beef sausage, basically the ballpark franks we know), frankfurters (smoky, with a nice snappy casing), *blutwurst* (blood sausage; more liquid than solid, and tasting strongly of clove), *leberwurst* (liver sausage, similar to the blood sausage in texture, but a bit stringier like braised beef), and a black-peppery bratwurst. It's here that we first became acquainted with the German practice of serving sausages with so much sauerkraut as to seem like a mistake or a joke or a dare. It's as though the sausages are but the croutons in a salad of sauerkraut. I understand it on an academic level—the acid in the cabbage (and the cider and the tableside urns of mustard) makes the fat in the meat more palatable. All of the sausages *did* seem especially rich, leaving our mouths shellacked with fat. But Christ, there was just so much kraut, and everyone around us finished all of theirs.

In any case, this was Walter's maiden voyage to Europe, and so the apfelwein-wirtschafts were also where he had his first sip of European alcohol. He did not appreciate the funk of the cider, comparing it unfavorably to "my own peepee," so I finished his glass, too.

WALTER GREEN: Chris loves drinking my peepee.

DAY TWO, STRASBOURG

CLK: I arrived to find Ying and Walter facedown across some tram tracks outside the Frankfurt train station and immediately worried that they hadn't understood that the *Apfelwein* is supposed to be diluted to taste with the sparkling water they provide in handsome earthenware jugs. But then Ying explained to me that they weren't facedown across the tram tracks because of the apfelwein but because they'd eaten an entire mountain of sauerkraut. I explained that the mountain of sauerkraut is supposed to be diluted to taste by the tradition of not eating all of the sauerkraut.

Already on the wrong side of Germany, we lit out on the train for France, alighting a few hours later in Strasbourg. En route, we regaled Walter with tales of Strasbourg's half-timbered splendor. But Walter, still dyspeptic from the uncut apfelwein and the uncut sauerkraut mountain, told us he was disappointed that, on his first trip to Europe, we hadn't taken him somewhere full-timbered.

WG: Was Strasbourg where I started using Tinder? I think it was. I was hoping to use the app to find someone to help me re-create that movie *Before Sunrise,* but with 100 percent more sausage. I went through a bunch of different bios over the course of our trip—some mentioning that I was traveling with two older men who were looking to eat encased meats, some not—to varying degrees of success. Varying between nonexistent and extremely low.

CY: Strasbourg is where we peaked, mealwise. The Alsace region has one spiritual foot in France and the other in Germany and the food is a happy intersection of the two. We arrived looking specifically for a plate of choucroute garnie—a super classic Alsatian casserole of fatty cuts of meat and sausages braised in wine, stock, and sauerkraut—and we found the platonic ideal of it at a hole-in-the-wall called Au Coin des Pucelles.

CLK: So after all of that Walter thought that we were telling him that Strasbourg was only half-Tindered. At any rate, we'd initially set out to eat choucroute at one restaurant, but our gracious Airbnb host recommended a place that the locals like better. Walter looked up from his full-Tindering to ask if he might help us get a

reservation. Our host called the restaurant for us. Even with our broken French we could understand him on the phone saying, "Yeah, yeah, they're foreigners, Americans, but I will tell them that before they visit your establishment they must shake the Camaro dust from their trousers and please to put on some shirts."

CY: We ordered two different choucroutes garnies—one pork version and one duck. As in Germany, the sauerkraut still came in an ungainly quantity, but this stuff was tempered by a slow simmer—still sour, but also savory. The sausages—two each of pork and duck—had an ultrafine emulsified grain and were profuse with pork fat. We giddily scooped up strands of sauerkraut with bites of sausage, duck confit, salty bacon, and pork belly, intermittently burning room in our bellies with shots of schnapps and gulps of dry Riesling. Any space we might have left in our bodies, we filled with *Parmentier de boudin noir aux pommes*—an outrageous shepherd's pie consisting of blood sausage and applesauce, fragrant with Christmas spices, topped with a browned layer of creamy mashed potato. Holy hell.

CLK: After dinner, we tried to shake off our torpor with a visit to the Strasbourg equivalent of New York's legendary Mudd Club. They used the same font. For much of dinner, Ying had talked about how the food we were eating represented a long-simmering historical compromise between Germany and France. I asked our bartender if, given the option, he'd rather speak to a foreigner in German, English, or French, and he said he'd rather the foreigners not speak to him at all.

DAY THREE, MUNICH

CY: Munich. Spiritual home of the beer hall. Site of Oktoberfest. We spent a couple hours halfheartedly poking around for some sort of off-the-beaten-path sausage underground, but gave in pretty quickly to Nürnberger Bratwurst Glöckl am Dom, one of a half dozen or so beer halls right in the thick of Munich's central district. As far as potential tourist traps go, this place wasn't bad. The clientele is almost entirely German, though the menu comes in four languages and we were seated at a large communal table with a group of three Japanese tourists.

GLK: The people of Munich are so taken by their own mythology that the more a given establishment looks like a Bavarian installation at Epcot, the more the locals love it—there's not really a difference between "tourists" and "locals" that way. There was a slight difference between tourists, locals, and the Japanese people at our table. At a beer hall whose specialty is a plate of fifty bratwursts, they ordered exactly three—to share.

CY: This place's namesake is the *Nürnberger Bratwurst*—a thin breakfast-sausage-size pork link grilled over beechwood. The sausage itself is a geographically protected product of Nuremberg (more on this later), but you can order them fifty at a time here. We ordered significantly fewer and they were tasty—snappy and juicy and simple—but the real eye-catcher was the *Käsekrainer,* a long, cheese-studded sausage that puts all other cheese sausages to shame. In my experience, the cheese in a cheese sausage tends to be blended into the meat, a mere background flavoring. With the käsekrainer, each slice reveals a tiny pocket of molten cheese that appears seemingly out of nowhere, like blood pooling on a cut you've just wiped clean.

GLK: Each of the Japanese guys had three bites of sausage. One of them even had the temerity to ask for a vegetable. The waiter didn't understand, so he pulled out a pocket translator. When the waiter still didn't understand, he did a Google Images search for vegetable. The waiter scrolled down for what seemed like an eternity, frowned, and finally shook his head. He pulled his other friend over to point at the screen, and the two of them shared a hearty laugh. Then they brought the Japanese tourists a mountain of sauerkraut.

CY: Feeling confident after our first stop, we pushed our luck with a pilgrimage to a more scene-y beer hall: Hofbräuhaus München. What a mistake.

GLK: I wore a HB Haus sweatshirt for years until I actually visited Oktoberfest and decided it was an event I henceforth wanted zero to do with. The members of the oompah band recognized Walter as a lost member of their jolly race, and tried to get him to run off with them.

WG: Even though deep down, in my heart of hearts, I would have preferred to go with those strange men, I stayed with Chris and Gideon out of devotion to our Sausage Quest. And 'cause they paid for my trip.

CY: We found redemption at our last stop of the night, Haxnbauer, where we arrived just in time to order a pair of *Schweinshaxe*—spit-roasted pork hocks. They sell these hulking gems by weight—little flags mounted on toothpicks indicate the price of each knuckle—and we asked for the biggest ones they had left. Despite how much beer and wurst we'd already consumed, those two mammoth specimens barely sufficed. We tugged ravenously with forks and fingers to pry off chunks of crackly skin and steamy meat until all that was left was the sad sound of clean bone rattling against porcelain plate.

DAY FOUR, NUREMBERG

CY: The next day, Gideon and I took a day trip to Nuremberg, a truly mind-bending city with astonishing examples of both medieval and National Socialist archi-

tecture. For a long stretch of the Holy Roman Empire, Nuremberg was one of the most important cities on earth. We came for the bratwursts.

CLK: We were lucky enough that the local museum was holding an exhibition about the historical relationship of the city to its most famous food. (For more about that, please see Drei im Weggla, page 21.)

CY: Visiting the Nazi Party rally grounds was probably the most profound emotional experience I've had in Europe. The sausages we had in Nuremberg were the weakest we had in Germany. At Hausbauerei Alstadthof, I ordered a house special of Nürnberger bratwursts suspended in a block of brown aspic shaped like an external hard drive. I

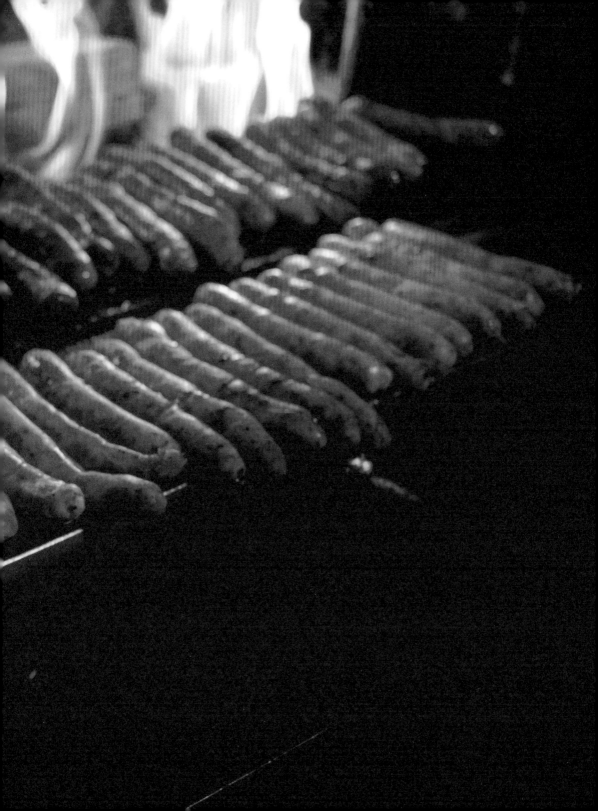

guess it's my fault for seeing a brick of cold sausage Jell-O on the menu and thinking, *Yes, that sounds good*. But even the warm brats were far inferior to the ones we had in Munich. And although we saw signs advertising *Drei im Weggla,* the local specialty sandwich of three bratwursts in a bun, on our visit, there was not a weggla to be seen.

DAY FIVE, MIESBACH

CY: We reunited with Walter and set out together the next day for Miesbach, where we'd heard reports of both exceptional weißwurst and a stand-out lung soup. We followed our leads to Metzgerei Holnburger, a small chain of butcher shops that kept coming up as the only place to go if you're looking for white sausage. *Weißwurst,* a cousin to French *boudin blanc,* is a fresh pork and veal sausage spiced with white pepper, cardamom, lemon zest, parsley, and mace. It's always served poached (often in a tureen with the poaching water), usually with a warm pretzel and a dollop of sweet brown mustard on the side. The prescribed method of consumption is either to cut a shallow incision down the length of the sausage and peel off the casing, or to clip off one end like a cigar and suck (*zuzeln*) the meat out. I've got a big soft spot in my heart for sausages like this—kind of squishy, balanced, and mild almost to the point of anonymity. Neither Gideon nor Walter were fans.

Plates of breaded fried spleen sausage and sour, pickled lung soup at the next restaurant received warmer acclaim from those two. And rightly so.

CLK: When we got to the restaurant around the corner, there was a cohort of local pensioners at the next table over; they were enjoying their elevenses over beer and lung. One of them laughed and pointed to Ying's camera and said something to the group about how we'd come all the way to Miesbach to order a schnitzel we could've had in Munich. Contrary to expectation, we proceeded in fact to order essentially all viscera. They raised their glasses in tribute. Walter, whose own viscera were beginning to rebel, ordered salad, which came

the standard German way: floating in a ten-thousand-calorie broth of dressing. Germans fear and distrust vegetables in winter, and will go to great lengths to subdue them.

WG: Me and Germans have that in common! But that's what I get for ordering a salad for the first time in my life. Anyway, I'm just here to say that weißwurst is awful, and so is anyone who likes it. When I was little, I saw some WHITE POOP, and I was like, *What the fuck is that!?* Then someone was like, *That's dried-up cat poop.* Weißwurst looks exactly like white cat poop. So . . . GOOD JOB, Miesbach!

Oh, and another thing: you're supposed to eat weißwurst before noon. Why? Because you want to ruin your whole day?

CLK: There's more about this topic in my more measured contribution (see page 37), but the idea is that it might've been dangerous—by which one could only mean that it was *definitely* dangerous—to consume fresh sausages that had been sitting around for too long, so, even long after the incursion of refrigeration, it's still the tradition that one stays on the safe side and only orders them in the morning.

WG: Hey, I've got an idea, let's have some *white lukewarm sausage* for breakfast! Okay . . .

DAYS SIX AND SEVEN, BURGENLAND AND VIENNA

CY: We arrived in Vienna, the terminus of our quest, late at night and set out the next morning for the Hungarian border. Our guide was an English expat named Richard who was running a sausage start-up from his apartment.

CLK: He invited us to come around at nine, and he was still in his pajamas. This didn't stop him from cooking us sixty sausages for breakfast. He cooked that many in part because all of them had reached their sell-by date, which is something that the Austrian authorities take very seriously. He was afraid the cops would come in and find expired sausages in his fridge. Also, perhaps out of fear of the authorities, he cooked the sausages for at least fifteen minutes to a side. Because they were his homemade sausages, and he'd gotten out of bed early for the occasion, we felt as though it would've been rude not to eat them all.

CY: Six or eight hours later, Richard drove us out to the eastern state of Burgenland to meet an acquaintance of his, Otmar Schürtz, an old-school butcher and sausage maker who'd agreed to show us how he was making award-winning *Blutwurst* from pigs raised on the other side of the Hungarian border. We tasted the sausages cold. Spongy and bread-like, they were unlike any other blood sausage we'd encountered west of Hungary. Schürtz gave us the rough formula for his creation: fifteen percent breadcrumbs, twenty to twenty-five percent fat, and the rest a mix of lungs, heart, tongue, skin, blood, garlic, and marjoram. Maybe because it was cold, or maybe because it wasn't served with a heap of sauerkraut, I found the blutwurst oddly refreshing. I didn't have time to put my finger on it, though. Schürtz shooed us out of the shop after half an hour—he had work to do—and we set sail again for Vienna.

CY: Back in Vienna, we felt pressed firmly against the limits of sausage consumption, so we putzed around the city, deftly avoiding any inadvertent encounters with wurst. Finally, late on our last night in town, wandering around near the opera house, we summoned the intestinal fortitude to try just one more käsekrainer, this one from Bitzinger, a handsome and beloved late-night *Würstelstand*. The three of us split a griddle-blistered cheesy sausage; it was most excellent.

CLK: We all had heart attacks on the plane rides home and died.

WG: Actually, on the flight home, the airline served a sausage sandwich and some Warsteiner beer. There was another meatless meal choice, too, but there was no way I could pass up the opportunity for one last sausage.

Sweden

Lisa Abend

It starts with a flatbread not dissimilar to an Old El Paso flour tortilla—the kind that, when you chew it, sticks to your teeth with the tenacity of plastic laminate. The bread is topped with ice cream scoops of instant mashed potatoes. Not just instant, in fact, but à la minute: The vendor whisks them into being from flakes right before your eyes. The hot dog, ostensibly the main event, is actually a bit of an afterthought, overwhelmed as it is by the mountains of potato-like substances and its own disturbing flaccidity. Streams of ketchup and mustard are squirted on top, and then comes the coup de grâce: shrimp salad the color of Pepto-Bismol and the texture of snot. In all likelihood, the shrimp salad will contain little or no shrimp at all, just bits of turnip or other filler vegetables cooked to a consistency vaguely reminiscent of shellfish.

It is *tunnbrödsrulle*, and it is unspeakably vile.

A lot of hot dogs get eaten in Scandinavia. They are the region's one semi-indigenous form of fast food, introduced at the 1930 Stockholm Exhibition and rising in popularity after the Second World War, when changing demographics and work habits made a cheap, readily available, and easy-to-prepare protein especially appealing. To this day, they are sold in most any highway gas station or inner-city convenience store. Hot dog carts dot the streets of Copenhagen, Oslo, and Stockholm. They are the food of choice for both workers with short lunch hours and revelers looking for something to soak up alcohol at two in the morning. It is from this tradition that the abominable tunnbrödsrulle arises.

There are, of course, many foods that outsiders to the local culture cannot understand, let alone enjoy. Marmite comes to mind. Peanut butter is repellent to most Europeans. Icelanders leave shark meat to rot for months (because rotten fish is so very much more delicious than fresh) to produce the delicacy *hákarl*. But all of these foods have explanations: a use for leftover brewer's yeast; a Depression-era source of cheap protein; fermentation leaches the local shark of its toxins.

There is no explanation for tunnbrödsrulle, at least not a fully satisfying one. The bread can be justified: Although most hot dogs in Sweden are served in a hollowed-out chunk of baguette, the tunnbrödsrulle is rolled in a flatbread (a *tunnbröd*) that is popular in the north, where harsh weather conditions favor a bread that can be consumed either fresh or dried. The potatoes can be similarly explained: Anything that adds calories and carbohydrates is welcome protection against the cold. But the shrimp salad? With ketchup and mustard? It defies reason, to say nothing of good taste. Why would anyone do that to a hot dog?

I went to Stockholm to find out.

I chose my first stand for its name, Ove's Hjulkorv, which, according to the linguists at Yelp, translates as "Ove's Penus." (How anyone arrived at that interpretation—or its spelling—is a mystery. As best as I can decipher, *hjulkorv* means "wheel sausage.") Located in the center of the city, Ove's pulls a steady stream of customers at lunch hour. The man inside was not actually Ove. Ove, who worked the stand for forty years, is dead. Gunnar was just helping out. He suggested I try some "special cucumbers" on my tunnbrödsrulle. When I accepted, he dipped a spoon into an economy-size jar of what looked suspiciously like Kraft relish, and tasted for himself. "Yeah," he said. "Those are good."

They were not good. They were sticky sweet, and slightly metallic tasting, and their verdant green stood in contrast to the pink gloppiness of everything else. Instant potatoes oozed from the bread when I tried to take a bite. It was the opposite of that old Catskill joke from *Annie Hall:* The food was terrible, and the portions were huge.

I asked Gunnar about the shrimp salad. "Yes, it is strange," he agreed amiably. A Nordic pause descended while he considered the subject in greater depth. Then, "You should do some research." A woman in line nodded appreciatively at the sagacity of this statement, then tried to help: "The bread comes from the north." Yes, I pressed, but the shrimp salad—where does it come from? She shrugged.

The tunnbrödsrulle at the next stand I tried, Nybrogrillen, located on the edge of Berzelii park, was much, much worse. Swedish hot dog stands keep their ketchup and mustard suspended in upside-down dispenser packs, like so many udders, for better squeezing. At Nybrogrillen, they did not have a good grip on theirs. The mustard came out in great streams, and yet was still insufficient to mask the overpowering flavor of the steam table in which the sausages were bobbing sadly. I literally gagged. When I mustered the fortitude, I asked about the goo that was masquerading as shrimp salad. "I don't know why we do that," came the considered answer. "Maybe we just like shrimp salad."

Stockholm's better sausage stands, it seems, don't serve tunnbrödsrulle at all. At Östermalms Korvspecialist, for example, the woman behind the counter merely shook her head pityingly when

I inquired after them, as if to say, *Can't you read the sign? We're specialists.*

And at Günter's, I was advised to not even mention the tunnbrödsrulle. Like Ove, Günter is no longer among us, but under his successor, the cart is still widely considered the best in the city. The line was so long at lunchtime on a Wednesday that it took forty minutes just to order. Ahead and behind me were construction workers, office managers, bohemian types, soldiers in uniform, and executives in skinny suits. They were all men; in a line of sixty-plus people waiting to order, I was the only woman. It was a true sausage fest.

Behind me, a security guard named Mikkel said he had been coming to Günter's since he was a child. It was he who had warned me about asking for a tunnbrödsrulle; I should also refrain, he added, from requesting ketchup. "You've

heard of the Soup Nazi?" he said with a discreet nod toward the guy in the cart. "He's the Sausage Nazi."

At Günter's, Mikkel usually ordered the Romersk Wurst (Roman sausage), but he admitted to enjoying a good tunnbrödsrulle from time to time. "What times are those?" I inquired. "Drunk times," he replied. "Tunnbrödsrulle is really good when you're drunk."

I should have known. When they're not serving lunch to the male half of the workforce, hot dog stands throughout Scandinavia exist to meet the carb-and-fat requirements of the wasted. Perhaps, I reasoned, a tunnbrödsrulle can only be appreciated with enough alcohol coursing through one's bloodstream. I resolved to get drunk, in order to see if I might move the meter.

But a strange thing happened on the way to getting blitzed. I went to a bar,

and ordered a cocktail made with ginger and smoky bourbon. It was delicious. I ordered another, and it too was delicious. Everything was going according to plan. I was cultivating a nice buzz, and thought I might have one more drink, or maybe move on to the natural wine bar around the corner before seeking out my next wiener. But that second drink was so good. Too good, actually. It induced an existential crisis of sorts. *Why,* I asked myself, *isn't everything delicious?* Why do bad things happen to good hot dogs? Why is there tunnbrödsrulle? I felt deflated and then nauseated by the prospect of facing another shrimp-sausage-and-potato burrito. I couldn't bring myself to do it. I paid the bill and went back to my hotel in defeat.

If I ever hoped to understand or appreciate the tunnbrödsrulle, it wasn't going to happen here. I would have to eat it from the hand of the one chef in Sweden who might make it palatable.

Magnus Nilsson is the flowing-tressed chef of Fäviken, a sixteen-seat restaurant located on a hunting estate in north-western Sweden. There, he and his staff grow, preserve, hunt, fish, and butcher many of the ingredients they serve; the rest—with a few exceptions—come from nearby producers. His cooking is precise, even austere, but because his ingredients are so good and his touch so deft, it is also extraordinarily delicious. Dining at Fäviken is a crash course in the pleasures of purity.

Nilsson is not, in other words, the first person you would turn to for an encased emulsified meat product. But about two years ago, he rescued a small sausage factory that was about to go out of business, renovated it, hired a tiny staff, and got to work making charcuterie, and not just the precious, air-cured stuff that you slice thin and serve on an artfully chiseled piece of slate. At Undersåkers Charkuteriefabrik, they make black pudding, smoked ham, and *falukorv*—a fat red sausage that Swedes like to serve (in yet another display of questionable taste) with macaroni cooked in milk.

So it was only a small step to hot dogs. In truth, they were something Nilsson had long been interested in; he registered the name for a hot dog stand—Korvkiosk—more than a decade ago. "It's always been something I wanted to do," he says. "I just really like hot dogs."

Both the charcuterie facility and the hot dog stand, which he opened in the nearby ski town of Åre in December 2014, are intended to bring good, well-raised ingredients to a public far broader than the one that can afford to eat at Fäviken. Because sausages are so popular in Sweden, they seemed a great place to start. "It's an obvious thing to do because the bar is so low," Nilsson says. "Changing some of the most basic things makes it so much better."

I remained skeptical that changing ingredients could really make a tunn-brödsrulle better. It seemed to me like a concept immune to elevation. Nevertheless, I went to Korvkiosk. Nilsson's head chef, Jesper Karlsson was there, manning the counter. He welcomed me in, and carefully laid a piece of brown kraft paper on the counter with thoughtful solemnity.

The flatbread, made by hand by a woman from a neighboring village and, as Nilsson put it, "violently expensive," came first. Jesper heated it on a plancha, then laid it atop the paper. The potatoes, a local variety from a nearby farm, were mashed with near-Robuchonian quantities of butter, then piped hot onto the bread. The hot dog is Nilsson's own recipe—pork and beef, with enough potato and cream to hold it together and enough spices to keep it interesting. It's topped with artful squiggles of ketchup and whole-grain mustard. Nilsson endeavors for every fully assembled hot dog they serve to be at least half vegetable—not counting the potato—so next came crisp shredded carrots, thinly sliced kale, and quick pickled cucumbers, all laid neatly side by side. And then, on cue, came the shrimp salad. "But it's fifty percent shrimp," Nilsson assured me. "And no carrageenan. So it doesn't have that mucus texture."

It looked almost good, which was more than I could say for any previous tunnbrödsrulle. I took a bite. The bread was warm and nicely chewy. The sausage had a good little kick to it. The vegetables added freshness and crunch. The shrimp salad was properly creamy and tasted of shrimp. "Wait!" Karlsson said. "I almost forgot the chocolate milk."

This is the moment in the story where the God of Sausages might have parted the clouds and revealed Himself in all His glory, the moment when the mustard-coated scales fell from my eyes. I wanted to like Magnus's tunnbrödsrulle. I wanted to take that unlovable union of meat and bread and shellfish and potato, wash it down with the traditional chocolate milk, and embrace it as the glorious monument to human ingenuity that it is.

And I was so close: I could tell

beyond a doubt that Korvkiosk's tunnbrödsrulle was of a higher order than any other I had tried. It tasted of food—of pork and shrimp and bread and real potatoes. It seemed almost wholesome. It didn't make me gag.

"It's a mystery, but it works really well," suggested Magnus.

It was then that I remembered my previous trip to Fäviken. I had been there to write a story about Nilsson, and had spent a Saturday in the kitchen with him, watching him clean scallops that had been plucked hours earlier from icy Norwegian waters. I saw his mind turn as he came up with a dessert made from the last of the raspberries he had grown and picked and fermented in lactic acid the summer before, and I observed as he butchered a cow that had lived on grass and happiness for all of its long life. So I was surprised to see him, late in the afternoon, set out a bowl of the crappiest kinds of crap candy for his staff to eat, citing Swedish tradition. I was surprised again late that night after service, when he and his staff sat down to a meal of Coke and homemade pizza. Pizza, it should be said, made with ketchup for sauce.

So no, Nilsson's tunnbrödsrulle wasn't bad. Taken in the proper cultural context—one that included a habit of crap candy on Saturdays and ketchup-sauced pizza—it might even have been good. But Magnus could see in my reaction that there was still something ultimately unknowable to outsiders about the shrimp salad and hot dog combination.

"Yeah," he said resignedly. "It's weird."

AGAINST HOMEMADE KETCHUP

Chris Ying

There are plenty of good, sensible reasons to make your own sausage. Or your own bread, your own charcuterie, your own cheese. By all means, stockpile your homemade marmalade, kimchi, chicken soup, and chowchow. Though I don't love it, I understand the appeal of home brewing.

Do *not* make your own ketchup. This goes for home cooks, but I'm looking specifically at you, restaurants.

I do not want your homemade ketchup. Even if it's made from heirloom tomatoes you grew in your aquaponic garden. Even if it's seasoned with bamboo salt and aged in bourbon barrels. Especially if it's curry flavored.

It's not that homemade ketchup tastes *bad*, per se; it's just that it always, *always* tastes worse than the bottled stuff.

Listen, if you have some kind of moral or nutritional objection to processed foods and don't want to serve store-bought products, fine. I assume you concede that your ketchup is worse than Henry John Heinz's. But if you're

masquerading your own ketchup as a *better* alternative, you're all 57 varieties of wrong.

Let's give up on the notion that you'll ever match the texture achieved by corporate food scientists. I have never encountered a noncommercial ketchup that had the same shiny-smooth gleam or cling-to-the-bottle, french-fry-coating viscosity as Heinz.

As for the taste of homemade ketchup, what are you trying to achieve exactly? You can't improve ketchup. It's an impeccable condiment—perfectly tart, sweet enough, deeply umami. Sure, you can do any number of things to change ketchup, but what's the point? You think the Mona Lisa could use a little rouge?

Lest you think I'm in the pocket of Big Ketchup, let me also register my strong objection to any commercial attempts to improve ketchup, too. If I want sriracha or balsamic vinegar on my fries, I'll do it myself.

Everybody stop fucking with my ketchup.

AFRiCA

From the origins of merguez to a sausage found in the tombs of ancient Egypt, African sausage varieties—while not exactly plentiful—are diverse and delicious.

Boerewors

WHERE: South Africa
MEAT: beef and pork
PREPARATION: grilled
SERVED: as is

In Afrikaans-inflected parts of southern Africa, people don't grill or barbecue, they *braai*. In South Africa in particular, grilling beef, pork, chicken, and game (springbok, kudu) over charcoal is a class-defying ritual that one finds in the ritzy, Napa Valley-esque wine wards as well as in the country's densely populated townships.

In Umlazi township, southwest of Durban, residential buildings are mixed in with—and often indistinguishable from—commercial ones. Behind brick walls and swinging metal gates are hidden thatch-roofed bars serving Castle lager and Savanna cider. And around winding roads studded with shipping containers converted into tuck shops, and homes of all sizes and styles, one might stumble across the odd parking lot in front of a large wooden porch covered in beer-branded umbrellas.

At the back of the porch will be a butcher counter, stocked with thinly sliced meats on the bone, poultry legs, and thick coils of unlinked sausage: *boerewors*.

Boerewors is a compound of the Afrikaans words *boer* (farmer) and *wors* (sausage), and hews close to its rustic descriptor. It's ground coarsely, plenty pork-fatty, and seasoned with salt and a few warm spices. Ask for a length of sausage, along with whatever other meats tickle your fancy, and the butcher will pile them onto a tray. Before a cook comes in to take your meat tray (without taking your name), he will season the boerewors the same way he seasons everything else—that is, haphazardly, with braai seasoning. Braai seasoning doesn't taste distinctively of any one spice, save for salt, but has a cumulative flavor that South Africans recognize as braai.

The grill man cooks all the meat well done over a grill on blocks. When your meat's ready, he'll find you on the patio, and bestow you with a cutting board stacked with the now-browned and glistening cuts of meat you selected. You'll elect to start with the sausage, trust me, piercing the casing with a satisfying snap and snarfing down a piece before the juices run out for someone else to sop up with a piece of bread. **—CHRIS YING**

Gatsby Sandwich

This is a clear-out-the-fridge concoction. As the story goes, when the owner of a suburban Cape Town fish-and-chips shop ran out of fish one day in the mid-1970s, he threw together a slapdash sandwich of whatever he could find for the queue of hungry workers: fried bologna (an extra-pink South African version known as "polony"), french fries, and achar (Indian-style pickles), all stuffed into a round Portuguese roll. How the sandwich acquired its name is one of the more tenuous and less comprehensible literary allusions. Evidently, the 1974 movie (starring Robert Redford as the eponymous antihero) had played recently at a local cinema, and the word Gatsby had caught on as local slang for "great." One of the workers declared the concoction a "Gatsby smash" and the sandwich was thus inextricably tied to the legacy of F. Scott Fitzgerald. Other shops in the Cape Flats area have expanded on the idea, with some offering upwards of thirty variations. Today, Gatsbys are generally

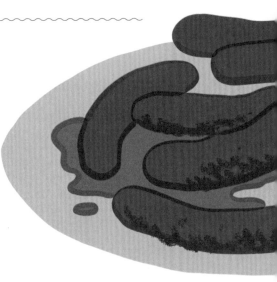

Moroccan Market Merguez

WHERE: Morocco
MEAT: lamb or beef
PREPARATION: grilled
SERVED: as is or stuffed in a roll, with harissa

Jemaa el Fna, the main market square of the old city in Marrakech, changes character gradually throughout the day: The morning and afternoon feature orange juice stalls, hawkers of plants and cacti, dried fruit and nut vendors, musicians in traditional garb, dudes with monkeys on chains, and snake charmers who will put a snake around your neck and refuse to take it off until you pay them (it's all in good fun, sort of). As the sun goes down, the square truly comes to life. Storytellers and singers replace the day's earlier entertainment; the locals, having sensed that most of the tourists have gone, begin to sold in long, baguette-like rolls for easier sharing.

WHERE: Cape Town, South Africa
MEAT: polony, traditionally
PREPARATION: various ways
SERVED: with fries in sauce

Mirqaz
(a.k.a. Merguez)

This lamb (and/or beef) sausage from the Berber communities of North Africa is usually spiced with sumac, cumin, aniseed, and harissa (which gives it a ruddy color), though fancier versions may contain preserved lemon or even crushed rose petals. *Mirqaz* can be eaten fresh, or sun-dried, fried, then stored in earthenware jugs of olive oil. The sausage pops up in tagines and couscous-based dishes throughout the Maghreb, and heavy emigration has taken it to France and beyond. You'll likely know it as merguez, the Frenchi-fied transliteration. In just about every Parisian quartier (more specifically

promenade and fill the square, while steam rises from dozens of food stalls that seem to have magi-cally popped up out of nowhere.

Enter the maze of stalls and you'll find kebabs of all kinds (except pork), fried fish, mussels, sheep's head, as well as various teas and soups. Find the busiest stall and take a seat, ignoring the pleas and supplications of the young men who work at less popular operations, each extremely persistent in trying to get your business. For thirty dirhams, about $3, order a plate of merguez, a spicy lamb sausage seasoned with paprika, fen-nel, and cumin (see a version from Mourad Lahlou, the Moroccan-American chef of Aziza in San Francisco, on page 184). A plate will have maybe ten sausages, each one the size of a fat finger, and will be served with *khobz,* the round, grainy Moroccan white bread. (Alternatively, you can have the sau-sages stuffed into the khobz and served as a sandwich.) Either way, you'll be drowning the greasy little suckers in spicy harissa and tomato sauce. When the sausages are gone, pick up the rest of your bread with your right hand (the left hand is reserved for less savory activities) and sop up any remaining grease and sauce. Or just order another round. **—LUCAS PETERSON**

Montmartre and the Marais) you can find carts peddling *merguez frites*: demi-baguettes split and stuffed with grill-blackened sausages, french fries, and a smear of mustard or fiery red harissa. That towering mess is the true street food of Paris.

WHERE: North Africa; France; almost everywhere, really (see also Moroccan Market Merguez, page 68)
MEAT: lamb, beef, or a combination
PREPARATION: grilled; or dried, fried, and stored in oil
SERVED: with couscous; in a tagine; or layered with fries in a spicy sandwich

Mombar Mahshy

A length of beef intestine stuffed with rice, cardamom, parsley, and mastic (the hardened resin of the mastic tree, which, when powderized, acts as a binding agent). Egyptians have been making and eating some version of *mombar mahshy* for something like five thousand years (there are reports of mombar mahshy remnants being found in ancient Egyptian tombs). Mombar has no defined shape or length; you'll see long, horseshoe-looking ones just as often as little, lumpy, almost meatball-looking versions. Traditional mombar mahshy has no meat inside, just rice, but in the relatively recent past, people have begun adding a mixture of beef and lamb. In the U.S. you're more likely to find the meatery version than its vegetarianish progenitor.

WHERE: Egypt
MEAT: traditionally none (just rice and spice), but can include beef and lamb

PREPARATION: grilled
SERVED: with lettuce and parsley, alongside larger meals

Mutura

Sometimes referred to as the "African sausage," *mutura* could technically be grouped under the banner of blood sausage, but it's really more of a home for whatever unwanted bits are around. It originates from celebrations where a whole animal (usually a goat) would be butchered. Scraps of meat, along with lungs, kidneys, and other organs are chopped fine and stuffed into the animal's intestines along with a bit of salted blood. The whole thing is boiled, then grilled until snappy. Served sliced or in a roll with *kachumbari*—a diced tomato and onion salsa—the sausage has since spread to the streets, becoming the preferred cheap protein source for Mombasa's residents.

WHERE: Kenya
MEAT: goat or cow (blood sausage)
PREPARATION: grilled
SERVED: sliced

Nigerian Sausage Roll

The next time you're stuck in a Lagos traffic jam and feeling peckish, roll down the window, and flag down a sausage-roll hawker (the guy darting between cars yelling "Gala! Gala! Gala!"). He's not inviting you to a black-tie reception, but rather selling one of Nigeria's favorite handheld snacks: minced beef seasoned with bouillon powder and baked in a pastry wrapper. Gala is the name of the country's most popular brand of packaged rolls, and has become a misnomer for the rolls themselves. At about twenty-five cents each, they're very economical, which is good because you'll have plenty of time to scarf a few in this gridlock. MOVE, dammit!

WHERE: Nigeria
MEAT: beef
PREPARATION: baked
SERVED: by itself as a snack

Osban

Osban (or *asban* or *usban*) is like a Muslim cross between haggis (page 24) and andouillette (page 13): a sausage designed to utilize just about every bit of the body of the lamb from which the majority of its filling is derived. Save for the animal's blood, which is *haram* (forbidden) in Islam, basically the whole animal is used. Stuffed in the sheep or lamb intestine, you're likely to find, in no particular order, pieces of heart, liver, kidney, spleen, tongue, and *liyya* (lamb fat), seasoned with parsley, mint, cilantro, and chili. Rounding out the stuffing is a grain, which can include rice, barley, couscous, and sometimes coarse bulgur. Osban's shape varies. The sausages can be short and thick, or forearm length and skinny, unless of course the particular osban you're eating is the sort that's been stuffed in a piece of reticulum—one of the chambers of the stomach of a cud-chewing animal—in which case your osban looks like a flabby softball. Osban's origin can be traced back to Libya and Tunisia, where it's typically served with couscous or rice, chickpeas, and pickled vegetables.

WHERE: Libya and Tunisia
MEAT: lamb offal
PREPARATION: poached
SERVED: with couscous, chickpeas, rice, pickles

ASiA

On one end of the Asian sausage spectrum are dazzling feats of whole-animal usage. On the other, an almost religious devotion to American-style hot dogs.

Cha Lua

Cha lua is the springy, off-white "Vietnamese ham" found on your standard banh mi. Very lean pork is pounded with potato starch, garlic, fish sauce, and baking powder until paste-like, then wrapped in banana leaves and boiled. It's popular year-round but particularly associated with Tet (Vietnamese New Year), when it graces altars throughout the country in honor of deceased relatives.

Variations include:

- *cha bi*—cha lua with shredded pork skin (steamed)
- *cha Hue*—cha lua with extra garlic and whole black peppercorns (boiled)
- *cha chien*—cha lua without the banana leaf (deep-fried)
- *cha que*—cha lua with a ton of powdered cinnamon (deep-fried)

WHERE: Vietnam
MEAT: pork
PREPARATION: boiled in a banana leaf
SERVED: in banh mi and many other dishes

Da Chang Bao Xiao Chang

The name of this sausage is a complete, grammatical sentence in Mandarin, though one you won't likely find in your phrase book: "A big intestine wraps around a small intestine." The "small intestine" (*xiao chang*) here refers to a simple grilled pork sausage, and the "big intestine" (*da chang*) to a larger sticky rice–filled sausage that bear-hugs the smaller sausage. (The barnyard funk that usually accompanies large intestines is present and accounted for.) Condiment options might include everything from simple soy sauce and wasabi to pickled mustard greens and peanut powder. This greasy treat is often enjoyed at Taiwan's night markets (try Shilin or Fengjia for the most options). Just don't get caught in the crossfire: The competition is notoriously fierce among *da chang bao xiao chang* vendors, and some stalls are outfitted with scathing signs and looped videos accusing neighboring stands of criminal acts.

WHERE: Taiwan
MEAT: pork
PREPARATION: grilled
SERVED: nestled in a larger sticky-rice "sausage," served with various condiments

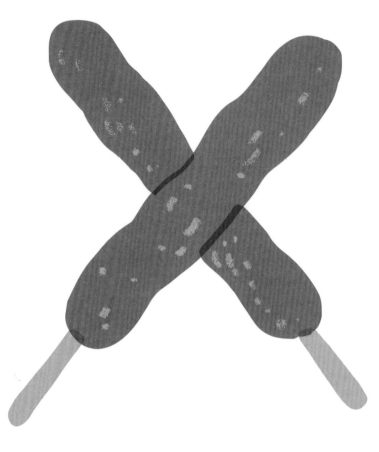

Arabiki Sausages

WHERE: Japan
MEAT: pork in sheep or pork casings
PREPARATION: smoked, then griddled or boiled
SERVED: with hot mustard

The sausages you find in Japan aren't as varied as they are in, say, New York, where you can get any kind of sausage from any part of the world. For much of the twentieth century the predominant Japanese sausage was a fish sausage called *gyo-niku* (*gyo* means "fish," *niku* means "meat"). Then, in the late seventies, companies started making Vienna sausages—the little ones in the cans—and they became popular. Really, really popular.

German-style sausages first arrived in Japan, as I understand it, via German soldiers who were captured after or around World War I and were compelled to divulge their wurst secrets. Germany is still the guiding star toward which all Japanese sausages tend to veer. In the eighties, a manufacturer introduced "Schau Essen" (translating to something like "show food") pork sausages: stubby smoked sausages in natural casings (something relatively new to Japanese diners, who were used to synthetic casings dyed bright red). Schau essen–type sausages have been the archetypal and ubiquitous Japanese sausage ever since.

Schau essen have a great snap when griddled and a juicy pop when boiled—they're served both ways. When you order them at a bar or *izakaya,* the cooks might score the sausage, skewer it, and cook it until the scored skin is blackened and crisp, but the sausage will still be juicy inside. They're known commonly as *arabiki* sausages in Japan, a term that refers to the coarseness of the grind (and that is also applied to coffee). They have a good amount of fat in them, too, so when you bite into them, they practically squirt their juices.

There are a number of different brands of arabiki sausages. Nippon Ham is one of the biggest pork producers in Japan and makes schau essen, but there are a lot of artisanal sausages as well. Down in Tokyo's department-store basement markets (*depachika*), you'll find sections where you can choose from a hundred different varieties. The size of the sausage varies, although they're usually about three inches long and maybe a little thicker than your average hot dog; but I used to buy a brand at my local supermarket called Ganko Oyaji (which means "stubborn old man") and those were pretty long. This past summer, my family ate Nippon Ham sausages for breakfast almost every morning—my six-year-old would walk three or four blocks from our house in Tokyo to a convenience store by himself with a handful of money to pick up his bag of schau essen sausages. I was so proud.

For me, sausage is a cook-at-home food, but there are actually a lot of pseudo-German beer halls in Japan where you can get your fix. I visited Kirin City, a restaurant in Osaka run by the Kirin Brewery. I was nervous that it was going to be cheesy, but it's a favorite haunt of my friend Shimazaki-san (of the Rock and Roll One ramen shop, who makes one of the best bowls of chicken *shio* in Japan), so we gave it a shot. And it was great. We ordered this platter of sausages—chorizo, weißwurst, Lyonnaise sausage, and a few others—and they were all so outstanding. We couldn't stop eating.

Perhaps we're seeing the first cracks in the schau-essen hegemony. All I know is that for as much Japanese sausage as I've eaten, which feels like a lot, it's still just the tip of what there is to eat and learn about. **–IVAN ORKIN**

Embutido

One side effect of the American occupation of the Philippines in the early twentieth century was the arrival of new ingredients for Pinoy cooks to play with, among them: canned smoked ham, Vienna sausages, cheddar cheese, and sweet pickle relish. Like the Planeteers, when these novelties combine their powers with those of ground pork, peppers, raisins, and hard-boiled eggs, they create the Captain Planet of forcemeats: *embutido*. Embutido is great steamed or baked, right out of the oven, brushed with banana ketchup. It's even better at Mission Chinese Food in New York, where chef Angela Dimayuga stuffs it inside of a chicken and roasts it to create a dish her Filipino grandmother taught her, known as *relleno manok*.

WHERE: Philippines
MEAT: pork, canned ham, and Vienna sausages
PREPARATION: steamed or baked in a loaf
SERVED: hot with banana ketchup; in (cold) slices on a sandwich

Gamja Dog

This entry comes in the form of a letter from one of our readers and loyal sausage acolytes.

Dear Sausage Boss,

The light tap-tap of poppy seeds falling from my hot dog bun onto the paper wrapper below and the ketchup dispenser's flatulence are the soundtrack to an indelible, edible pastime. There I was, naively eating a hot dog and fries separately, taking the time to dip each fry into a small paper thimble.

The "Gamja (potato) Dog" is a practical, portable homage to the American classic, and it raised some questions. Why had I wasted all that time and effort eating them separately? Does gravity work differently in Seoul? Sadly, I did not sample the Gamja Dog, so I can only infer that encased meat was encased in the fries.

Yours,
Matt Cohn

WHERE: South Korea
MEAT: standard-issue hot dogs
PREPARED: entombed in french fries, deep-fried
SERVED WITH: ketchup or hot sauce

Goan Chouriço

Cuisine in Goa, India's smallest and wealthiest state, has a markedly Portuguese accent—the result of nearly five hundred years of colonial occupation. Consider the Goan chouriço: a fatty pork sausage heavily spiced with cumin, cloves, cinnamon, and fiery dried chilies. The mixture is flavored with coconut-sap vinegar, cured briefly with saltpeter, then stuffed into pork casings and smoked over burning grass. Often the meat is strung into beads: The locals call these rosary sausages. The chouriço is usually dried in the sun for several months before finding its way into a crusty *pão* (Goan bread) or dishes like *pulao* (rice pilaf).

WHERE: India, particularly the state of Goa
MEAT: pork
PREPARATION: cured, smoked, dried
SERVED: on bread or with rice

Kazak Pigs in a Blanket

WHERE: Russia, Ukraine, and elsewhere
MEAT: mostly pork, but sometimes mixed with beef or chicken
PREPARATION: microwaved
SERVED: in wax paper or a repurposed milk carton

The sheer prevalence of the *sosiska v testye*—"sausage in dough," or, in an unfortunate homonymic mistranslation spotted in at least one international airport, "hot dog inside your father-in-law"—makes it the go-to to-go sausage for Russians.

The hot dog is tucked into a yeast-risen dough or into a laminated pastry, covered in an egg wash and sesame seeds—or not. The sosiska v testye is sold at *stolovaya* (cafeterias) and snack stands in the passages underneath wide boulevards and in phone booth–like kiosks on the street—and at a surprising number of newsstands.

All kinds of accidents can occur during the consumption of the sosiska v testye. The dough acts as a koozie for the meat mass, a convenient carrying case on the go—this is a good thing. But, as we know, microwaves work by heating up liquids, and the liquids inside hot dogs and dough are heat-conducive oils and fats. A layered pastry dough freshly removed from the microwave may surprise the holder with its temperature, inducing a squeeze reaction. The layers could collapse under the weight of one's grip, leading to a squished, disappointed sausage, and a burned, greasy hand. Upon the heat-induced squeezing action, the sausage may go flying out of the sausage hole the way slippery soap squirms loose around a shower. This disaster can be curbed with the use of little wax paper bags, or by serving sosiska v testye inside a used, cleaned, trimmed milk carton.

The restaurant chain Стардог!s (Stardog!s) website recommends "eating the sosiska v testye on the go, sitting in car: and don't be afraid to get your clothes dirty! Without question: our most convenient hot dog." No disagreement here.

—HARRY LEEDS

Hong Chang

This specialty of Harbin in Heilong-jiang Province came to being when the Trans-Siberian Railway brought a taste for Eastern European flavors to northern China. Since the early twentieth century, this garlicky smoked pork sausage has been manufactured in and around the city. It resembles kielbasa more than the shriveled candlestick one thinks of when they think of Chinese sausage. It's traditionally eaten with *khleb*, a chewy Russian bread.

WHERE: northeast China
MEAT: pork
PREPARATION: cured and smoked
SERVED: with khleb (Russian bread)

Kanom Tokyo

Kanom Tokyo refers to small, crepe-like pancakes that have popped up on Thai streets over the past two decades. Cooked on a griddle, stuffed, rolled, and piled high to attract customers, they often trend sweet—*sangkhaya* (coconut cream) and *sai pueak* (taro paste) are particularly popular as fillings—but can also switch-hit as savory. You'll find the same slightly sweet crepes spread with chili sauce and wrapped around cocktail wieners, like a Thai pig in a blanket. According to Thai chef Kris Yenbamroong of Night+Market in L.A., there's also version called the "phiset," which means "special"—a larger crepe with crumbled sausage and egg beaten into it, topped with Maggi and a liberal hit of white pepper.

WHERE: Thailand
MEAT: pork cocktail wieners
PREPARATION: boiled, then swaddled in a griddled crepe
SERVED: with chili sauce

Khao Pad American

Khao pad american (literally "American fried rice") sounds at first like a parody dish: fried rice sweetened with ketchup, raisins, and sugar, and then topped with a meat lover's mixed bag of chicken, ham, eggs—all fried in butter—and deep-fried hot dog "blossoms" (see the recipe for Wiener Blossoms, page 205). But the concoction isn't satire; it originated with the U.S. armed forces stationed in Thailand during the Vietnam War, when Thai cooks kindly cobbled together a dish of all the things our homesick boys longed for on one plate. Almost half a century later, khao pad american is still popular, especially with young, drunk people (it's often offered in university cafeterias).

WHERE: Thailand
MEAT: American-style hot dogs (beef, pork, and mechanically separated poultry)
PREPARATION: notched with an X at each end, so they "blossom" when fried
SERVED: with very sweet fried rice, fried chicken, ham, and a fried egg

Lap Cheong

The catchall term *lap cheong* covers a wide array of Chinese sausages—both fresh and cooked—but most commonly refers to the wrinkled, waxy, crimson, hard sausages you may have seen diced in dim sum dishes or sliced into coins and tossed in fried rice. A trip to a well-stocked Asian grocery store will reveal a wide selection, including versions made with beef, chicken, duck, liver (duck or pork), and blood. The meat in lap cheong is coarsely diced, marbled with white flecks of fat, and seasoned with Chinese rose wine, which gives it its signature candy-like sweetness. These sausages are flavor bombs, and lend themselves well to seasoning other dishes. In fact, if you've seen it anywhere, you've likely seen lap cheong cooked, as the drying and smoking process leaves them too tough to eat in their natural state. Thus, although lap cheong should probably be filed under salumi—a subject this book dares not broach for fear of the size of the can of worms it would open—their desire to be cooked allows them safe harbor in this collection.

WHERE: southern China
MEAT: usually pork, but also beef, poultry, seafood, blood, and liver
PREPARATION: cured, air-dried, and smoked
SERVED: by itself or in innumerable Chinese dishes

Longganisa

Longganisa came to the Philippines by way of Spanish ships in the 1500s. The Spanish planted *longaniza* (their traditional pork sausage with garlic and cumin and paprika) in Filipino soil, and it grew into longganisa, a family of sausage with dozens of variations, some almost unrecognizable to the original.

Longganisa can be encased and short-looking like ape thumbs, or skinless in loose patties. It can be smoked, or it can be dried. And longganisa can be made of pork, but it can also be made of chicken or beef or even tuna. But, while a longganisa's exact ingredients may vary from region to region, they generally fall into one of two categories: salty (*de recado*) and sweet (*hamonado*). In the city of Guinobatan, the longganisa can be especially thin; the ones from Guagua tend to be saltier and made with more vinegar; the ones in Lucban, heavy on garlic and oregano; Alaminos's longganisa are secured at either end with a toothpick; Vigan's is like Lucban's, but stubbier. At one point in time you could get a longganisa breakfast burger at McDonald's, with rice formed into patties acting as buns, and egg (classic McMuffin disc style). Basically, there's no wrong way to make longganisa.

WHERE: Philippines
MEAT: pork or chicken or beef or fish (like tuna)
PREPARED: smoked, cured, grilled, poached
SERVED: with eggs and rice, and pickled things; sometimes chopped up and added to *pancit* (stir-fried noodles)

Makanek

These fat, thumb-shaped Lebanese lamb sausages are redolent of clove, cinnamon, and nutmeg. (In Christian pockets of Lebanon, you might also find versions made with *haram* ingredients like pork and red wine.) "One of the most important ingredients," says Joseph Abboud, chef of Rumi in Melbourne, "is a type of lamb tail fat, which comes from a particular breed of sheep that has fat tails." Restaurants and home cooks serve *maka-nek* as part of a larger spread of dishes. After grilling or pan-frying, they're often squirted with lemon juice and drenched in a healthy glug of *debs el remmen* (pomegranate molasses). Otherwise, they can be found quickly stewed with tomato or bundled into a sandwich with tomato and pickles.

WHERE: Lebanon
MEAT: lamb, beef, or a combination (and, rarely, pork)
PREPARATION: grilled or pan-fried
SERVED: with lemon juice and pomegranate molasses; as a sandwich; or stewed with tomato

Mum

WHERE: northern Thailand
MEAT: beef and beef offal
PREPARATION: stuffed (sometimes in gall-bladders) with beef and rice, and sun-dried
SERVED: raw, grilled, or fried, with garlic and chilies

On any road trip through Isan, the vast region of Thailand bordering Laos and Cambodia, long vertical rows of sausage hanging from simple roadside frames are a common sight. Most of these are *sai krok isan* (see recipe, page 193)— sausages that are universally popular throughout Thailand.

But every once in a while, in my early years traveling in the northeast, I'd

spot larger, heavier, deep red-brown balls among the lighter hued sai krok: *mum* (or sometimes *mam*). I never saw them anywhere outside Isan, and in fact even there it seemed that mum territory was confined to Chaiyaphum, Khon Kaen, and Kalasin provinces.

The relative rarity of this sausage piqued my interest, so when a northeastern Thai acquaintance in Chiang Mai mentioned that she knew a couple who made mum at Khamthiang Market, I persuaded her to take me to meet them.

Wijit Sikaew and her husband run a rustic Isan eatery in the market called Somtam Kalasin, which consists of little more than some wood poles supporting a grass-and-palm-thatched roof over a dirt floor. A couple of charcoal pots and a worktable in a back corner make up the kitchen. Wijit led me over to a large bucket covered with a well-worn white cloth and pulled the cloth aside to reveal a mess of raw chopped meat. She gestured for me to have a taste.

I grabbed a pinch, rolled it in my fingers, sniffed it, and gingerly placed it in my mouth. First, a sturdy wave of tartness followed by savory fresh beef tones and a slight iron finish. Wijit explained that the addition of beef liver accounts for the iron flavor as well as the deep red color.

Wijit listed her recipe for me: eight kilos of hand-chopped beef and a kilo of liver, a half kilo of *khao khua* (toasted sticky rice, pounded to a coarse powder), a plate of cooked white rice, salt, and MSG. She lets the mixture age for a day, then squeezes out excess moisture before stuffing it into casings: cow bladders for larger ball sausages, intestines for smaller links.

Once the links are stuffed, she hangs them in the sun for five or six days, to let the contents dry and ferment. Even after one day in the sun, the beef will be noticeably sour.

Some of Wijit's clientele eat the links raw, but most order them either grilled or fried. I tried a fat grilled link, and was blown away by how different it was from the Thai sausages I know. Mum is dry, almost like a crumbly salami, with none of the fat globules or oiliness commonly found in Thai pork sausages.

Over years of speaking to Isan cooks, I've found there are as many homegrown mum recipes as there are mum makers. Many add garlic to the mix. Others incorporate spleen into the filling, or stuff the sausage in gallbladders to up the funk factor. Some refuse to add rice, which speeds up the fermentation, but, according to them, dilutes the richness of the beef. Some mum experts swear by a careful regimen of three days of sun-drying followed by two days in the shade, which they claim yields the perfect level of acidity and prevents excessive drying.

If you manage to find it, remember that, as with sai krok isan, there's a prescribed way of eating mum: always with chunks of fresh garlic and whole bird's eye chilies. Some northeasterners also like to spice it up further with fresh young ginger slices. Just look around and do as the locals do.

—JOE CUMMINGS

Ngoh Hiang

WHERE: Singapore, Malaysia, Indonesia
MEAT: pork (and sometimes shrimp)
PREPARATION: fried
SERVED: with vermicelli for breakfast, or with meat sauce for dipping as a snack

***Ngoh hiang* (five spice) is a roll of minced pork** that's been seasoned with five-spice powder, wrapped in bean-curd skin, and deep-fried. Its roots are in Teochew and Hokkien dialect groups, and it's now popular in Singapore, Malaysia, and some parts of Indonesia. Back in the day in Singapore, ngoh hiang was popular during street *wayang* (theater) festivals, but today it's mostly restricted to hawker centers. It's often served alongside a selection of other fritters with *bee hoon* (rice vermicelli) as breakfast, or just as a teatime nibble with a side of gooey meat sauce and hot pink chili sauce.

People in Singapore don't really associate hawker centers with getting drunk, so ngoh hiang isn't exactly a drinking sausage, but I do love eating it with beer. I also like it when the vendors first chop the roll into coins before deep-frying, so it's crisp on all sides. The only thing is, the filling needs to be able to stand up to the frying. It should have plenty of fat so it stays juicy, and enough five-spice powder so that it's robust and fragrant.

Otherwise, there are a great many different ways to remix ngoh hiang. Xin Dong Fang on Old Airport Road sells ngoh hiang exclusively, nothing else, and makes the sausage by hand, adding distinctive little bits of crunchy water chestnut to the mix. Lao Zhong Zhong Five Spice does a classic Teochew-style ngoh hiang. Mashed yam is folded into the sausage, giving it a subtle sweetness. And they're open till eleven at night—late by Singapore standards—which means you can do some drinking before your ngoh hiang after all. **—TRIS MARLIS**

Opka Hesip

WHERE: Xinjiang, China
MEAT: lamb offal (and rice)
PREPARATION: boiled
SERVED: with chunks of stuffed sheep's lung and steaming stock

In the old Silk Road city of Kashgar, street vendors stack long, pale sausages, one on top of another, to build curved walls of meat, held in place by wooden skewers and perched on top of great flabby lobes of sheep's lungs. Some skewer sheep's hearts along the wall in an artistic flourish. When a passerby places an order, the vendors chop a length of sausage and a few pieces of yellow lung into a bowl and souse them in stock from a simmering pot.

Opka hesip—stuffed lung and sausage—is a favorite snack of the Uyghur people, the Turkic Muslims who inhabit the Xinjiang region in the far northwest of China. The lung-and-sausage vendors can be found in the backstreets and night markets of the old city, scattered among sellers of pigeon soup and sheep's heads, of cumin-scented kebabs and steaming dumplings. They make their sausage by stuffing a sheep's intestines with its chopped heart, liver, and fat, bulked out by rice and seasoned with chopped onion, salt, dried chilies, and cumin, boiling it until cooked. It's something like a Uyghur haggis, with its mix of grain and offal, galvanized by spices, but with a milder flavor than its Scottish cousin.

The sausage's twin sister, stuffed lung, is made by a process that resembles a surrealist installation. A pair of glistening fresh lungs is hung on a wall by its windpipe. Improbable quantities of a thin batter made from wheat starch, oil, egg, and salt are then funneled into the windpipe, until the lungs, hissing gently, swell to grotesque proportions. At this point, the windpipe is stoppered with a plug of wheat gluten, and the lungs are hurled into a vat of boiling water to be cooked.

Cooked, the sausages are pleasantly piquant, the lung a strange hybrid of savory custard and offal that appeals, surprisingly, to those who like English puddings.

—**FUCHSIA DUNLOP**

Sai Krok Isan

WHERE: throughout Thailand
MEAT: pork
PREPARATION: grilled
SERVED: with an assortment of fresh chilies, cabbage, and
  herbs

Like New Orleans, the northeastern chunk of Thailand
bordering Laos and Cambodia is famous for music and
cuisine that stand in stark contrast to the rest of the country.
Molam bands pump out raucous melodies and fiery rhythms
that rival those of zydeco. Bangkok's Korean-copy boy bands
don't cut it here and neither does the comparatively tame
central Thai cuisine of green curries and pad thai.

The cooking of Isan (what most Thais call the northeast)
revels in a grand display of fresh herbs, fresh chilies, and a
stinging tang that comes not only from the liberal use of lime
and mint in such classic northeastern dishes as *somtam* and
larb but also from the fermentation of meat and fish.

While Isan dishes are popular throughout the country,
perhaps none is as ubiquitous as *sai krok isan* (Isan sausage),
which achieves its brilliantly sour and deeply savory flavor
from a few days of natural fermentation at room temperature.
Also known as *sai krok priaw* (sour sausage), the links are
stuffed with pork and rice and usually twisted into tidy round
balls, although they may also be given a slightly elongated
shape, or, much less frequently, formed into coils like the sai
ua (page 88) of Chiang Mai.

Recipes vary throughout the region. The ratio of pork to
sticky rice, particularly, changes from cook to cook. Although
purists abhor it, some sausage makers substitute bean thread
noodles for sticky rice. The addition of *pla ra*—a pungently
aromatic sauce made from freshwater fish, rice husks, and
dried chili flakes—makes for an even stronger-flavored
sausage.

As you travel through the Isan countryside, look for
strands of sausage dangling like beaded curtains from clotheslines along the side of the road, drying and fermenting in the
open air. Smoke rising from grills off to the side will lead you
to al fresco dining areas where you can sample the little flavor
bombs. Fresh off the grill, the glistening sausages are served

along with stacks of raw cabbage, roasted peanuts, whole bird chilies, sliced garlic, and cilantro. The prescribed routine is to wrap a little bit of everything in one of the leaves and stuff the whole thing into your mouth. The best sai krok isan have a pleasant, lasting tang and a slightly creamy texture derived from the fermented sticky rice and pork fat. Grilling adds a layer of smoke, and the fresh accompaniments supply crunch and heat. (In restaurants that serve them, the sausages will often be halved and fried, rather than grilled, and served with the same range of accompaniments.)

Sometimes you might encounter a simpler accessory plate of just whole bird chilies and garlic. In this case, shove a bird chili, pointy end first, into the sausage, and then place a slice of garlic into the hole made by the chili. Pop the whole thing into your mouth and wait for the multiple explosions. **—JOE CUMMINGS**

Naem

If we had to guess at *naem*'s origin story, it'd go something like this: Cook accidentally leaves raw pork out for days at room temperature, comes back, eats it, doesn't die. Thus, naem. Naem is, if you haven't deduced, raw pork allowed to ferment at room temperature for about five days. Lean pork is blended with skin, garlic, bird's eye chilies, sticky rice, salt, and sugar, then wrapped in banana leaves or plastic and left alone for bacteria to do their work fermenting the sausage and producing mouth-puckering lactic acid. Naem is frequently eaten raw, sliced straight off the pale-pink log, with shallots, chilies, ginger, and peanuts, or in salads. But it can also be found fried, grilled, or stir-fried with eggs or rice.

WHERE: Thailand
MEAT: pork
PREPARATION: stuffed in banana leaves and fermented
SERVED: raw or cooked and incorporated into various dishes

Thai Hot Dogs

WHERE: Thailand
MEAT: American-style hot dogs (beef, pork, and mechanically separated poultry)
PREPARATION: griddled, boiled, stir-fried, baked, or deep-fried
SERVED: in khao pad American (page 78), kanom Tokyo (page 78), or Waffle Hot Dogs (page 204)

When Krispy Kreme opened its first branch in a swanky Bangkok mall a couple of years ago, it had to install cordons to keep the hour-long lines from turning ugly. The same sort of ropes now keep the crowds back at the Garrett outlet in Bangkok, which dispenses flavored popcorn all the way from the Windy City. That Thais love good food is a well-documented fact, but that they love sugary, salty, greasy, processed junk food is their dirty little secret.

While star chefs and ambassadors of Thai cuisine wax poetic about things like the terroir of coastal salt marshes in Samut Songkhram and the pleasures of artisanal dried tofu sheets and candied bael fruit, they tend to thumb their noses at the lowbrow stuff

Nem Nuong

This fatty, skewered, uncased pork sausage, a specialty of the Khanh Hoa province along the south-central coast of Vietnam, is a marriage of recognizable Southeast Asian ingredients (shallot, garlic, star anise, roasted-rice powder) and unexpected additions (red food coloring and Alsa, a specific French brand of single-acting baking powder). The mixture is shaped by hand, either into tightly packed logs or meatballs, then skewered (sometimes on lemongrass stalks) and grilled. The texture of *nem nuong* can be dense almost to the point of squeakiness, and the color can range from breakfast-sausage brown to grilled-SPAM bronze. Nem nuong is often found atop bowls of rice or vermicelli, but it's probably best enjoyed wrapped up with herbs and other accessories in rice paper (*goi cuon*), with a side dish of liver dipping sauce. (See the recipe for nem nuong on page 227.)

WHERE: Vietnam
MEAT: pork
PREPARATION: skewered and grilled
SERVED: wrapped in rice paper with dipping sauce, or in various rice- or noodle-based dishes

that proliferates in Bangkok's alleyways. Look closely at any street-food market, and you'll see bricks of instant ramen to be served in soups or flash-boiled and tossed into mixed salads; thick-cut fluffy white bread as a vehicle for margarine and jam; sticky puddles of condensed milk; and most prominent of all, hot dogs, whole, sliced, or diced, and more often than not deep-fried.

On any given day, my local supermarket bakery weaves hot dogs into puff pastry and bread dough in no fewer than a dozen lurid combinations. (Nori-holy-basil-sausage bun, anybody? Or how about a soft roll wrapped around a frankfurter and topped with Chinese dried pork floss, cheese, and mayonnaise?) Hot dogs are everywhere, dipped in waffle batter and griddled on a stick, or lined up end-to-end and baked into the circumference of chain-restaurant pizza crusts. A few years back while waiting for my sister to convince a Siam Square dressmaker to sew the wedding dress she wanted, I bonded with my brother-in-law-to-be over a surrealistic "pizza danish," a spiraled flaky pastry base topped with sliced franks, barbecue sauce, processed cheese, and a scattering of diced bell peppers. The dress was ultimately a failure but the brother-in-law was a keeper. The pizza danish has sadly disappeared from the coffee shop's menu.

Hot dogs in simpler form can be found in food stalls throughout Bangkok, often artfully incised so the sausages bloom like flowers when grilled or deep-fried, and meant to be eaten slathered with sweet chili sauce right out of the bag. *Khai jeow* vendors offer sliced wieners among the fillings for their fried omelets. Khao pad American ("American fried rice," page 78)—a ubiquitous local combination plate that bears resemblance to a county-fair version of Indonesian or Malaysian *nasi goreng*—features ketchup-laden fried rice alongside bacon, fried chicken, hot dogs, and a fried egg. Nobody said that dining has to be sophisticated to be delicious.

—VINCENT VICHIT VADAKAN

Sai Ua

Though it originates in the far northern provinces of Thailand, this sausage is celebrated all over the country for its heady fragrance and powerful flavor. Minced pork in a natural intestine casing is punched up with red curry paste, galangal, lemongrass, soy sauce, chilies, kaffir lime leaves, and shrimp paste. *Sai ua* is usually available at open markets and street stalls, where long spiral coils are grilled over a coconut-husk fire and served with sticky rice and herbs.

WHERE: Thailand
MEAT: pork
PREPARATION: grilled
SERVED: by itself or with rice and herbs

Som Moo

Laotian "sour pork" sausage is essentially the same as Thailand's fermented naem (page 86), though perhaps even more savory: Before being hung to ferment, the mixture of pork and pork skin gets a heavy-handed sprinkling of MSG, which even home cooks use liberally in Laos.

WHERE: Laos
MEAT: pork
PREPARATION: fermented, then eaten raw or cooked
SERVED: as is; or in rice dishes and salads

Sundae

Order a *sundae* (pronounced soon-dae) in Korea and you won't get a treacly ice cream treat but rather a grizzly amalgamation of vegetables, cellophane noodles, and blood packed into a pig intestine. Steamed and then sliced, this night-market delicacy is often dunked in *gochujang* (chili paste) to counter the metallic tang of its iron-rich filling. Steamed liver, lungs, and other off-cuts are popular accompaniments. Sundae can also come boiled in a soup with cabbage (served, in a reusable hard plastic bowl, right there on the street), stir-fried with chili paste and onions, or eaten on its own.

WHERE: North and South Korea
MEAT: pork (variations can include seafood)
PREPARATION: boiled or steamed
SERVED: sliced, in soup, or stir-fried

Waffle Hot Dogs

Yet more evidence of the hot dog legacy left behind by American GIs stationed in Thailand during the Vietnam War. Waffle hot dogs are basically corn dogs, but sweeter and softer. Thai street vendors skewer store-bought hot dogs, dip them in waffle batter, then lock them in dedicated waffle-hot-dog presses. Drizzled with mayonnaise, ketchup, or sweet chili sauce, they sell for just a few baht each.

WHERE: Thailand
MEAT: American-style hot dogs (beef, pork, and mechanically separated poultry)
PREPARATION: griddled in a special waffle-hot-dog contraption
SERVED: with ketchup, mayonnaise, and/ or sweet chili sauce

Xiang Chang

WHERE: Taiwan
MEAT: pork
PREPARATION: griddled
SERVED: skewered, sliced, or wrapped in rice

It's startling, at first, to come across the Taiwanese street sausage. There it is, under the harsh glare of buzzing bulbs: grilled and greasy, red and spicy, almost vulgar in length and meaty tumescence. *Xiang chang*, or "fragrant sausage," is a coarse-grained fatty pork sausage spiced with black bean paste, soy sauce, and five-spice powder, and sweetened with sugar. Some open-air market stands make no concessions to convenience, impaling the whole sausage on a skewer and handing it over. Navigating the teeming night market while gnawing on a foot of steaming-hot sausage ends, inevitably, with stained shirts and disappointment. Other stands are kinder, slicing the sausage before skewering it. It's also sometimes offered with a dizzying choice of condiments: You can go for the mundane (like mayonnaise) or the bizarre (like chopped kiwi in fluorescent-green syrup). A good middle ground is the Da Chang Bao Xiao Chang (page 73), or "big sausage wrap little sausage"—this creation finds the xiang chang (the little sausage) nestled in a bun made of densely packed sticky rice (the big sausage), topped with pickled vegetables and chili sauce. The entire night-market experience in each bite. **—RYAN HEALEY**

Thailand

Chris Ying

Thai garage rock sounds a lot like early Modest Mouse.

The thought dribbles into and out of my consciousness like a bead of sweat running down my face.

It's hot in Bangkok.

My wife and I are having dinner at an Isan (northeastern Thai) restaurant called Sabai Jai Kai Yang. We're seated on a covered patio on woven stools around a waxy wooden table; a tiered series of dimly lit fish tanks trickles behind us. The music is coming from an adjacent room—it's hard to tell if there's actually a band playing live or if the tinny-sounding guitar is just recorded that way. Thick, hot air passes through the restaurant from all sides.

Did I mention it's hot? It's so hot.

The restaurant was the choice of our dining companion, an expat musician named Joe Cummings. Joe's face is a map of Thailand's backstreets. He looks like a later-but-not-late-stage version of David Carradine, who incidentally died in Bangkok under questionable and supposedly lurid circumstances, about which Joe has deep insider knowledge pried from an employee at the hotel where the actor perished. Joe fills us in while we wait for our food, then regales us with a story about hanging out with Harry Styles, who was in town last week with One Direction and wanted to "meet some real people."

This is all by way of saying that if you're an English-speaking visitor to Thailand, Joe's the guy you want showing you around. He wrote the Thailand installments of the *Lonely Planet* guide for years, speaks fluent Thai, and knows the cure for whatever ails you. At the

moment, that's a beer tower filled with icy Chang brand beer. (A beer tower, in case you've never seen one, is a specialty of more civilized parts of the world: a three-foot-tall, suds-filled plastic cylinder that looks like an oversized bong with a spigot.)

Our first course is something I've been waiting forever to try in its native habitat, a dish that's simple and seems almost stupid if done poorly or out of context. *Kai yang* is just grilled chicken, usually served with sticky rice and a sweet chili sauce. The chicken gets a soak in fish sauce, soy, sugar, lemongrass, and spices before being charred bronze and crisp over charcoal.

Chicken in Asia is so much more chickeny than in the States. There's a nice hint of backyard-barbecue smokiness and, if you squint your taste buds, you can sense the marinade. But the predominant flavor is chicken, which would be a dis Stateside but is a compliment here. It comes with a side plate piled high with fresh herbs, crunchy green beans, chilies, cabbage leaves, and lettuces. I follow Joe's lead, alternating and combining bites of fresh vegetable, chicken dunked in sauce, and warm rice. The thought of using utensils never crosses my mind, but I do wish that napkins in Asia didn't always have

to be so gauzy and tissue paper–like. I amass a collection of crumpled wads that would rival that of a teenage boy home alone for the weekend.

The only other thing we want or need to eat tonight is *sai krok isan* (Isan sausage). These Ping-Pong-ball-size sausages originated in northern Thailand but are eaten all over the country. You'll find them drying on roadside clotheslines where they dangle like strings of oversized Buddhist prayer beads. When it's time to cook them, they get skewered two at a time, with the piece of twine that separates each link removed. The two sausages remain connected by a thin bridge of intestine and resemble two cells that haven't quite finished dividing. They're grilled over charcoal right on the street or sidewalk, often on bike-mounted grills.

On the plate, the sausages are mahogany orbs with a little nub of meat poking out of either end where they were separated from their neighbors. Joe shows us how to impale each sausage with the pointy end of a small Thai chili, wrap it in cabbage with a few bits of crunchy fried peanuts, a cube of ginger, and a slice of garlic, then eat it like a taco.

It's sour—a running theme among Thai sausages—and smoky. The casing is thin and snappy. The filling—a mix of pork and sticky rice—has a texture that lies somewhere really wonderful between crumbly and juicy. I'm hooked immediately, and answer without hesitation when Joe asks, "Should we get more sausage?"

"Yeah, of course."

I can see how one gets swallowed up by this place. You can't stay removed from Bangkok's ceaseless energy. The traffic is inescapable; the smells, sounds, and tastes unavoidable. Good luck dressing in anything that's not loose and breathable—the heat and humidity wilt you like the pages of a book in the shower. This city bends visitors to its will. Even the backpackers who have only spent a couple nights partying hard on Khao San Road look tattered, as though they've been here for months and will never summon the strength to leave.

We meet up with another American, Vincent, a writer and book editor, who's much newer to Thailand than Joe. He's from California, and arrived in Bangkok by way of Paris and Rome. Native Thais and longtime residents don't seem to sweat, no matter how oppressive the weather. Like us, Vincent still does.

He takes us for a tour of a few hawker centers and a weekly market near Srinakharinwirot University that caters to students and nearby office workers on their lunch break.

We assemble a piecemeal lunch to take back to Vincent's apartment:* pork that's been air-dried and then deep-fried, rendering it chewy and sweet; slices of rose apple and papaya and nodes of jackfruit; curries; grilled pork cutlets; tangy *larb* topped with fried catfish flakes; sticky rice grilled in bamboo; more Isan sausage.

While we're gathering lunch, I spy one of the sausages I've been looking for—a pig in a blanket (*kanom Tokyo*). It's a beauty. A latticework of thin layers of pancake batter envelops a standard-issue store-bought frankfurter. I eat it on the spot, among the throngs of people pushing past me as I do.

Thais have an idiosyncratic affection for American-style hot dogs. They show up in places where drunk/junk food is served, waffle-battered and fried like corn dogs, or split, fried, and served with fried rice. Along with a larb pizza, the pig in a blanket is one of the more novel foods I ate in Thailand. The pizza turns out to be pretty great—a nice intersection of East and West. But both the pig and the blanket are squishy and sweet. It's one of the more Instagrammable foods I've seen, but alas, not that delicious.

Back at Vincent's apartment, we lay out our spread on the dining table. With few exceptions, everything we've brought back from the market is outstanding. I only pause intermittently to get up and stand in front of the air-conditioning. Just as I'm creeping up to the precipice of uncomfortable fullness, Vincent insists we try his homemade pineapple

---

* With each purchase, we add to a growing collection of plastic bags. The use of plastic packaging in the street markets is ultraliberal and really off-putting. Plastic clamshell containers get tied off in plastic bags, then slipped inside another plastic bag. There's some cognitive dissonance between seeing what you want to eat sizzling hot on the grill, and then being handed a double-bagged box you can't see. When we ask the vendors not to use a bag, they look at us incredulously and proceed to bag our food anyway.

chutney and help him get rid of some leftovers—Brazilian-style mashed potato croquettes from last night's dinner party.

We eat gratefully but don't linger. We're already late for our next sausage date.

Prin Polsuk is the head chef of Nahm, David Thompson's heralded flagship restaurant in the Metropolitan hotel.

Everybody I talk to in Bangkok has an opinion about Nahm—not about the food, which is unimpeachable, but of the restaurant's (and Thompson's) place in Thai culture. David Thompson is white, originally from Australia. His journey to acceptance (or not) as a chef cooking Thai food in Bangkok is the story most people want to tell you when you inquire after Nahm.

Though his reasons for relocating to Bangkok were unambitious ("I fell in love with the food and the boys"), Thompson is the apotheosis of the expat. He's the one who made it big in a foreign land, assimilating so well as to sell the local cuisine back to the locals and have them like it. His success, as most people tell it, boils down to two things: One, he pulls no punches when it comes to cooking for an upscale, often Western clientele. (He and others refer to the authentic spice level they reach for as "Thai spicy.") Two, he has an advanced, scholarly understanding of traditional Thai foodways.

The latter is owed, at least in some part, to the fact that he's surrounded himself with Thai cooks, learning and teaching at the same time.

"Prin and I met seven or eight years ago in Bangkok. I was interviewing Thais for a job at Nahm in London," Thompson says. "I had this instinctive feeling he was just right. We've worked

together ever since. Prin is in charge of Nahm's kitchen. I have had several chefs who have been in the position, but Prin is the first one who also puts dishes on the menu. His contribution is much, much more than just a head chef. We work on the menu as equals, as collaborators."

When we meet Prin, I'm relieved to see signs of perspiration on his T-shirt. I guess Thais do sweat. He's waiting for us outside of Or Tor Kor Market. He's got a boyish face and a furrowed brow that combine to give him a distinctly mischievous quality. We get straight to it.

Or Tor Kor Market seems to be more of a shopping market than a street-food market. You come here to buy rice and spices in bulk, meat and seafood, fermented goods, fruit, herbs, vegetables. But there are plenty of stalls serving food and a cluster of tables where you can sit and eat. It's not overrun with tourists looking for pad thai, and we're here during the midafternoon lull, so it's especially quiet. As far as diners go, it's just us, on the prowl for sausage.

Prin leads us on a meandering tour of the market, stopping here and there to show us specialties—giant water bugs for grinding into *nam prik*, fragrant *maprang* (the "plum mango"), palm sugar—and to pick up different sausages. In about half an hour, he cobbles together a meaty survey.

There's *sai ua* from Chiang Mai, which comes in longer coils than its fellow northern Thai *sai krok isan*. The grain is coarser, too, and seasoned with curry paste and turmeric. We buy a section of already grilled sausage from a stack resting on a banana leaf. It's spicier than I expect, and suffused with smoke.

At another stand, a woman deftly flips skewers of chubby, finger-length *sai krok woon sen* over a small yakitori-style grill. Sai krok woon sen is a lot of filler—60:40 meat to glass noodles, Prin estimates. They're fermented in the open air for at least one night, giving them a nice acidic bite. We bundle slices of the salty, garlicky sausage in cabbage leaves with ginger and chili. The rice inside makes it a bit like eating Cajun boudin—sticky, funky, delicious boudin.

Finally, my favorite sausage of the day: *sai krok plaa naem*. The sausage is sweeter than the others I've tried, filled with very finely ground pork, curry paste, and peanuts, and gently grilled. It's a more refined sai krok ("really palace food," as Thompson describes it), native to Bangkok. Later on, I deduce that the region's river-veined topography accounts for the peanuts, as well as the way this sausage is served: wrapped in a leaf of *cha phlu* (a.k.a. wild betel, *Piper sarmentosum*) with a curl of gelatinous pork skin, shallot, garlic, chili, and fluffy fish powder (*plaa naem*). The powder is made by pounding or grinding the flesh of grilled snakehead fish, which are abundant in the Chao Phraya river basin.

We chat a little longer and make another lap around the market, then Prin has to get back to service. I tell him thanks and that we'll see him for dinner tomorrow night. He tells us to come hungry.

The Metropolitan is a sleek, polished hotel and Nahm is a big, beautiful restaurant, warmly lit, with dark floors and dramatic pillars that look like oversized geometric *trompos* of al pastor. The kitchen is bright and busy with cooks in clean white chef coats. But, acting as our guide again, Prin prefers to point out the charming, homey touches that appear like small tufts of grass growing between the seams in a sidewalk: "This is my office and where we do special projects," he says, unveiling a closet-size room redolent of fermentation and mostly filled with containers and dry goods. He cracks open a tub of some sinister-looking potion and smiles. We wheel through the rest of the kitchen, spotting more Thai flourishes in the otherwise Western-looking landscape. In the corner of one of the back prep rooms, there's a gigantic rice-pounding mortar carved out of a tree trunk. And hanging like shot puts above the stainless steel

pass on the hot line are some special treats that Prin has made just for us: *mum,* a beef offal sausage that he keeps telling me is flavored with "the green one." It takes me several tries to decipher that what he's talking about is bile.

Back in the dining room, Prin takes the ordering reins and proceeds to crush us with food. After a few canapés, we get our mum—poached, sliced, and tossed with herbs, garlic, shallot, and chili. It's gamy but not overwhelmingly so. It's very lean—there's no fat in mum—and elegant in its way. I expected it to punch me in the mouth but it's really pleasant and not at all threatening. It does, however, stand out from the rest of the meal, which is a careful orchestration. Prin explains that balance in a Thai banquet is achieved on the whole rather than in individual dishes. One thing's spicy, another is cooling. A dish of cured catfish relish might be salty, but the accompanying rice is unseasoned.

Mum doesn't quite fit into a puzzle like this. It's an event unto itself—something sought out by devotees and celebrated for its own splendor.

David Thompson's not in the kitchen tonight; he's in Singapore opening a new restaurant, Long Chim, where I saw him a couple of days ago, and he set us up with Prin. He told me that Prin would take me around Bangkok and show me some "kookier stuff," mum, in particular. "It's fermented beef and offal sausage with blood. You eat it with raw garlic and beer," he said.

"Could there be a better way to connect with your primordial nature?"

AUSTRALiA

By their own admission, Australians love crappy sausages. Still, the "snag" holds an important place in Aussie food culture.

Bull Boar Sausage

Drawn by the promise of gold, a whole community of Italian and Italian-speaking Swiss settlers arrived in the hills of Victoria, outside Melbourne, in the 1850s. Most never found the fortunes they sought, but they did make their mark on the local cuisine: They created bull boar sausage, which, as the name implies, is equal parts beef and pork. It is flavored with garlic, wine, and pie spices like cinnamon and nutmeg. It's particularly revered in Hepburn Springs, a little spa town that's home to a 150-year-old macaroni factory and the site of the annual Swiss-Italian Festa.

WHERE: Victoria, Australia
MEAT: pork and beef
PREPARATION: boiled or grilled
SERVED: by itself

Devon

Devon is a smallgood (Aussie for charcuterie/lunch meat) also known in different parts of the country as polony, luncheon, Fritz, Belgium, or bung. Like other lunchable forcemeats—American baloney is a very close cousin—it consists of unglamorous cuts of pork and beef filled out with cereals and starches, then chemically flavored and preserved. For many, Devon is the ghost of cafeteria lunches past. In the '70s and '80s, seemingly every kid Down Under was sent to school with the same sandwich: buttered white bread with tomato sauce (ketchup) and a few slices of Devon.

WHERE: Australia and New Zealand
MEAT: beef and pork
PREPARATION: cold
SERVED: on white bread with butter and ketchup

Kanga Bangas

Despite kangaroo meat's nutritional benefits (it's almost fat-free) and very low environmental impact (the bouncy marsupials run wild and rampant), some seventy percent of it is still exported to Europe and Russia, and much of the rest is turned into pet food. Those Australians who do eat kangaroo are rewarded with a mild, not-too-gamy flavor, like a cross between filet mignon and squab. (Bet you'd pay good money to see that conception.) But kangaroo is most commonly sold in sausage form under the brand name Kanga Bangas (*banga* from the British "banger"). When grilled with onions and wedged in bread, they make a Dr. Seussian sandwich: a Kanga Banga sanga, if you will.

WHERE: Australia (and exported to Europe and Russia)
MEAT: kangaroo
PREPARATION: grilled or baked
SERVED: by itself or in a sanga (sandwich)

The Bronte Barbie

WHERE: Australia
MEAT: thin beef snags (sausages)
PREPARATION: grilled, always grilled
SERVED: with onions, ketchup, beer, and goon

Everything Paul Hogan said in the eighties about Australia is true. Some of us wrestle crocodiles. We wear budgie smugglers (that's a Speedo), which we invented solely so we can wear as little as possible in public while still looking staunch. That teensy switchblade you call a "knife" is merely a toothpick by our standards. And we love barbies (okay, barbecues). It's as close to a defining cultural trait as we get.

The parking-lot sausage sizzle (see page 106) is our church of encased meat. But there's more than one place to worship at the altar of the Bad Sausage, and in fact it's where you'll see Australia at its best—the real melting pot.

The scene: any warm Saturday morning on Bronte Beach. The surf rolls in across one of Sydney's most dangerous seashores. Its treacherous rips, undertow, hidden reefs, and shore breaks mean the crowds are more likely loitering just outside the reach of the water than in it. The rolling green lawns off the back of the pristine white sand provide shade and wind protection: prime real estate for an all-in brawl-in of crosscultural barbecuing.

There are your prawn-loving, Speedo-wearing, tanned-to-boot-leather bottle blondes throwing back beers, burning onions, and laying out snags (sorry, *sausages*). Over on the hill, several Turkish families have lugged in their own *mangals*—portable metal boxes on legs—on which they're cooking shish kebab and *sujuk* sausages, while the kids dip hot chips (that's french fries to y'all) in tubs of hummus.

Strapping groups of Brazilians shirt off and do pretty much everything you expect them to: kick a football more successfully than anyone else on the beach while executing some flawless capoeira and forming a drum circle while eating steak. Korean international students line the freestanding communal barbecues with foil and somehow magic up a pretty impressive-looking *bokkeumbap*. Anyone that can execute fried rice at the beach is working on levels I'll never understand, but wish I could.

Every Sydney beach worth its salt offers free barbecuing facilities. The massive stainless steel hot boxes activate at the push of a button and stand sentry around the park. Now, these are a public facility very kindly run by the local council. I can neither confirm nor deny that an old boyfriend of mine would, on occasion, take a late-night drunken weave down to the beach, turn the barbecues on, wait for them to heat up, and then urinate on them. Folks, this is the very reason you always come armed with at least one beer to clean the barbecue before using it.

Back in the light of day, successfully procuring said barbecue is one part lingering to two parts menacing and a little bit of bribery thrown in for good measure. Sometimes it's the offer of a slightly better piece of meat, other times you're sacrificing part of a six-pack. The quintessential Aussie barbecue is a lot of things to a lot of people, but a classic bogan (a.k.a. redneck a.k.a. Donald Trump's wig in a Speedo a.k.a. everything that is near or surrounding Kid Rock) barbecue will always have the following: sliced white bread, thin beef sausages, onions, tomato sauce (ketchup to you), beer, and goon.

Yes, at some point in our lives, most of us have had a love affair with The Sack. Cheap boxed wine, a.k.a. goon, is as deeply ingrained in Aussie outdoor-eating culture as a good sausage sandwich. And it just so happens that the two are a match made in, well, not heaven but certainly Australia.

The greatest thing you can do with this fine product requires a rotary clothes-line. First, take your goon sacks out of their boxes—you'll need at least four of varying colors and quality, depending on how many people are playing—then attach them securely to the clothesline. Arrange your friends around the perimeter. Now—and this is the important part, everything depends on this—everyone has to scream GOON! OF! FORTUNE! as the clothesline spins. Whatever sack stops in front of you, you must suckle from like a calf from a teat. The game continues until the goon's all gone. Some people also claim that Wheel of Goon is an acceptable variation.

But they would be wrong. **—MYFFY RIGBY**

Sausage Sizzle

WHERE: Australia, all over (but most of all at Bunnings Warehouse stores)
MEAT: the cheapest, thinnest sausage sold at the supermarket (pork, sometimes beef)
PREPARATION: grilled on a gas-fired griddle (alla plancha, if you will)
SERVED: on white bread, under chopped onions and ketchup

On any given weekend at school fetes, on roadsides, at the beach, and in the bush, moms and dads are standing over barbies, grilling snags, slapping the charred remains into single slices of soft white bread (diagonal positioning of the sausage across the slice is preferred by the sausage-sizzle connoisseur), covering them with chopped onions that are miraculously burnt and raw at the same time, and then smothering the lot in ketchup.

In recent years, the sausage sizzle has become a mainstay in the car parks of Bunnings Warehouse stores—the popular hardware/garden-supply chain provides the tent, tables, and the barbie free to community groups for fund-raising. Your Girl Guide troop or junior cricket team or whatever brings the food, burns the snags, and keeps the profits, which can run to four figures at the bigger stores on weekends. Sure, Australia also has slightly more involved, culinarily high-minded sausage traditions (the sharply spiced pork-and-beef Bull Boar Sausage [page 103] invented by Swiss-Italian settlers in the goldfields of Victoria in the nineteenth century, being the key example), but the Bunnings sausage sizzle is now such a staple of Saturday mornings in the country that for most Australians the mere sight of hardware triggers a Pavlovian association of onions cooking in fat, and vice versa. It's probably the closest thing we have, too, to a real street food. The pop and crunch of a hot cheap snag under a cool blanket of tomato sauce (ketchup) is a beautiful thing, especially ahead of a morning spent looking at axes, shade cloth, and drought-resistant succulents. **–PAT NOURSE**

NO BEANS IN THE CHILI

Chris Ying

I firmly believe that there is no place for beans in hot dog chili. It is my understanding that this might be a contentious opinion, so let's look at this empirically.

If you survey everybody about their opinions of beans in chili:

- *Some people will support removing beans from all chili.*

- *More people will support removing it from hot dog chili only. Not all people.*

But we are concerned specifically with chili dogs, so we must keep in mind that:

- *Some people like chili, but don't like hot dogs. They can be omitted from consideration, because it doesn't matter to them if there are beans on chili dogs or not.*

- *Some people "don't like" chili dogs. At least some percentage of these people would change their minds if they tried a chili dog without beans.*

- *Some people don't eat meat. I assume they would prefer beans (vegetarian) not be wasted in chili (not vegetarian).*

Thus, the percentage of relevant people in favor of eliminating beans from their chili is much closer to 100 percent than we originally thought. The numbers are on our side.

- *One might estimate the percentage of people who wouldn't mind eliminating beans from hot dog chili to be roughly the same as the percentage of people in favor of eliminating the penny from circulation.*

- *Nobody wants pennies in their hot dog chili, because pennies have a very incongruous texture.*

- *Beans also have a very incongruous texture.*

Here are more hard facts and statistics about beans:

- *Beans make you fart.*

- *Farts alienate those around you, regardless of whether they are pro- or antibean.*

I am not fundamentalist about this; I am open to compromise. Some people distinguish between the chili that goes in a bowl and the chili that goes on hot dogs by referring to the latter as "sauce" and not "chili." I am open to this distinction, as I think that even fewer people will want beans in their "sauce," while "chili" will continue to have beans.

But we have all reached the same conclusion that beans do not belong on chili dogs.

NORTH AMERICA

Like fugitives on the lam, frankfurters, andouille, boudin, and Italian sausage all assumed new identities when they arrived on American shores. They also spun off some wholly new creations.

Ách'ii'

This entry comes in the form of a letter from one of our readers and loyal sausage acolytes.

My contribution to the great sausage database: *ách'ii'*, a Navajo specialty. It's more of a proto-sausage, a concoction from tube-meat prehistory: nothing more than sheep intestines coiled around a strip of lamb fat (although any self-respecting Navajo would say "mutton"). It's grilled and sold at flea markets all over the Navajo Nation, with a chewy grilled tortilla and an optional strip of roasted green chile. I know ách'ii' best from Gallup, New Mexico, where the Saturday flea market has plenty of stands selling it and other Navajo food. The flavor is mostly what you'd expect: sheep-funk, a hint of fresh grass, plus grease and distinctly intestinal bounciness, which may not sound great, but it tastes precisely of the place it's from, and of some of the deeper food roots in America. (I'm not Navajo myself—I imagine it tastes much better if your grandma made it for you, or if you'd been going to the Gallup flea every week with your family since birth.)

WHERE: Navajo Nation (Arizona, Utah, New Mexico)
MEAT: mutton
PREPARATION: grilled
SERVED: wrapped in a chewy flour tortilla, with green chile and/or chopped tomato

Andouille

Like Boudin (page 110), andouille is an example of the ways in which the long voyage from France to Canada to the Louisiana bayou transmogrified classic French dishes. Traditional *andouille,* a tripe-filled smoked sausage best loved (sliced cold and thin) in Normandy and Brittany, lost its offaly touch when it went Cajun. For American andouille, cubed (or very coarsely ground) pork is packed into beef casings with garlic and peppery seasonings, and smoked over pecan wood. Its perfume can be detected throughout Cajun and Creole cuisine—in beans and jambalaya and gumbo and étouffée. LaPlace, Louisiana, about twenty minutes west of Louis Armstrong International Airport, is the Andouille Mothership, home to Jacob's, Bailey's, and Wayne Jacob's smokehouses, all fine purveyors of awn-doo-ee.

WHERE: Louisana
MEAT: pork
PREPARATION: grilled or stewed
SERVED: as is, or in numerous Louisiana dishes

Boudin

Hardship builds character, and so it is with boudin. Somewhere between arriving in Nova Scotia with French colonists (Acadians), being pushed out by the English, and landing in Louisiana, where Acadian became Cajun, *boudin blanc* got a little rougher and a little spicier. Listen to someone speak Louisiana French and you get some sense of the difference between the New World version and the old. Cajun boudin is a specialty of local grocery stores and boucheries—communal pig cookouts, basically, where friends and family gather together to kill and make the very most they can out of a whole animal. Boudin recipes vary wildly from cook to cook, but when most people in southern Louisiana hear "boudin," their imaginations turn immediately to thick links stuffed with soft-squishy pork, liver, rice, aromatics, and peppery spices. *Boudin noir* exists here too, but when it arrived in Cajun country, it became red boudin—still made with blood, if slightly less poetic. And of course there are also boudin balls, like arancini, orbs of ricey filling breaded and deep-fried crisp.

WHERE: Louisiana
MEAT: pork
PREPARATION: poached, grilled, or smoked
SERVED: as is, to be squeezed out of the casing directly into your mouth; uncased and fried as boudin balls

Breakfast Sausage

Jimmy Dean grew up poor on a farm in Plainview, Texas. His mother ran a bar-bershop out of their home to make ends meet and Dean walked around wearing shirts made from sugar sacks. Every fall, Dean and his grandfather slaughtered a hog and made their own sausage. After serving in the Air Force, Dean spent the '40s and '50s building a name for himself as a country music star of radio and television. He'd remain a big shot for decades to come and had a huge hit with "Big Bad John," which told the story of a mythical coal miner who "stood six foot six and weighed 245, kinda broad at his shoulder and narrow at the hip." How'd John get to be so big and bad? By eating Jimmy Dean sausage, no doubt. In 1969, Dean was picking at a gristly piece of sausage in his teeth, and felt the call to produce a better breakfast meat. Tubes of Jimmy's sausage hit grocery store refrigerators soon after, and American breakfast tables were never the same. Jimmy Dean breakfast sausage now comes linked or loose, uncooked, precooked, frozen, in a microwavable bowl, skewered and stuffed in pancakes, or breakfast-sandwiched. This reflects the myriad ways Americans take their morning meat, Jimmy Dean variety or no: pan-fried on the side, baked with eggs and cheese in a casserole, stirred into gravy, rolled up in pancakes (or sprinkled directly into the batter), and, frankly, however else we want, dammit, so long as it's flavored with sage and/or maple syrup.

WHERE: USA
MEAT: pork
PREPARATION: Cooked in a skillet or baked
SERVED: with eggs; in a breakfast sandwich; in a casserole; next to pancakes

Butifarra Chiapaneca

WHERE: southern Mexico
MEAT: pork
PREPARATION: poached or simmered
SERVED: with salsa and shredded carrot

Thirty miles from the Guatemalan border, in the southernmost state (and one of the poorest) in Mexico, nestled into the central highlands, is the city of Comitán de Dominguez. Zapatistas protect these misty hills of dense jungle dotted with coffee fields and small towns that are bisected by narrow, tortuous roads. Guatemala is visible on the horizon where the dark green of the forest meets gray sky.

In the markets of Comitán, the state's tropical bounty—multiple varieties of bananas, pineapples, vanilla beans, and cacao pods—is on offer, beside smoked hams and mortadellas, garlands of dried salamis in their moldy skins, and hard cow's milk cheeses—evidence of overlapping Spanish, French, German, and Italian influences. Women in brightly embroidered blouses sell tamales and *atole* alongside sliced cold cuts. It's a delightfully discordant bricolage of cuisine and culture.

One of the local prizes is *butifarra chiapaneca,* a fresh sausage with lineage traceable back to Catalonia, where it is served with fava beans and crusty bread. In Chiapas, there are two versions, a white butifarra, which is pale and poached, and *butifarra negra,* turned black with blood. Both are pork sausages, seasoned with warm spices and splashed with brandy or *comiteco,* the local *aguardiente,* then stuffed into natural casings and simmered until the coils become taut. Loosely emulsified, the sausages are freckled with pockets of fat and unleash flavors of fresh bay and ground anise. The black butifarra is more supple than the white one, wine-dark, iron-rich with flickers of nutmeg, clove, and black pepper. The white is milder, more porcine, and carries the faintest murmur of spice, sliced open to reveal an inside richly speckled like Venetian marble. At lengthy, midday *comidas,* the sausages are often served simply, unseared, warm to room temperature, with toothpicks. Or, as with most proteins in Comitán, on a plate flanked by a potent dried chili salsa and a thicket of shredded carrot. While Europeans might decree a wedge of lemon with their blood sausage, the natural accompaniment here is a halved lime. **—SCARLETT LINDEMAN**

North America

111

Chicago-Style Hot Dog

WHERE: Chicago
MEAT: all-beef hot dog
PREPARATION: steamed
SERVED: on a poppyseed bun, with tomatoes, mustard, neon green relish,
   dill pickle, onions, sport peppers, celery salt

For all you hear about Chicagoans and their midwestern-bred congeniality, ask them for ketchup on a hot dog and watch their expression turn. Bad idea. You may as well have spit on Michael Jordan and told him he carried Pippen's jockstrap. In Chicago, civic pride and decades of unwavering tradition have fenced off ketchup as sacrilege. The reasoning: It doesn't belong on a Chicago-style hot dog, which is to say, the one *true* hot dog.

They have a point. The hallmark of a Chicago hot dog is its rigid assemblage of condiments, and the slightest deviation from its delicate balance renders the style null and void. (Rare is the Chicagoan who customizes this hot dog, an all-or-nothing proposition.) The wiener must be all-beef. The steamed bun must be poppyseed. There are seven required toppings: tomato slices, a spear of dill pickle, chopped onions, whole sport peppers, neon green relish, mustard, and a dash of celery salt. These are ingredients of Greek, Italian, German, and Jewish heritage, a reflection of Chicago's population in the early twentieth century when this style of hot dog took form. It rose from the proletariat class because it was inexpensive, a sandwich bulked up with cheap produce and enjoyed across ethnic lines in all corners of the city. If ever terroir could be applied to a hot dog, *this* is Chicago encapsulated.

So what makes this treatment, known to Chicagoans as "dragged through the garden," singular in its deliciousness? You're getting the spectrum of taste sensations. There's piquancy from peppers, sweetness from the relish and tomatoes, the sharp bite of pickles, a bitter undertow of onions and mustard, and umami from the beef. (Ketchup, purists will say, would just be gilding the wiener lily.) The Chicago dog also offers a mélange of textures: Every bite guarantees some crunch, some squish, some soppiness. The funny thing is, even for Chicagoans, it's difficult to differentiate between Chicago dogs from different restaurants. That's because the Chicago hot dog experience is specific and unyielding. Or put another way, perfection next to perfection is impossible to tell apart. **–KEVIN PANG**

Chicago Dog, Deconstructed

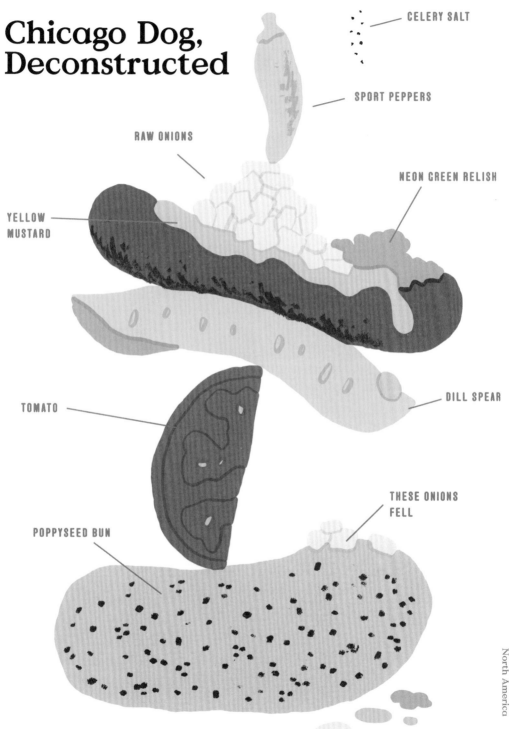

CELERY SALT

SPORT PEPPERS

RAW ONIONS

NEON GREEN RELISH

YELLOW
MUSTARD

TOMATO

DILL SPEAR

THESE ONIONS
FELL

POPPYSEED BUN

Chorizo

WHERE: Cuba, Mexico, Puerto Rico
MEAT: pork
PREPARATION: grilled or fried

SERVED: with eggs or queso fundido; as a filling for tacos, burritos, and *tortas*; as a popular pizza topping in Puerto Rico

Chorizo is more than just a sausage in Mexico. It's a proudly nationalistic, inescapable part of Mexican life.

For months, I lived above one of those informal, public social clubs called *cafeterías* in Mexico City, where every morning locals would shuffle in for a quick breakfast, which often included eggs with chorizo. The scents that drifted upstairs were, as you can expect, intoxicating and maddening.

All over the streets of Mexico, vendors grill local chorizo over charcoal fire as part of their popular mixed-grill *platos,* or they griddle and hash them with potatoes for delectable tacos. Butcher counters proudly display strings of *bolitas*—handsome little orbs of fiery-red chorizo—tempting all who stroll by.

There's just something special about the distinctive texture and flavor of this sausage. It's fresh and a little crumbly, unlike the cured-and-sliceable Spanish chorizo, and it's boldly aromatic with a balanced blend of spices and just enough vinegar to brighten the pronounced flavor of the chili.

Chorizo helps elevate common foods—eggs, a bowl of beans, potatoes, simple sandwiches—into satisfying, savory meals. Although it's not common throughout Mexico, I love pairing chorizo with wild mushrooms. They're perfect cohorts. At my restaurant, Frontera Grill in Chicago, we top our classic queso fundido—a taco filling of melted cheese—with crispy chorizo and garlicky roasted peppers, and we regularly use the sausage as a filling for *gorditas*. At Xoco, our next-door corner street-food place, our chorizo and cheese torta is wildly popular, which is really no surprise—a quick spread of black beans and a little chorizo will make any sandwich taste better.

At the restaurants, we use a recipe inspired by the fresh chorizo found in Oaxaca, which many would argue is Mexico's best. In Yucatán, they opt to smoke their achiote-laced version into skinny *longaniza,* which contains no chili. There's also a fair amount of charcuterie in Chiapas. The mountainous elevation and climate (and Spanish influence) makes it conducive for curing, which is why you'll find a diverse array of smoked and fresh Spanish-style meats, from *butifarra* to tasty hams.

Of the traditional varieties, though, one of my favorites is the chorizo from Toluca, some versions of which use ancho and pasilla chilies, a touch of ginger and nutmeg, along with other spices to produce a super-interesting and flavorful sausage. Some *carniceros* include nuts, raisins, or a shot of booze. (In his cookbook, *Toluca del Chorizo*, Tolucan author Alfonso Sánchez García declared, with just a touch of bombast, that the superiority of the Tolucan earth, the health of its hogs, the herbs and spices and careful process by which the sausage is made, "constitute the artistic contribution of the Tolucan pork butchers to the singularity of their chorizo.") **—RICK BAYLESS**

~~~~~~

Chorizo Verde

From high up in the city of Toluca—the capital of Mexican chorizo—comes this verdant spin on the dark red sausage we know. Sometime in the middle of the last century, Tolucan sausage makers tried swapping the dried and roasted chilies that give chorizo its signature vermilion tint for ingredients like fresh cilantro and parsley, chard, spinach, roasted poblano or jalapeño chilies, and tomatillo. Some recipes now call for almonds, rice, vinegar, potatoes, or spinach powder, which stains certain specimens a shade of bright green worthy of St. Paddy.

WHERE: Mexico
MEAT: pork
PREPARATION: pan-fried
SERVED: in tacos and tortas

Corndog

Several different men have staked paternity claims to the corndog. One, an Oregonian man named George Boying-ton said that he was the first to skewer, cornmeal-batter, and deep-fry hot dogs in 1942 after rain ruined a batch of buns during a picnic. Two thousand miles south in Texas, the Fletcher brothers were reputed to have given up their careers as vaudevillians that same year to sell "corny dogs" at America's biggest state fair in Dallas. To this day, the lightly sweet, salty, crunchy, pleasantly gritty corndog remains the quintessential portable meal of American fairgrounds (and boardwalks, ballparks, and certain school cafeterias). As anyone who's ever suffered a corndog burn on the roof of his or her mouth can attest, a corndog's shell—a hush puppy, basically—is also the world's most effective insulation material.

WHERE: America!
MEAT: pork and/or beef
PREPARATION: battered and deep-fried
SERVED: with mustard or ketchup

Coney Island Dog

WHERE: Detroit and upstate New York
MEAT: pork and beef

PREPARATION: griddled or grilled
SERVED: covered in meat sauce

In Detroit, the Coney is both the city's signature dish and shorthand for the establishments that serve it. Coneys are eaten any time of day by just about every strata of society. They can be found all over the city and suburbs in the same way that New York slices are indigenous to every borough. You're just as likely to find a Coney at a 24-hour drive-thru armed with bulletproof glass on the East Side as you are to have one in a bright and shiny outlet, alongside tweens with their parents' credit cards in the super affluent Oakland County suburb of Birmingham.

The Coney might be mistaken for any other chili dog if not for the details. The hot dogs come from either Dearborn Sausage in Dearborn, just outside of Detroit, or Koegel Meats in Flint. Buns are usually produced by Metropolitan Baking Co. in Hamtramck. The dogs are topped with a generous ladleful of all-meat chili. The meat sauce is usually made with beef, but in Flint, they use ground beef heart. Others use ground hot dogs in the sauce. The chili is always bean-free. No, beans would be blasphemous, as would ketchup. Each Coney is finished with a handful of diced onions and a couple of ribbons of yellow salad mustard.

The dogs are always grilled, no boiling, deep-frying, broiling, or baking. You can also tell a true Coney when you bite into it, a snapping sensation that comes from the natural casing.

The Coney's provenance is rooted in the early twentieth century, when Greek and Macedonian immigrants started opening restaurants selling a mix of America-nized Greek food and Coney dogs. (Today at most of these joints, along with your Coney, you can get a gyro soaked in tzatziki, a baby Greek salad, or a saganaki fried cheese plate.) There's some debate as to whether the very first Coney dog shops popped up in Michigan or Indiana, but we Michiganders tend to ignore any such frivolous claims from our southern neighbors. The Coney dog is a Detroit specialty.

At the very least, it was Detroit where Coneys found their audience. Their rise paralleled the beginnings of the automotive industry, when getting hot, cheap, fast sustenance into the hands of workers became a priority. The city was inundated with lunch counters, chop suey spots, and Coneys. The Keros brothers, Constantine "Gust" and William, opened one of the first, American Coney Island, in a narrow flatiron building downtown. A family spat led to the opening of Lafayette Coney Island next door. Over the decades, as Detroit gave way to suburban sprawl, these diners have multiplied and spawned new chains.

The Coney has also spread and diversified. Venture outside of Detroit, to Flint or Jackson, and you'll find a drier meat sauce. Farther north, the sauce has a more pronounced ketchup base. And in a classic case of coming full circle, a variation of the Coney has a strong following in New York, specifically upstate where it's known as a Michigan hot dog. The Michigan is also popular in Montreal and other parts of Quebec.

As for the etymology of the name Coney, things get a little confusing because of the existence of that other favorite son of Coney Island, the Nathan's hot dog. It seems that the immigrant entrepreneurs who invented the Coney wanted to fold themselves into American culture and named their creation after the Brooklyn amusement park—the supposed birthplace of the hot dog—where they'd visited on their way to the Midwest. How were they to know that Nathan Handwerker would go on to open the world's most famous hot dog chain in Coney Island?

—SERENA DANIELS

Italian Sausage

If you've ever purchased sausage from a grocery-store butcher case in America, you may have wondered how the entirety of the Italian sausage canon was reduced to a choice between Hot and Sweet. The answer begins with US soldiers returning from the Italian theater following the end of World War II. While fighting in southern Italy and Sicily, our boys developed a taste for *salciccia fresca*: fresh pork sausage seasoned with salt, pepper, and fennel. Upon landing back in the States, the guys sought out their new favorite sausage in the Little Italys of New York, Philly, and Chicago. It was only a matter of time before the broader sausage market felt the demand. In the '50s and '60s, the popularity of so-called "Italian Sausages" flavored with garlic and fennel—plus red pepper flakes (hot) or without (sweet)—skyrocketed. After that, they were as much a part of Italian-American cuisine as canned breadcrumbs, spaghetti and meatballs, checkered tablecloths, and chicken parm.

WHERE: USA
MEAT: pork
PREPARATION: grilled, poached, or braised
SERVED: with peppers and onions, over pasta or polenta

Dirty Water Dog

WHERE: New York (mainly Midtown, and then parks, museums, and other places where there are tourists)
MEAT: beef
PREPARATION: simmered
SERVED: in a bun, condiments loaded on top

The "dirty water dog" is what New Yorkers call street-vended hot dogs. They are of mediocre provenance—Sabrett is one of the underwhelming names you may see emblazoned on the sellers' carts' umbrellas—and they luxuriate in a murky, meaty hot tub—the "dirty water"—until a tourist or other new arrival to the city buys one. They are served in buns that are magnificently charmless, devoid of flavor, and always stale in a way that makes them start to disintegrate only seconds after you've (over)paid for them. There is limp sauerkraut available that you should probably hide the dog beneath, and a strange ketchupy, oniony relish thing that you shouldn't. The mustard, brownish and spicyish, is probably the best thing about the whole affair.

—PETER MEEHAN

And here a Lucky Peach *reader responds to Peter Meehan's characterization of the Dirty Water Dog:*

February 17, 2014

Dear LUCKY PEACH

I disagree with your article "Dirty Water dog".
I disagree that New York Hot dogs are not good.
I think that New York Hot dog are good.
I have eaten a lot of Hot dogs in my
I life, Hot dogs are always good. Everywhere!

Sincerely,
Rehaan Ansaria
1st grade
Cambridge, MA

Danger Dog

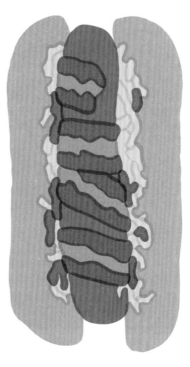

WHERE: Mission District, San Francisco
MEAT: ? (and bacon)
PREPARATION: griddled on a cookie sheet
SERVED: in a bun, onions and peppers on top

The San Francisco Danger Dog is one that you buy after you've had four too many drinks at your favorite dive bar and need to recover your wits so you can walk home. Or—and this has only ever happened to me once—the gratis Danger Dog that a vendor hands to you at the very, very tail end of the night, when he's getting rid of his goods, and after you've badly (but honorably) lost several rounds of beer pong. In this moment, he is more than mere hot dog vendor—he's an angel sent from heaven, handing you this foil-swaddled foodstuff that glistens virtuously in the moonlight.

The Danger Dog, a.k.a. Mission Dog, is a bacon-wrapped hot dog. It's called the Tijuana Dog in San Diego, the Hot Dog Estilo Sonora in Tijuana, the Sonora Dog in Arizona and New Mexico (see Sonoran-Style Hot Dog, page 123), and Dirty Dog or Border Dog elsewhere. After Americans brought the first hot dogs to Mexico in the mid-1940s, the story goes, some enterprising Mexicans thought to wrap the dogs in bacon and sold them from a stand in Mexico City, starting in the mid-1950s.

San Francisco visitors, here's how to ID a Danger Dog operation. First, you will smell it. You will see a lady or gentleman perched behind a cookie sheet set over a propane burner. There will be, atop the cookie sheet and to one side, a heap of sliced onions and bell peppers cooked to perfect limpness and sweetness. The vendor will push these around with tongs, while scraping up the stuck browned parts and squeeze-bottling oil to slicken the pan. On the other side of the sheet, the wieners will be sizzling, thin-sliced bacon wound round and round them, like tubular meat mummies. The browned wieners go in buns, where they are crowned with the onion-pepper medley. Condiments (ketchup, mustard, mayo, sometimes Thousand Island dressing) are left up to the consumer. **–RACHEL KHONG**

Maxwell Street Polish

Less distinctive than the Second City's flashier sausage export (See Kevin Pang's exposition on the Chicago-style hot dog, page 112), the Maxwell Street Polish was born on the corner of its namesake and Halstead in Chicago in 1943 at a hot dog stand (what's now known as Jim's Original). The proprietor, a Macedonian immigrant named Jim Stefanovic, topped a kielbasa with grilled onions, sport peppers, and bright yellow mustard, and named it for the neighborhood. The sausage in a Maxwell Street Polish has become something of a regionally specific variation of kielbasa, with multiple Chicago-based manufacturers (Vienna Beef, Daisy, Bobak, Leon's) each offering its own beef or beef-and-pork Maxwell Street Polish sausages. (Most seem to be characterized by their length more than anything else.)

WHERE: Chicago
MEAT: pork or beef, or a combination
PREPARATION: boiled, then grilled
SERVED: with onions, sport peppers, fries; in a brown paper bag

Mini Chili-Cheese Dog

The Berkshires are home to a number of hot doggeries specializing in minuscule chili dogs. But Jack's Hot Dog Stand in North Adams, Massachusetts, is the high practitioner of the teeny-tiny chili doggy. Jack's opened around the same time that Greek immigrants were opening Coneys in Detroit (see page 116), putting it right up there with the progenitors of the American chili dog. Jack's dogs are bigger than some of their truly mini Berkshires brethren, which can sometimes measure just over finger length, but not so large that a hungry hungry hippo can't take down a half dozen without thinking about it. The chili is cooked down to its savory essence (meat, no beans); the cheese is white American; the bread is squishy supermarket style. Acceptable additions are mustard and onions.

WHERE: North Adams, MA
MEAT: beef
PREPARATION: steamed
SERVED: in a squishy bun, topped with chili, cheese, mustard, and onions

Pigs in a Blanket

Americans tend not to enjoy being reminded that the meat we're eating comes from an animal, but we don't seem to mind when the image is an adorable one of a pig snuggled cozily in a blanket. The pig, of course, refers to sausages—cocktail wieners or breakfast links, usually—wrapped in dough blankets and baked, or rolled up in griddled pancakes at the breakfast table. In Germany, a pig in a blanket is known as "sausage in a dressing gown"; in Israel, "Moses in the Ark." The American version became popular in the late 1950s after a recipe was published in a Betty Crocker cookbook.

WHERE: USA
MEAT: beef and/or pork
PREPARATION: baked or griddled
SERVED: as is, or with syrup at breakfast

Klub

MEAT: pork blood
WHERE: the Upper Midwest (via Norway)
PREPARATION: boiled, then poached in milk or pan-fried
SERVED: with mashed rutabaga or topped with sugar

In the decades bookending the turn of the twentieth century, a wave of Norwegian immigrants arrived on American shores and made their way to the Upper Midwest, where the Homestead Acts granted them sections of land in return for a commitment to farming.

One immigrant who took advantage of this was Bernt Hagen, a wheat farmer who came over from Norway in 1876 and settled outside of Grand Forks, North Dakota. Bernt's great-great-grandson is my husband, Nick, who is the reason why, despite my heritage being about as far from Norwegian as can be, I find myself invested in Norwegian cuisine.

It's so good! I love their heavy use of cardamom and almonds. I could eat their fluffy potato flatbread, *lefse*, every day, and my wimpy taste buds don't ever have to worry about being surprised with any sort of spicy food. For the first year and a half that I lived in the Upper Midwest, nothing could stop me from trying anything thrown my way.

And then blod klub happened. I just can't warm up to blod klub.

Seattle Hot Dog

In the 1980s in the Emerald City neighborhood of Pioneer Square, a serendipitous ménage à trois between drunk people, hot dogs, and local bagel culture produced a famous child. Someone (either at a hot dog stand or a bagel shop—reports vary) started serving hot dogs on day-old bialys schmeared with cream cheese to liquored-up revelers. At some point, grilled onions came into the fold, the hot dogs were split down the middle and grilled after being poached, the cream cheese started getting piped on like caulking, and the bialys were replaced by regular buns. Seattle-style dogs are sold in and around Safeco Field, as well as at pretty much every hot dog stand downtown. The actual dog can be a classic hot dog or a Polish sausage, and additional toppings can include sriracha, mustard, sauerkraut, and jalapeños.

WHERE: Seattle
PREPARATION: boiled and grilled
MEAT: pork and beef, usually
SERVED: with cream cheese, onions; various toppings

The children and grandchildren of that initial wave of Norwegian immigrants remember eating klub during the Great Depression, when meat was scarce. Some look back on their klubing days with nostalgia, as it reminds them of their parents and life on the farm, while others are glad they distanced themselves from the stuff when they could. Lovers of klub describe it as sweet, buttery, and meaty without the toughness of a steak, while haters cringe over memories of chewy, metallic, ugly masses of congealed blood.

Klub—sometimes referred to as *kumla* or *raspeboller,* in addition to *blod klub,* which helps differentiate it from its close relative, the potato klub (a dumpling)—typically consists of cow or pig's blood mixed with shredded potatoes, flour (white, wheat, rye, or a mixture), spices like cinnamon, allspice, ginger, and cloves, and cubes of pork fat or suet. The mixture is typically either shaped into hockey puck–sized patties or stuffed into a muslin bag to form a large cylinder before being boiled until firm.

In Norway (where the klub is almost identical to its American descendant) the sausage is served with various other meats and mashed rutabaga. Stateside Norwegians take their klub for breakfast, pan-fried in butter, and sometimes topped with sugar or syrup or an egg. It's one of those dishes where every family has a different recipe passed down through the generations and every family's is the best.

Today the tradition is kept alive in the Upper Midwest in the winter when local meat markets sell both pre-made klub and buckets of blood for klub-making parties held at churches and in home kitchens around town. Huge batches of the thick, rubbery blood mixture that looks deceptively like red velvet cake batter are formed into portions, some of which are eaten for a group supper right out of the boiler. Leftovers are cooled and packed away in the freezer (or, in the olden days, a snow-covered uninsulated building). One by one, the klub is defrosted, sliced, and then fried in butter (or poached in milk) for a breakfast that takes the full day to digest.

—MOLLY YEH

Sonoran-Style Hot Dog

While we can't definitely tell you where the Sonoran is from (the Mexican province of the same name or the American Southwest, where it flourishes), we can tell you where it's going: straight to your thighs. Like its cousin the Danger Dog (page 120), the Sonoran is wrapped in bacon before being griddled or grilled. The Sonoran bun is a *bolillo*—more commonly seen as a vessel for *tortas*—so the sausage tends not to poke out of the ends, but rather stays snug in the hollow that's carved out for it. With toppings, it looks like an overstuffed clutch. Those toppings include some combination of red and/or green salsa, grilled or raw white onion, cheese, pinto beans, chopped tomatoes, mustard, a tasteful squeeze of mayonnaise, pickled jalapeños, and—fuck it—a whole second bacon-wrapped hot dog. On the side expect some kind of char-roasted pepper.

WHERE: southwest U.S., northwest Mexico
MEAT: pork or beef
PREPARATION: wrapped in bacon; griddled
SERVED: on a bolillo roll with toppings

Spam Musubi

Invented in the 1930s, SPAM (the name is a head-on collision of the words *spiced* and *ham* and the product of a national naming contest held by the Hormel Company in 1937) is perhaps the world's best-known canned forcemeat. It lodged itself in the American consciousness during World War II, when fresh meat was scarce. SPAM remained the king of comfort foods in Hawaii long after the war ended, maybe because SPAM pairs so nice with rice, or maybe because the state lives in perpetual anxiety of being cut off from supplies. On the islands, SPAM makes appearances with eggs, chopped into fried rice, in bowls of noodle soup, and, most famously, sliced thin, pan-fried, and draped over a small brick of cooked rice. It's a riff on the ubiquitous handheld Japanese snack, *omusubi* (a.k.a. *onigiri*), a rice ball filled with various proteins or vegetables, often wrapped in a sheet of nori. Hawaiians, who comprise almost as many people of Japanese descent as Caucasians, love their Spam musubi. You'll find it wrapped in plastic and held under heat lamps at convenience and grocery stores, sometimes gilded with slices of avocado or sheets of egg omelet.

WHERE: Hawaii
MEAT: pork and ham
PREPARATION: griddled
SERVED: atop a block of cooked rice, sometimes wrapped in nori

Vienna Sausages

Brought to you by the titans of industrialized cuisine, Vienna sausages come in tightly packed cans of short, skinless links usually made of pork, but also sometimes a mix of pork, beef, veal, and/or chicken. They come in different flavors—smoked, barbecue, spicy—but are always smooth, soft, and perfectly cylindrical. This is deep convenience/survivalist stuff, mostly reserved for campers, latchkey kids, and the similarly displaced and desperate. They have little or nothing to do with sausages from Austria—yet another example of a geographical moniker being applied to a wildly nonspecific foodstuff. But before you get judgy about it, let's talk about wieners. The term *wiener,* which most Americans feel comfortable tossing around to refer to pretty much all forms of tube meat, comes from Wien, the German word for Vienna. So in a way, all sausages are Vienna sausages to us.

WHERE: USA, Cuba, Philippines
MEAT: pork (sometimes beef, veal, or chicken)
PREPARATION: canned
SERVED: straight out of the can; or with/in crackers, noodles, potato salad

Taylor Pork Roll

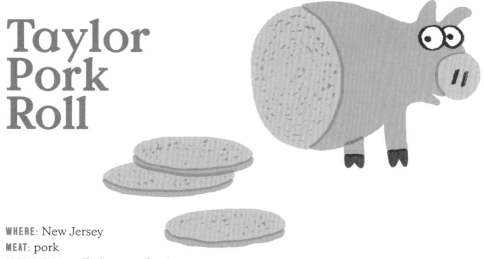

WHERE: New Jersey
MEAT: pork
PREPARATION: grilled or pan-fried
SERVED: on a burger or an egg-and-cheese sandwich

Of the seemingly endless array of pork "products"—we use the quotation marks to convey a meat of uncertain (and probably better for being uncertain) origin—the Taylor Pork Roll is one of the least known.

Almost nobody outside the Northeast has ever heard of it, much less tried it; nearly all those familiar with the product came in contact with it for the first time in or around New Jersey. The product's exact origins are unclear, but we do know that one John Taylor began producing his pork roll in the 1850s. There was a similar product on the market at the time, and in the wake of Taylor's success other pork roll companies emerged to compete. In 1910, Taylor brought suit against them, and a legal case ruled that "pork roll" could not be trademarked.

The product became known as Taylor Ham, though to this day many Jerseyites have essentially overturned the court order: they still refer to it as Taylor Pork Roll. Why it never became more than a regional delicacy is something of a mystery. One possible answer is that even for packaged forcemeat, it's not particularly distinctive, like SPAM or Canadian bacon. In appearance, the slices somewhat resemble bologna, but its composition is saltier and fattier.

The best way to appreciate the Taylor Pork Roll is to grill it or pan-fry it, so that some of the fat is leached out and the edges begin to brown a little. Not only does this concentrate the flavor, but it also intensifies the best quality of Taylor Pork Roll: the rich, porky residue it leaves on the tongue.

In Jersey, it is not uncommon to add a slice of Taylor Pork Roll to a burger, much the way the rest of America would a slice or two of bacon (this is known either as a Trenton Burger or Jersey Burger), or to an egg-and-cheese sandwich (sometimes referred to as a Jersey Breakfast). In Trenton, the déclassé delicacy exerts a special hold on the populace: the town held its first ever Pork Roll Festival in 2014. **—TODD KLIMAN**

North America

STUCK-UP SAUSAGE iS WHAT'S WRONG WiTH YOUR RED BEANS AND RiCE

As told to Peter Meehan by Jonathan Gold

The best way to make red beans and rice is to use the cheapest sausage you can find. I know this by hard-won experience. Perhaps you have had only mediocre versions of the dish and this idea makes it seem even less desirable. I've had mostly mediocre versions of it except in New Orleans itself, where you eat it every Monday with hot sauce and you're happy because it costs almost nothing or was thrown in with your drink. Then you realize it is one of the great dishes in America, the cassoulet of South Louisiana.

I do not make red beans in the traditional way. I put them in a clay pot, stick it in a 250-degree oven for five hours, and go about my day. You don't have to look at it—it's a Monday dish, what you're supposed to cook while you're doing your wash. Once the laundry is off the line, the beans are perfect and creamy and luscious and the meat, that very cheap sausage, is transformed. There's something about cheap sausage that is honored by a low-and-slow cooking process.

I have, of course, made red beans with expensive sausages—the ones at the specialty butcher shops, those made by Bruce Aidells, the special andouille that the New Orleans Fish Market in Los Angeles brings in from Louisiana. They all fall apart. But when you use the incredibly cheap stuff—in L.A., the brands would be Farmer John Hot Louisiana Brand Smoked Sausage (only sold in African-American neighborhoods) or these unreal-red off-brand sausages that I don't imagine contain any parts of the pig that you would be comfortable mentioning in polite society—and they bring the dish to life.

Those last hot links are unspeakable as a stand-alone meat product, but somehow when you slice them up and cook them in a batch of beans, they develop this magnificent, soft, almost loose texture at the end and they have a lot of good flavor from all the obviously industrial-grade chilies, garlic and onion powder, modified cornstarch, and whatever the hell else they're putting in there.

While I'm opening up about my sausage proclivities to you, I'll tell you the other thing I do with red beans and rice: I try to put as many kinds of fat in there as I can. There are some people who always admonish that the entire point of red beans is the beans and that you shouldn't put too much stuff in there. Those people are, of course, wrong.

Typically, I'll take some duck or goose fat or whatever sort of poultry fat I have lying around (I freeze poultry fat; it's just a magical substance, why would you throw it away?) and use it to sauté celery, onion, and peppers. Then I'll put in big handfuls of diced slab bacon and add the beans. I may stick in a ham hock or a ham bone and some pancetta—it adds a vague, haunting peppery funkiness—or guanciale, whatever the case may be. And there's also, almost always, some of the rich, roasty lard that is the by-product of making carnitas, which is also my favorite cooking medium for fried chicken. If I haven't made carnitas recently, I sometimes buy the lard from the local Mexican supermarket, which sells it on weekends, still half-molten, in huge, leaky plastic tubs. There's really no such thing as leftover goose fat, but if you have some goose to put in there, that's great too.

As for the beans themselves, I use Camellia beans, which are cheap and commonplace in Louisiana, and a bit more expensive here. There are people who say that to get the best red beans, you have to use the cheapest possible beans. Pableaux Johnson, one of New Orleans's most prominent red beans and rice evangelists, is of that school. He goes around the country and makes red beans and rice on Mondays, and I think if he were in your town, he would go to the bodega and use whatever red beans were there. There's a brand called Bayou Magic that will get you a fairly righteous version of the dish if you don't want to mess with the seasoning.

And then there's the rice. I use a cheap, superfragrant basmati rice from India,* but it becomes magical if you cook it with enough salt and butter, which is something one tends not to do if you're used to cooking rice for Asian dishes. But when you're doing something like red beans and rice you want a rice that has some flavor kickback, because the rice is served separately. You'll spoon some rice into a bowl and then some red beans over the top of it.

There are people who cook the rice in the bean broth. But they are wrong too, missing out on the contrast of meaty beans studded with transformed sausage playing off of buttered aromatic rice.

---

* It's Royal brand, if you care, but only because that's the brand the local Armenian butcher sells. It used to come in big burlap bags. Now it comes in plastic printed to look like burlap, which may be aesthetically displeasing but means that the rice is far less likely to harbor the occasional tiny bug.

Texas

Amelia Gray

"Smell that post oak," Dad says as we park behind the smoker at Freedmen's. "I'd like to live in that little shack."

Barbecue can define a region or a city block better than any map. And at barbecue joints and church picnics across generations, my family has built our own story in smoked meats. My father is a consummate home cook with a bathtub-size smoker and a cooler dedicated to resting the pork shoulders and beef briskets that emerge, tender and perfectly spiced. My earliest memories feature the man slow-smoking ribs in a red Weber kettle and driving the family to wait in the car line at Oehler's Mallard Creek BBQ Barn for chopped pork soaked in Carolina-style vinegar sauce. His own savory scrapbook begins with his mother smoking turkey on a Hasty-Bake grill in northeastern Oklahoma. In the '70s he moved to Dallas, met a pretty girl, and invested in a Brinkmann, using the wet smoker with a water pan to make ribs marinated in pineapple juice and a flavor of Lea & Perrins that's not around anymore. Loyalty is held sacred in barbecue: by family, by company, by ingredient. If our family tree bore flowers, the buds would smell of mesquite smoke.

Texas has its own barbecue story, its own family of pitmasters and flavors. The family might grow and change, rebel against its fathers and strike out on their own, but they all live under the blue skies of the Republic. It's a proud family, one with a story, and their crest is what you might call the Holy Trinity: ribs, brisket, and sausage.

WHICH IS TO SAY: IT GOES WAY BACK

The Texan's love of sausage goes back to early statehood, when acres of grassland stretched uninterrupted by the thorny mesquite that would ultimately invade the low country. When they weren't eating sausage, they were writing about it; the *Texas Ranger,* a weekly from the town of Washington, presented in March of 1854 a juicy sausage metaphor to workers' rights: "Labor to be well and satisfactorily done must be well and satisfactorily paid for. Bargains have too [*sic*] ends to them, like a sausage; and like a sausage, they should be palatable at both extremities—not stuffed mit [*sic*] shweet [*sic*] pork at one end, and minced goat-tail at t'other."

The first mention of chorizo in Texas records is found in an 1890 restaurant ad in the Spanish weekly newspaper *El Regidor,* where proprietor Juan Jiménez offers chorizo, *champurrado,* and chili con carne at his table, "the very first West of the Plaza de la Leña." And Daniel Vaughn, *Texas Monthly*'s barbecue editor and a man without whom no story on Texas barbecue would be complete, notes that sausage is mentioned in the first advertisement for barbecue in an October 1878 edition of the *Brenham Weekly Banner:* "A Bastrop butcher keeps on hand at his stall a stock of ready barbecued meats and cooked sausages."

Sausage making was a homesteader's trade and the logical end for scraps of meat and fat, made in the style of whatever old country to which one aligned. The home of Texas-German sausage on the commercial market found its heart in Elgin, twenty-five miles east of Austin. The earliest settlers brought their recipes from Germany and Mexico, while the Czechs brought a garlicky link to the table. Weekly import registries printed in the paper teased notice of sausage imported from Bologna, too steep for a settler's wage. William J. Moon opened up a storefront in 1886, selling a spicy "hot guts" sausage that made him

famous. His Southside Market stuffs links to this day. Fourteen years later, Charles Kreuz Sr. opened Kreuz Market in Lockhart, thirty miles south of the capital city.

Dad stood up from the school-desk table at Sonny Bryan's Smokehouse in Dallas to bring his bride to Tucson in 1979, but he never really left Texas barbecue. When I first came to Texas for school twenty-five years later, the whole family made the trip in support, and Dad parked the U-Haul at a Best Western in Lockhart with a mind to sample the city's barbecue strip. It was fun at first to take down ribs and Big Red at Smitty's or Black's, sopping up the remains of a plate with white bread. But by the end of the week, Dad was a lone soldier, going for brisket breakfast tacos while the rest of us ate fruit salad and tried not to absorb too much of the pervasive odor of smoked meat that clung to his clothes when he returned. Three years later, my folks returned and took me out for graduation dinner to the Salt Lick in Driftwood, where we filled our plates with sausage and cobbler.

I still have a place in my heart—a place no doubt weakened by saturated fat—for those legendary places. Still, given the chance to sample sausage around Austin, I wanted to try some new contenders, picking two food trucks and a storefront based on buzz that was surely hard-earned in a city that has begun to be known for its buzz. It has been more than ten years since that Lockhart week and untold barbecue dinners in between. Still, when I told Dad I wanted to sample the best sausage shops in Austin, he dropped everything to make the trip from Arizona, bringing a small black book in which he might make notes of times and temperatures, the type of wood going, each of the sauces and rubs. I told him to wear short sleeves. Our first stop in the morning would have us making sausage at Freedmen's Bar.

EIGHTY POUNDS OF MEAT IN THE HANDS OF EVAN LEROY

Evan LeRoy is a Renaissance man of meats. In addition to his role as pitmaster and executive chef of Freedmen's, he cofounded the Austin Barbecue Society. For its first party, he worked an Indian theme, serving smoked lamb vindaloo as a main course after a smoked spinach and kale *saag* with a housemade, lightly smoked paneer cheese. At Freedmen's he serves that Holy Trinity of brisket, pork spareribs, and housemade sausage and a barbecue Benedict for Sunday brunch. "There's so many ways to do this simple thing," he says, testing a slab of meat with a practiced two fingers. "That's the great thing about barbecue." And he does it well; he had to start locking up the shed's windows overnight, he says, because people were coming in to steal the heavy slabs right out of the smoker.

But we weren't here for the smoker's brisket or ribs or pulled pork, those

meaty tent poles of the pitmaster's circus. We were there for the sausage. I was looking for snappy casings, a balance of meat and fat that glistens without gushing, and flavors that either support or challenge the German standard raised by the local legends in Elgin and Lockhart. Sausage in Texas is an ongoing conversation with as many accents as acres, and I wanted to get to know the local dialect of Austin once again.

Making sausage is part of Evan's ethical philosophy of using as much of the animal as possible. It's an economical choice as well, using scraps and fats they would throw out otherwise. This is the genesis and true spirit of sausage making, when every ounce is of the essence. He has everything weighed and ready by the time we arrive, the beef and pork trimmed and chilling in two big tubs. (Culling these scraps from the larger cuts of meat is apparently the worst part of what is already a time-consuming endeavor, hacking at a mountain of brisket and pork. We were spared that duty for the day.)

Evan uses sixty pounds of beef and pork and twenty pounds of fat, plugging in meat and spice into a basic ratio he has marked on a piece of printer paper slipped into a laminated sleeve. This

eighty-pound batch will last the weekend. A few scoops of ice are mixed in; grinding the mix with ice efficiently distributes moisture and keeps the mix stone-cold and the fat solid until the moment it goes into the smoker. The ice-cold ground meat is mixed thoroughly by hand so nobody gets a mouthful of caraway seed.

Once Evan sets us up, he heads off to check on his prep cook Gary, an old hand who has spent the morning heartily bitching about the decision to keep the salt upstairs, forcing him to hump it one flight up whenever he needs to season something. He leaves me and Dad with the grinding and mixing grunt work, the both of us feeling a little like the saps Tom Sawyer convinced to paint that fence. We're elbow-deep in the stuff by eight in the morning, hands plunged into the tub, fat speckling wrists and forearms, clothes studded with flecks of meat. Dad worries aloud about the pork in his watch. We keep mixing, nothing if not obedient. Also hungry, having skipped breakfast in anticipation.

Evan returns to give us a casing lesson, which he slides like a scrunched sock over the nozzle of the extruder. The goal is to keep the casing smooth as it exits the machine, allowing just enough meat to emerge for a firm pack that doesn't stretch the boundaries of the intestine. One hand cranks the plunger down on the meat, while the other guides the outgoing sausage, guiding the mixture slowly enough to ensure fewer air bubbles, which would expand when hot and burst. It's a complicated endeavor and a little porny. After a few rounds of this and no hope that I'll pick up the action, I feel it's time to step out for a brisk walk around the restaurant.

A man named George Franklin laid the foundation for Freedmen's in 1869. A former slave, he built his home a solid four stones thick, which bought him a bit of well-deserved security and helped to ensure the structure would remain one of the last standing in the Wheatville freedmen community. The place has since housed a church, a grocery store, a publishing house, and a private home, all while keeping its foundation intact, which is no small feat for the loft-happy West Campus neighborhood in which it's nestled like a gilt stocking tucked in the back of a sock drawer.

Evan grew up in Austin but returned only a few years ago, leaving a job at Hill Country Barbecue Market in Manhattan to come here when he felt it was time to get serious about smoking in the actual Hill Country. "If you're going to compete in the barbecue world, this is where you've gotta be," he says. He opened Freedmen's in 2012, serving the standards in his own style—a

133

moist and tender brisket sliced a little thicker than usual, nestled beside slabs of rich pork belly. His sausage takes on the flavors of the moment, integrating the materials he has on hand.

Back in the prep room, Evan reels out thick four-foot spirals. He doesn't hang his sausage to cook it, rather placing them directly on the grill. When he gives us the chance to try stuffing one we let him down immediately: Dad keeps a death grip on the casing as I press too quickly. The thin membrane bursts and we're left with a five-inch nub, which Evan ties off and throws on the grill before loading up the machine again, patient as a choir teacher.

Gary arrives to tease us and, in trying to change the subject, I learn he once owned three places of his own in San Marcos, Texas, including a place that happened to serve my favorite iteration of King Ranch Chicken. (Perhaps the best meal named after a despot since

General Tso, King Ranch is an incredible comfort-food casserole best when it involves the standard cream of mushroom soup and store-bought tortilla strips—dressing it up with fresh vegetables or meat other than the day's leftover chicken would be a little like putting a bow tie on a turd.) "Best King Ranch anywhere!" Gary confirms.

"Bullshit," Evan says, laughing.

"I'll take you on," Gary says, puffing up to his boss. "I will kick your ass at King Ranch Chicken, little brother, you don't even know." He gets into talking about a wedding he catered with nothing but backstrap done different ways. He got burned out on owning but walked in one day at Freedmen's a few years later and asked for a prep job. "You don't walk away from this business," he says.

By the time the place opens at 11 a.m., we've all worked up a good animal stink, a combination of our hard labor and the product we're laboring over. We've finished the sausages and sampled our malformed personal specimen, which Evan had cleaned up and packed properly before tying off. After only an hour on the grill, the casing has a snap that means a good solid filling, a uniform texture, and proper time in the smoker.

Dad and I split the bar's take on an Old Fashioned—think smoked orange and smoked pecan bitters—along with a little of everything Freedmen's offers. Evan heads back into the kitchen to finish prep as we confront the Holy Trinity and its supplicants: thick slabs of brisket, pork belly, ribs nestled against a springy focaccia bread, spicy pimento cheese, slaw, pickles, potato salad, beets under a knob of goat cheese, everything made in-house. The sausage is bursting with flavor that finds a nice balance in the piquant sauce served alongside. This is the Platonic ideal of Texas-German sausage, excelling within the gory bounds of its casing to set the standard by which others might be judged.

Evan leaves us alone to eat, giving us time to both ask for a takeout box and then eat everything we have placed in the takeout box. He returns just as we're philosophizing again about the deceptive simplicity of barbecue. He wipes his hands on his apron, thinking about it. "Yeah," he says. "It's not that hard to do right, but it's very easy to screw up." He has his work cut out for him; in the next few years, he has his sights set on projects even closer to his belief in the material efficiency of every meal; he wants to bind farm and table closer than ever, microsourcing his materials. As for Dad and me, our future is a little more immediate: It's time for more barbecue.

ESAUL RAMOS GOES FROM HOME GRILL TO BIG TIME

We take Cesar Chavez Street over to La Barbecue, a trailer caravan in a food truck lot on the Eastside comprising three big smokers and a prep/cashier trailer, fronted by a big tub of icy-cold drinks—the tooth-stripping acidic sugar of red cream soda is efficient against pork fat. We're met by Pitmaster Esaul Ramos, a young guy with an easy charm. Robert Sierra of San Marcos's S&S Pit Crew calls him El Mexican Johnny Cash, the hardest-working pitmaster he knows.

Despite being new to town, E fits in as a true Eastsider, riding his bike to work. He's a people person who strikes up conversation with tourists who have the time to stand in line for hours—La Barbecue's trailer complex has achieved legendary status in three short years, opened by John Lewis, who has since fled the state to open up a new joint in South Carolina. E shows us around the caravan, calling out instructions to his prep guys in Spanish as he throws his weight back to lift the smoker's heavy steel hatch.

His sausage man Frank had already finished grinding and stuffing the hot guts for the day, the short, fat links bright red with spices and filling a bus tub, ready for their hours hanging in the smoker. There's beef hearts and liver in these guts in addition to the standard brisket and fat trimmings. Frank begins at two in the morning before it gets too hot out. The neighboring people of Austin can sleep better knowing that, nearby, a man is silently grinding beef hearts.

The neighbor thing is actually a point

of contention. A few months ago, the city started the process of creating an ordinance against the barbecue smoke that was created by the fifty restaurants in Austin with smokers, a move that would require the rigs to be fit with smoke scrubbers. It threw a hot coal under the community; Aaron Franklin argued that the scrubbers would change the way the cookers smoked, that his Franklin Barbecue would have to close or move, and that the resolution would "destroy Austin barbecue." As perhaps the most celebrated pitmaster in America, Franklin and his brand-new James Beard Award carry a lot of weight with the council. Coincidentally or not, the committee unanimously voted against the ordinance.

It was good news for the pitmasters of Austin, who are suddenly finding themselves thrust onto center stage. La Barbecue is no exception. "Maybe one day we can venture off," Esaul says, talking about experimenting with different sausage flavors. He looks up to guys who experiment with flavor and texture while keeping the product uniformly good. I try the same thing with him I tried with Evan, suggesting that sausage is a study in elevated simplicity, but calling his craft easy doesn't go over as well. "That's a bold statement," he says. "I think sausage and brisket are the two most complex things that we have here." He glances at the tub. "Frank has mastered the art of making this sausage that's so consistently good every day, you can tell when he did it." For a moment I'm afraid he's going to make me repeat what I said about sausage being easy in front of Frank.

"I mean, it's easy the way chess is easy," I backpedal, picturing the bishop moving to take a pawn who has belittled the lifeblood of the hardest-working pitmaster in Austin.

E is a generous man, but he suffers no fools. He laughs it off and shows us out of his office.

Unfortunately that bus tub of fresh links hasn't yet come anywhere near the smoker, and they're out of cooked sausage for the day. It's a common condition by early afternoon at the trucks. E has his eye on a storefront, an expanded menu, and a bigger team. Air-conditioning, if they're lucky. For now, we'll have to come back in the morning, when he promises to toss a few through our open window. We enjoy another gorgeous spread of the remaining meats, slices of brisket thick with fresh pepper beside ribs and turkey, hearty sides of beans and onions. The plate is a study in spice, and the hot guts we sample the next morning will only add to that palette. I wonder if the sausage in Elgin used to bring this kind of heat years ago, before they sold in the grocery stores; with smaller batches and a loyal fan base, La Barbecue has more room to push the limits. We end the lunch hour with a Big Red and head back to our Airbnb. I take a desperate shower while Dad snacks on ribs as he watches a vampire movie in order to get in the mood for an evening of mixing, grinding, and casing with Tom Micklethwait.

MICKLETHWAIT SELLS OUT

By noon, sometimes. The brisket and ribs last a little longer at Micklethwait Craft Meats but the sausage, a small batch in short supply, is often gone about an hour after the register fires up in the morning. Since 2012, the little trailer has planted a flag on Rosewood, supported by the philosophy of fresh herbs, unique ingredients, and a dessert menu that finds its way into most of its Yelp reviews. It's all guided by Tom Micklethwait who, by the time we arrive at sundown, isn't really in the mood to talk. "Ready to make some sausage?" he asks, barely breaking stride as he carries the ubiquitous bus tub into the pale yellow trailer painted with oak leaves and acorns.

Once inside, I understand his trepidation. Three people lined up side by side in his prep area leaves little room to breathe, let alone work. But he makes the best of it, chopping up garlic, tossing in a spice blend including cardamom, celery powder, mustard seed, and ground clove. He's using beef today, though he might make one with pork or duck, whatever's around. The process appears automatic and slightly somnambulant, as if you placed your hand

on his shoulder he might wake confused, gripping a jug of coriander.

Daniel Vaughn says, "Nobody in Texas barbecue is as creative with sausage recipes as Tom Micklethwait." Today, Tom frowns at his pantry while his grill man works with the smoker and a small group of diners finishes their brisket and beers and heads home. He goes to the back garden for a handful of fresh sage. He answers questions with the enthusiasm of a record store clerk who's been interrupted on his lunch break, but his meat speaks for itself. People rave about his curry goat and jalapeño cheddar sausage, his pork belly andouille, his Thai chili beef, and his chorizo.

With a diet like that, you'd think getting in and out of the trailer would become a problem, but Tom doesn't

make a habit of his own stash. Though Austin and its visitors seem to be enjoying the fatty fruits of their labor, the sausage men keep things in moderation. E grills chicken on his off days, while Evan digs into veggie tacos and speaks fondly about a dish of seared calamari with olives and blood oranges at Italic, a new Italian place in the Warehouse District. Tom raves about the cioppino at Clark's Oyster Bar and gets out to try other barbecue in town "maybe three or four times this year." They're happy to be where they are, sated with praise rather than meat, riding the wave of a city beginning to form its identity around traditions that once defined the towns nearby.

Tom warms up a little when we offer to do the hand-mixing for him. By now I find the process soothing and only a little disconcerting, like massaging the inside of a dead body. We discuss his concept for a graphic novel with a brisket hero styled like a young Tom Cruise with salt and pepper sidekicks. "Brisky Business," he says. He speaks fondly of a quail sausage he made from a twenty-pound batch of birds he bought off a friend at a game ranch. It was hard to trim enough meat from about fifty tiny quail breasts but the result was excellent. He brings out the grinder, their second: "The first one died in an explosion." Dad leans down to smell the tub of meat, always curious. (I'm reminded of a childhood trip to the Jack Daniel's distillery, where he conducted a similar study over a two-story vat of bubbling corn mash and nearly fell in.)

None of the guys we talked to wanted to hang their hat on the four-walled legacies they've already built. Tom is no exception; he's opening a deli truck with thick slabs of house-cured meat on that bread he's been spending his days perfecting. Meanwhile he's working the catering circuit, serving sausage to the Hill Country's lovely meat brides of June.

It's cooling down by the time we step out of Tom's trailer. He gifts us a loaf of the earthy, fresh rye bread he made earlier that day. A couple days later we swing by for a few Saint Arnold ale kielbasa-style beerwursts and a beef-and-pork hot gut served sliced and wrapped in brown paper. Mickelthwait's sausages are the wild card of the bunch we've tried, proof that to stake your claim in Texas barbecue, you need to carve out your own niche and balance your smoker in that niche to the best of your ability. The coarser texture of these sausages would work well tucked into a corn tortilla with sour cream and salsa, and I make plans to do just that later, taking a few home with us wrapped in spare paper. Something for the road, as we point our greased-up rental car toward the airport, another tour of Texas meats complete.

Though this one seems to have affected us a little more: Dad's ready to buy a grinder. He's talking about his ideal mix: garlic and jalapeño chilies, mustard and fennel seeds, red chili flakes, coriander, and cardamom. A few more weeks out, he's considering a food truck as a retirement plan. And the legacy continues.

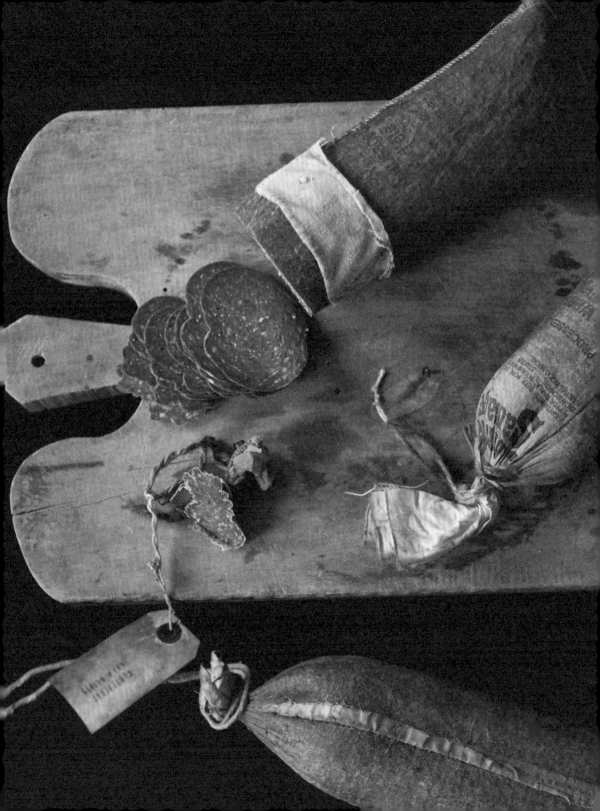

Canada

Adam Leith Gollner

"This is it, the Conestogo," old Jim Hodgson announced, guiding us over the low-lying bridge in his banged-up Oldsmobile. The Conestogo River meanders its way through rural Ontario's Mennonite country, a watery reminder that this community traces its roots back to the American township of Conestoga, Pennsylvania. Mennonite pioneers first started fording their way up to Canada's Conestogo after the American Revolution, using covered Conestoga wagons. Traces of those ancient carriages can still be seen all over Waterloo County: horse and buggy remains the preferred means of transport in these parts.

Old Order Mennonites today don't use cars, electricity, the Internet, deodorant, or any other modern conveniences. Despite living only an hour and a half away from downtown Toronto, on the fringes of what has become suburban sprawl, they continue to exist pretty much the way they did centuries ago. In the foreword to *The Trail of the Conestoga,* Bertha Mabel Dunham's 1924 account of the Mennonite exodus to Canada, Prime Minister William Mackenzie King wrote, "If we go back to early days, we shall find that the problems which perplex us are no greater than those they successfully solved."

I'd traveled here in search of one of those perplexing things the Mennonites long ago solved: the perfect summer sausage. A summer sausage is essentially a preindustrial smoked sausage. The name refers to the fact that it is made during warm weather, and that it can be preserved without refrigeration. It's how people ate dried sausage before the advent of supermarkets and cold storage.

And a proper Waterloo County Mennonite summer sausage (not the bogus imitation stuff sold in big-box stores) still tastes better than any other fermented sausage food scientists have figured out how to make in modern times. Unfortunately, health inspection requirements have made it pretty much impossible to buy the real thing anymore—unless, of course, you make a pilgrimage down the back roads of rural Ontario.

"Maybe that's the place Stemmler was talking about?" Hodgson wondered aloud, pointing toward a stone smokehouse next to a barn. Some freshly stacked wood indicated it was still in use.

Stemmler's directions couldn't have been simpler: Go north at the main intersection in Heidelberg and take a right down the first concession into the farmland. There'd be a river, then a sign.

But we didn't know what a concession was supposed to look like. Like any other country road, apparently? And the only sign we'd seen so far read KEEP AWAY FROM BARN in red spray paint. I'd felt sure we'd gone the wrong way until the river appeared, just like Stemmler told us it would.

So we took him at his word and continued on, drifting deeper into the Mennonite heartland, into the green aorta of summertime. Hodgson was in the middle of telling me how you can tell that a farm is really Old Order by the lack of electrical lines on the property when we saw it: a rusting placard with a white pig silhouetted against a yellow backdrop. The word *butchering* was spelled out in cursive red letters on the pig's body. Hodgson hit the brakes, and we turned onto the dirt lane leading to the house.

A forty-something Mennonite man stood at the end of the driveway watching us approach. He had dark hair, a dusty black sun hat, black overalls, and a blue plaid shirt. He scrutinized us through lucid blue eyes. Coming to a stop next to him, I rolled down the passenger-side window and asked if he happened to have any summer sausage for sale.

"No!" he responded immediately, almost instinctively.

"No?" I checked, a hint of dismay tinting my voice.

"We do, ah, whole carcasses, not, ah, small pieces," the Mennonite explained, with some finality. There was a Germanic lilt to the way he spoke, but mostly he sounded like someone from long ago.

"Does anybody around here sell any homemade summer sausages?" I persisted.

He looked into the car with those piercing eyes, trying to ascertain, he later revealed, whether we were inspectors or cops. Mennonites don't dislike interacting with outsiders, but they do find meddlers bothersome.

Hodgson started explaining a bit more. "So Mister Stemmler told us to come out this way and—"

"Stemmler?" the Mennonite man interrupted, pronouncing it the way the inhabitants of *Deliverance*'s leafier realms might have. He came closer, put one knee in the dirt next to the car, and tucked his fingers into his britches. "Oh, Stemmler Meats send you here?"

"Stemmler sent us onto this road because he said there were some people who make homemade summer sausage around here," I clarified.

The man looked to his right, toward the barn, where an older man in the exact same outfit—black sun hat, black overalls, blue plaid shirt—stood watching us. The elder Mennonite walked over and leaned right up to the passenger-side window, looming over the younger man. A dense shock of gray hair was bursting from his ear hole. It looked like a two-inch-long black-and-white bushfire spreading out of his brain.

"What are you looking for?" he asked, pointedly.

"We're looking for summer sausage!" I said, flush with the sort of almost pathetic optimism reporters like me employ as a strategy for cajoling people like him into letting us enter their world.

"Well, they make summer sausage in Canada," he offered.

"Well, that means we're in the right place," I parried.

The man smiled patiently. We shook hands and he told us his name: Cleason Weber.

"Stemmler Meats send 'em out here," the first guy explained. "Stemmler's don't make the old original summer sausage there."

"Ach, you want the original one?" Weber asked.

We nodded. He sized us up, then shook his head. "You can't really get it the true old way anymore," he explained, slowly. "The reason is, the government has their rules and regulations and—"

"I know, I know," Hodgson interjected. "They're always giving people a hard time, but we're not government, eh? I'm a Cress, so I'm related to the old Mennonites by extraction. My great-great-grandfather built the first farm in St. Jacobs. Do you know Edna Staebler there? I'm her nephew."

They both looked impressed at the Cress connection, but neither of the men had heard of Edna Staebler. I knew her, of course. She was the main reason I'd traveled out here in search of summer sausage, and the reason I was seated next to her nephew Jim Hodgson. In 1968, Staebler published a collection of down-home Mennonite recipes and folklore called *Food That Really Schmecks*. Nobody expected a book about Waterloo County culinary traditions to become a bestseller, but Schmecks became an instant classic, selling many tens of thousands of copies, going through numerous editions and printings. (It remains in print to this day.) Sequels ensued: *Schmecks Appeal* and *More Food That Really Schmecks*. Staebler used her earnings to start a foundation that hands out an annual award to the best debut book of creative nonfiction published that year by a young Canadian writer. Staebler died in 2006 at the age of 100.

Staebler's books were based on immersive reporting she did in the home of the Martins, an Old Order Mennonite family. The mother, Bevvy Martin, specialized in timeless dishes like drepsley soup (droplet-like flour-egg dumplings in a meat broth), schnippled bean salad (boiled green beans cut thin, on the bias, a.k.a. "schnippled," and served in a dressing made of sour cream, vinegar, and sugar) and fetschpatze ("fat sparrows," a type of batter that takes on bird-like shapes when fried in hot lard). "You might need more cream" is a typical recipe directive. Her desserts were fairy-tale concoctions: shoofly pie, hurry sponge cake, and various items "popular at Mennonite funerals."

Alongside these time-tested recipes, the book contained numerous anecdotes about Mennonite life, as well as home remedies. A mixture of two-thirds goose schmaltz and one-third turpentine is to be rubbed on congested chests. Recovery from a lightning strike, Staebler wrote, entails showering in cold water for two hours. "If the patient does not show signs of life," she added, "put salt in the water and continue to shower for an hour longer."

Part of the joy of reading Staebler's work is discovering how Mennonites speak—they have a vernacular all their own, a mish-mash of German dialects, Dutch Low Saxon, and New World slang. Good-schmecking food is food that tastes good. You eat "till everything is all" (meaning until there is nothing left). *Schnitzing* is the word for cutting up apples to dry.

Staebler's books are gems of folk literature. Always seeking the humanity in her subjects, she depicted her characters as generous, funny, peace loving, respectful, and full of the sort of dignity that comes from working hard and living off the land. Staebler brought to life a world of idyllic dance socials and Old Order farmers making dandelion wine.

An early moment in the original *Food That Really Schmecks* concerns summer sausage, which the Martin family held among their favorite things of all. "It is beef and pork ground real fine with

seasoning and saltpeter," explains Bevvy Martin, "then stuffed tight in cotton bags the size of a lady's stocking and smoked for a week with maple smoke."

Her shy ten-year-old son Amsey told Staebler that he and the family "couldn't live without summer sausage." Bevvy corrects him: "Ach, we could live without only we rather wouldn't."

What had become of Amsey? If he was ten years old in the mid-1960s, when Staebler was writing the book, he would now be close to sixty—and he'd be the perfect person to speak with about summer sausage. Of course, tracking down Amsey Martin in Waterloo County might be easier if Old Order Mennonites used telephones.

As it turns out, Bevvy Martin's real name was Libby Kramer. For the purposes of her book, Staebler changed Libby's and her son's names to common Mennonite names.

Staebler was survived by her niece Barbara Wurtele (née Hodgson), a landscape painter in Waterloo County. I asked her over the phone about where I might get ahold of the Kramers/Martins.

"They would be long gone," she told me. She said that the best bet would be to head to the St. Jacobs Farmers' Market in Ontario, the nodal point where Mennonite life intersects with the rest of the world. "There are tons of vendors at the market on Saturdays, and you'll find lots of summer sausage being sold." She also suggested I try speaking with her brother, Jim Hodgson, who she said would know more about summer sausage than she did.

And so it was that I found myself

waiting for Jim Hodgson at St. Jacobs market on a busy Saturday afternoon. There were hundreds of vendors out, selling everything from shoes to crocheted doilies to animal pelts. The turnout was as multicultural as the Greater Toronto Area itself—Southeast Asian couples snacked on Salvadoran *pupusas* while Middle Eastern families bought fabric from Senegalese *schmatta* guys. Dour women in prayer bonnets sold *doner kebabs* to a line of First Nations kids, Pakistani seniors, and Mennonite men all wearing the same suspenders and shirts and straw hats.

The corridors through the market were seriously overcrowded. Shoppers milling around would stop to peruse a stall, causing everything behind them to come to a standstill. Locals trying to get their shopping done were getting frustrated by big-city visitors having a lazy day in the country.

Around a dozen vendors had summer sausage for sale in the market, but all of them were made at processing plants. I asked one butcher whether it was possible to get homemade summer sausage the way Amsey Martin would've eaten it. "Nobody is making summer sausages in the barn and smoking them in the old shed out back anymore," he explained. "I mean maybe some people do it, but you'd never be able to sell that to the public. If health inspectors found out, you'd be shut down."

When Jim Hodgson arrived, he informed me that he had no idea how to attempt (a) getting in touch with Amsey or anyone else related to the Martin/Kramer clan, and (b) tracking down any authentic home-style Mennonite summer sausage. He suggested I just pick up any of the summer sausages for sale.* "This is some of the best summer sausage in the world here in Waterloo County," he said. "I grew up on it, right? Although I don't really eat it anymore." He pointed to his few remaining teeth.

Hodgson then took me to Stemmler's Meat & Cheese, in the nearby town of Heidelberg. He said they were famous not just for their nitrate-free summer sausage (delicious) but also for their smoked pork chops and their ham hocks and their special head cheese and their smoked pig jowls and their pickled sausages and their elderberry pies and their zucchini bread and about twenty other things that I lost track of, but most of all they are famous for their pig tails, he said.

"It's old recipes here that go way back," Hodgson said. "Pig tails like

---

* Of the health-inspector-certified summer sausages I picked up, the version by A. F. Weber was better than the version by Noah Martin's, but the best summer sausage I found at the market was the one by N. S. Martin.

this, you won't see that anywhere else in Canada. They're divine. They're like candy."

He handed me a box of frozen pig tails that I later heated up in the oven to divine result.

As we strolled through the aisles, I asked a bonnet-wearing Mennonite employee if I could take some photos of the store and she went to check with the owner. Kevin Stemmler himself came out to see us a few minutes later. Upon learning that Jim Hodgson was related to Edna Staebler, he immediately said he'd be happy to speak with us. "Edna used to be a good customer of ours," Stemmler explained. He suggested we go back into his office to discuss summer sausage there.

As we walked, he noticed the package of frozen pig tails I held in my hands and asked if I'd ever tried them before. I shook my head. "They're a lot like ribs," Stemmler said. "We basically marinate the tails in a brown-sugar-and-molasses-based sauce. You just roast this container in the oven for one and a half hours and you're ready to go. People love pig tails around here. It schmecks good." I was so happy to hear him say those words.

Our discussion grew more guarded once the subject turned to the Stemmler's summer sausage. "We make summer sausage here using a very old formula and very old techniques," Stemmler said, in the store's back office. "The formula we use is over a hundred years old. We discovered the formula accidentally and it is so good that we've been producing it this way ever since."

I could tell by the deliberate way he chose his words that he was being careful not to overshare. "Is it a secret formula?" I asked, half jokingly.

"Yeah, kind of," he replied entirely seriously. "I don't want to give away anything, but, uh . . ."

"Could you give me any information at all about it?"

"Like I say, it's a simple recipe with four or five ingredients besides the beef and the pork. And that's it."

I looked at him beseechingly.

"What can I tell you?" he said, shaking his head but smiling. "Look, it starts with the saltpeter, which you need for the preservative. You got salt, pepper, sugar, and other spices that grow here locally. Then there's drying, smoking, and cooking. We rely very much on bacterial cultures. The trademark flavor profile in the sausage comes from the bacteria, not from the spicing."[*]

Stemmler diverted our conversation

---

[*] As he spoke, it occurred to me that Stemmler's reticence to share manufacturing details wasn't exactly unjustified. There's a lot of money at stake in Mennonite traditions. For example: the sausage master Noah Martin (who passed away in 1990) became so renowned for his summer sausage that his descendants managed to sell the rights to his name to companies that still market Noah Martin's sausage even though he and his family have nothing to do with it. And in 1984, there was a major legal battle between Nabisco and Procter & Gamble over the intellectual property rights to cookies capable of being simultaneously crispy and chewy. Mennonites had figured out a solution to that organoleptic "textural dichotomy" long before multinational corporations embarked on the "Great Cookie War," as it came to be known (Procter & Gamble, Duncan Hines's parent company, ended up winning a $125 million settlement). In fact, a cookie recipe from *Food That Really Schmecks* ended up being a reference in the original patent filing by Procter & Gamble: Bevvy Martin's Rigglevake cookies. (*Rigglevake* is an Ontario Mennonite word for "railway.")

away from sensitive summer sausage IP talk by launching into a zymological look at meat fermentation. Strains of bacteria like *Pediococcus* play an important part in summer-sausage crafting. These beneficial microorganisms generate lactic acid and help increase gel formation in the sausage while also affecting the taste of the sausage. "The bacteria eats the sugar and leaves acids behind," he pointed out. "That's how you get that tang in your summer sausage, the acidic flavor, you know, that sour kick we like around here. We ferment the meat for twenty-four hours and then we cold-smoke the sausages for a couple of days. We want the bacteria to thrive. Then we cook it at the end to make it safe."

"Is that how Mennonites do it as well?" I inquired.

"In a way," he said, hesitantly. "They often use a less precise process called back 'slopping.' How that works is, you take an old batch of summer sausage that was really good, and you use some of that product in the new sausage you're making. That way, the bacteria gets passed on naturally. But that's a very old technique, and there are much more precise methods nowadays. We're inspected closely here, so we have to have science behind us. What they're doing isn't unsafe, but we absolutely couldn't do it in this store."

"Does anyone still do it that way?"

"Sure. Old Order Mennonites do it that way. Slopping is still the way they do it at home."

"Do they ever sell it?"

"Technically they probably shouldn't be, but they do sometimes. If you drive down some of the county roads around here, you might see summer sausage on farm gate signs."

Down by the Conestogo, the elder Mennonite, Cleason Weber, said he didn't know of anyone who would have homemade summer sausage for sale on a Saturday afternoon. There was one place, maybe, but they would only *sell* them— they wouldn't know much about *making* them.

"Where do you guys get your summer sausage from?" Hodgson asked.

"Us? We make it, of course."

"You make your own?" I exclaimed.

"Yes," said the younger Mennonite. "But we've got nothing to advertise about it."

"You wanna know how it's made?" inquired Weber.

We nodded.

"Well, what I use is pork and beef. For a hundred pounds of meat you would use three pounds of salt, two and a half pounds of sugar, and six to eight ounces of pepper, and your garlic. You mix that and spice it. And then you add your pickle cure, which is the same thing as saltpeter, only less potent. And then you smoke it in your smoker for a whole week or ten days."

Having finally relented to the fact that we weren't undercover government agents, he took us out back to see his smoker, a beautiful walk-in brick-and-stone shed charred with soot and blackened meat juices. There were some wood chips and other tree bits on the floor— from cherry trees, he noted. "Cherry-wood makes the best summer sausage. Not maple. And other woods can make the sausage taste bitter."

He walked away for a moment and then came back with one of his own summer sausages. The real deal! That which Amsey couldn't live without. It was almost two feet long and gave off a smoky, slightly fruity perfume redolent of a camping trip in paradise.

We spoke about how it differed from those available at the market. He said it mainly had to do with a longer, kinder, higher-quality smoking period. He also told me that he doesn't see any need to add any live bacteria. "The one reason for some of that stuff is that the white hats, the inspection guys, they think that natural summer sausage is gonna make you sick and they wanna protect themselves and that's what they're after," Weber said. "Whereas for me, I'm sixty-four years old and I haven't croaked yet from summer sausage. I smoke 'em for ten days. And smoking is a preservative—that preserves your meat. There's natural enzymes in your wood that preserves the bacteria."

I thought of Edna Staebler, who lived happily to the age of one hundred, and the Martin and Kramer families, wherever they may be. All their down-home remedies and lovely recipes would be considered deeply unhealthy by urbanites, yet these people seemed more than fine to me. "Us Old Order Mennonites, when you have to take us away to a hospital, the nurses they en-choy working with us people," Weber said. "Like, we're chust totally a different package."

I shot some photos of him and the sausage and the smoker, and then showed him what he looked like on the display screen. He liked the images, but asked me not to publish any photos of his face. "It's important for us to not be part of the system," he clarified. "Like my church wouldn't be pleased if they saw a photo of me in a magazine there. We believe in nonresistance, right?"

I didn't quite understand what he meant by "nonresistance," but later learned that the Mennonite philosophy of pacifism and humility goes beyond declining to participate in any violent activity—it also entails a commitment to avoid anything that might be perceived as self-glorifying. Being meek and modest is essential to the Mennonite identity, and the possibility that he could be construed as having posed in the photos would be taken as an affront by his congregation.

Still, seeing as I'd already been taking photos with him, I decided to push my luck even further. I asked whether he'd be willing to part with any of the sausage—for money of course. He looked down at it, then up at me, then down at the sausage again. He thought about it, scratched his head, and thought about it some more.

"There's no obligation," I added. "Just thought I'd ask—but please feel free to say no."

He nodded slowly, but didn't respond. A full minute went by. I wasn't sure what variables he was weighing. Had I put him in a difficult position? "Really, it's not necessary," I blurted out, uneasy with the lengthy silence. "I'm sorry I asked."

"No, it's fine. This would give you an idea of what it really tastes like. And it's not like my family will go hungry if we sell it to you . . ."

"We could split it?" I suggested. "You could just sell me a small piece if you want?"

He moved his fingers along the length of the sausage. Two of his fingers were missing above the knuckles—a telltale sign of a lifelong butcher. Using those stubby fingertips, he measured sections of the summer sausage, doing calculations in his head.

"He doesn't want to sell it," Hodgson said, growing impatient. "Come on, Adam, let's go."

I thanked Weber for his time, and insisted he forget about my request. But as I went to shake his hand, he thrust the summer sausage toward me and said, "Give me thirty dollars and it's yours."

I did so gladly; it ended up being so worth it. I could've lived without it, but I would've rather not. It tasted smokier, more vibrant, and slightly sweeter than the others I'd purchased at the market. It wasn't too far from a Pick salami from Hungary, albeit infused with a delicate cherrywood smoke aroma. The crustulated ring of deeper aged, smoked meat on the outside combined with the moist, soft center in a perfect textural dichotomy of schmeckdom.

That conjunction of opposites felt emblematic of something greater—different cultures and eras coming together in mutual respect and nonresistance, possibly. It wasn't just a cold cut; it was a clothbound emissary from the ancient future.

I brought it home with me. I kept it on a bookshelf in the back room where, true to form, it stayed fresh in its sock without the need for refrigeration. I gave some to friends and family and loved ones. It was summer, it was sausage, and then, in no time, it was *all*.

SOUTH AMERiCA

Repurposed and remixed Spanish and Portuguese imports, and an exuberant fascination with seeing just how much stuff one can fit on top of a sausage before it stops being a sausage.

Butifarra Soledeñas

In the city of Soledad, Colombia, vendors walk the streets tapping their knives against the sides of metal tins, calling out, "Buti, buti, buti!" It's not that Bubba Sparxxx's "Ms. New Booty" took an especially long time to reach northern Colombia; they're hawking *butifarras soledeñas*, descendants of Catalonian *botifarra* that come in long necklaces of small, spherical pork orbs. (They look similar to Sai Krok Isan, page 84, except grayer.) Should you wish to indulge, the vendor will slice off a few links from the chain and squeeze fresh lime juice onto the sausage balls before handing them over (perhaps with a *bollo de yucca*, a corn husk filled with mashed yucca). Peel back the casing of the sausage and dig in. If you're still hungry, follow your ears to more *buti*.

WHERE: Colombia
MEAT: beef and pork
PREPARATION: boiled
SERVED: sliced, with lime and yucca on the side

Cachorro Quente

It makes sense that the country that is home to Carnival would also be home to *cachorro quente*, a gluttonously redecorated Brazilian take on a hot dog. The cachorro quente starts out innocently enough—a soft white bun plus a steamed or boiled sausage—then takes a turn for the insane when toppings enter the equation. Tomatoes, corn, bacon bits, ground beef, mashed potatoes, quail eggs, ketchup, mustard, mayonnaise, grated cheese, *batata palha* (fried slivers of potato). It goes without saying, but a cachorro quente is best consumed long after the sun goes down, when darkness conceals the sins layered atop the unsuspecting white bun.

WHERE: Brazil
MEAT: beef
PREPARATION: grilled
SERVED: on a bun, loaded with toppings

Completo

The Chilean *completo* (see recipe, page 198) is, as the name promises, complete. A grinder roll provides the structural support for a standard boiled hot dog, chopped tomatoes, chopped avocados, and—this is the essential ingredient— more mayonnaise than seems possible or advisable. This relatively tame take on the completo is known as *el italiano* because of its colors, which are similar to those of the Italian flag. But to make it even more completo, add more toppings: green salsa, bacon, sauerkraut, melted cheese. There's no wrong way, but remember the *mayonesa* is the star of this show.

WHERE: Chile
MEAT: beef
PREPARATION: boiled
SERVED: in a bun, loaded with lots of toppings, especially mayo

Feijoada

The national dish of Brazil is also quintessential poverty food, created by slaves in the state of Bahia. Like sausage, it's designed to make the best of the cheap cuts you've been dealt—ears, feet, tails, tongues—along with whatever forms of salted, dried, or smoked meats you've stored away. A starch stretcher, it turns a pile of beans into a rib-sticking stew for a family and almost always includes a couple forms of sausage: usually *paio*, a cured pork-loin sausage, and whatever fresh or smoked *linguiça* is available (this was once a Portuguese colony after all). Served with traditional accompaniments like orange slices, sautéed collard greens, and rice or *farofa* (toasted manioc flour), it becomes *feijoada completa,* a feast served family- style for Saturday lunch or on special occasions.

WHERE: Brazil
MEAT: linguiça and piggy parts
PREPARATION: stewed with beans and cheap cuts of meat

SERVED: with oranges, greens, and farofa

Linguiça

Linguiça is the catchall term for smoked sausages in Brazil, inherited from the country's Portuguese colonizers. Different types serve different needs: spicy *linguiça calabresa* for pizza, *linguiça toscana* for feijoada, and especially garlicky *linguiça portuguesa* for grilling.

WHERE: Brazil
MEAT: pork
PREPARATION: hot- or cold-smoked
SERVED: grilled, sliced for pizza, or stewed in feijoada

Choripán

WHERE: Argentina
MEAT: pork
PREPARATION: griddled
SERVED: sliced lengthwise, stuffed in a bad baguette with chimichurri

Here you are, stranded on a desolate strip of torn-up grass and concrete between the domestic airport and the Río de la Plata, on the outskirts of Buenos Aires. It seemed like a good idea at the time, demanding the taxi driver stop when you first spotted the bright lights and smoke of these *choripán* carts on your way back from the clubs just on the other side of the airport. It still seemed like a good idea as you devoured the sandwich, slathered with chimichurri, hot and greasy—equal parts meat and fat, really—as the day-old French bread soaks up the juices, smoky and sweet, that spilled from the just-griddled sausage. It was somehow too much and just enough—perfect for your current state of mind. Fellow clubgoers mix with night-shift truckers—all walks of life are present and accounted

Morcilla

Morcilla is a Spanish-style blood sausage, a mix of pork fat and blood, rice, and onion, plus whatever flourishes are specific to the regions where it's found, of which there are a great many. Morcilla (or sometimes *moronga*) has left its bloody impression on most of Latin America and the Caribbean. In Argentina, you can find it grilled, split down the middle, and nestled in a roll for a variation on choripán (below) called *morcipanmorcipán*. In Uruguay, it's part of a full *asado* (or *parrillada*, a mixed grill). And in Puerto Rico, morcilla is a Christmas favorite.

WHERE: Spain and wherever Spanish explorers made

MEAT: pork
PREPARATION: boiled, grilled, fried, pan-fried
SERVED: as is; with numerous masa-based vehicles (tortillas, *gorditas, arepas*); in sandwiches

Morcilla Dulce

Oh god, there's . . . blood . . . everywheeeeerrrrreeee! Morcilla (left), Spanish-style blood sausage, is splattered wherever Spanish colonists set foot around the globe. It's even gotten into the sweets. Like most blood sausages, *morcilla dulce* is an almost black sausage that owes its color and heady flavor to the blood of a pig, but it's marked for the idiosyncratic addition of sugar, grapes,

for here on this sliver of land. And it all seemed like a good idea until the moment the choripán was gone. Now, thanks to the choripán's sobering alchemy of carbs and fat, you're tired and too full and just want to go home.

You wake up the next morning and wonder, Was that all a dream? Your nagging nausea and searing heartburn suggest that it was not, but you brave the morning sun's judgmental glare and decide to find out for sure. Two bus transfers and a treacherous walk across a highway later, you're back. The cook invites you behind the griddle to watch the process. He slices generic French bread lengthwise and sets it on a griddle to toast. Same goes for the chorizo. (It occurs to you only then that choripán is simply a portmanteau of chorizo and *pan*.) The meat sizzles and smokes, and when it's just seared, it's done. The cook slips it into the crisp bread and hands it over. Now it's up to you. Trying to re-create last night's hazy excess, you go all in: a slick of garlicky red chimichurri, a pile of fluorescent pickled cabbage, a heap of raw onions. This time, though, the harsh truth of daylight reveals the truth about choripán: It's too much and not enough. The bread is stale, the chorizo unsettlingly greasy and underwhelmingly mild, the chimichurri more oily than fiery. The magic of the night before is gone.

But maybe that's beside the point. Choripán is best experienced like Buenos Aires itself: after dark, after a bottle or three of Malbec, after dancing until the sun begins to rise. Choripán can't be judged in the light of day. Like so many great street sausages, it belongs to the night. **—RYAN HEALEY**

raisins, orange peel, nuts, and/or chocolate. Morcillas dulces can be found at Uruguayan grillouts (*asados* or *parrillas*) and in other Spanish-inflected parts of the world like Argentina and the Canary Islands.

WHERE: Uruguay, Argentina, Canary Islands
MEAT: pork blood
PREPARATION: grilled
SERVED: as is

Mortadella Sandwich

São Paulo's mortadella sandwich is a history lesson and heart attack in one. The heart attack is this: a half pound of warm mortadella, sliced thin, stacked as thick as a dictionary, and blanketed with a thick cover of just-melted cheese, squished into a soft chunk of Italian bread. The history lesson explains how the sainted sausage of Bologna found a home in South America: Brazil's early twentieth-century immigration policies allowed millions of Italians to move there and work the country's coffee plantations. As a result, today, much of Brazil's population has Italian roots; in São Paulo, home of this mortadella monster, it's closer to sixty percent. And this sandwich, found in delis and outdoor *mercados,* is an overstuffed benefit of that legacy.

WHERE: São Paulo, Brazil
MEAT: pork
PREPARATION: sliced
SERVED: in a sandwich

Pancho

Uruguay's entry in the Rose Parade of over-the-top decorated South American hot dogs is the *pancho*. Sold from *carritos*—steel trailers that dot Uruguayan streets—the unadorned pancho is an extralong hot dog whose nose and tail tend to poke out beyond the confines of its bun. But a fully loaded pancho might run over with corn kernels, onion, melted cheese, relish, and *salsa golf*—a mix of mayonnaise and ketchup.

WHERE: Uruguay
MEAT: beef and/or pork
PREPARATION: boiled, grilled
SERVED: with corn, cheese, and sauces

Salchipapas

In Lima, Peru, they've taken a staple of the American diet—a hot dog and fries—and improved on it. *Salchipapas,* a portmanteau of *salchicha* (sausage) and *papas* (potatoes), is better than the sum of its dialectical parts. Peruvian street vendors chop sausage into bite-size chunks and toss them with fries. Then they combine two other American staples—ketchup and mayonnaise—call it *salsa rosada,* and drizzle it on top. (For maximum convenience, some vendors preload the salsa into a small plastic cup and top it with the salchipapas.) With its critical combination of salt, fat, and sauce, it's no wonder salchipapas has conquered most of South America.

WHERE: Lima
MEAT: beef
PREPARATION: pan-fried
SERVED: sliced, with fries

LET YOUR SAUSAGE LOOSE

Dip your toes into sausage making, by leaving the casing out of the equation. All you have to do is grind meat and seasonings together, and presto chango: sausage.

Mexican Chorizo

MAKES ABOUT 2½ POUNDS

Like parmesan or balsamic vinegar, Mexican chorizo is one of those foods that Americans fell in love with and lured into our grocery stores, only to then corrupt it into a confused version of itself. In most supermarket refrigerated aisles, you'll find two chorizos on offer: firmer dried sausages (Spanish-style) and squishy, usually plastic-wrapped tubes of "Mexican" chorizo that melt into a soupy mess once it hits the pan. This is not what you want with your eggs or your potatoes (or your Brussels sprouts or your Thanksgiving stuffing!). Use this tangy, herbaceous one instead, the real deal, provided by none other than the inimitable *maestro de la cocina mexicana* Rick Bayless.

1½ lbs	boneless pork shoulder (without fat cap), cut into 1" pieces	**1 T**	fresh marjoram leaves or 1 t dried
½ lb	pork fatback, cut into ½" cubes	**1 t**	dried oregano (preferably Mexican)
12	medium (about 6 oz) ancho chilies, stemmed and seeded	**½ t**	ground cinnamon (preferably freshly ground Mexican canela)
2	bay leaves	**pinch**	ground cloves
1 T	fresh thyme leaves or 1 t dried	**+**	kosher salt
		⅓ C	cider vinegar

1 Freeze the pork and pork fat while you prepare the seasonings.

2 Tear the chilies into flat pieces and toast them in a dry, heavy skillet over medium heat, pressing them flat with a spatula until they are aromatic, about 10 seconds per side. Place them in a bowl, cover with water, and place a small plate on top to keep them submerged. Let soak for 20 minutes.

3 Drain the anchos and transfer to a food processor or blender. Pulverize the bay leaves in a mortar or spice grinder, then add to the food processor along with the thyme, marjoram, oregano, cinnamon, cloves, and 2 teaspoons salt. Add the vinegar and 2 tablespoons water and process until smooth, adding a little more water if necessary to keep everything from escaping the blades. Press the mixture through a medium-mesh sieve into a large bowl.

4 Coarsely grind the meat either through the largest die of a meat grinder or by pulsing it in a food processor (the blade needs to be sharp to avoid mashing the meat). Add the meat to the seasonings and mix thoroughly. Cover and refrigerate overnight.

5 Cook off a small patty to taste for seasoning, and adjust accordingly. Refrigerated, the chorizo keeps for about a week. Cook in a skillet over medium heat, stirring to break up any clumps, until fully cooked through, about 15 minutes. It freezes well.

Green Chili Chorizo

MAKES 1½ POUNDS

Do you like green eggs and ham?
I do not like them, Sam-I-am.
I do not like green eggs and ham.

Would you like them with Rick Bayless's green chorizo?
Oh. Yeah, duh.

1	large poblano chili	**1½ lbs**	ground pork (you'll need pork that's a little fatty—25 to 30%—and preferably coarsely ground)
2–3	serrano chilies, stemmed and roughly chopped		
1	medium bunch cilantro, tough lower stems cut off, leafy part roughly chopped (about 1½ C)	**1 T**	spinach powder (available online)
		2 t	kosher salt

---

1 Roast the poblano chili directly over a gas flame or 4 inches below a very hot electric broiler, turning regularly until blistered and blackened all over, about 5 minutes for an open flame, about 10 minutes for the broiler. Cool until handle-able, rub off the blackened skin, tear open, and pull out the stem and seed pod. Quickly rinse to remove any seeds or bits of skin. Roughly chop and scoop into a food processor, along with the serranos and cilantro. Pulse until uniformly chopped, then run the machine until you have a coarse purée.

2 Place the pork in a large bowl and add the chili mixture, spinach powder, and salt and mix together—your hand is the most efficient utensil for working the seasonings thoroughly into the meat. Cover and refrigerate for several hours before cooking.

3 To cook: Heat a skillet over medium heat and add the chorizo, stirring regularly and breaking up any clumps, until cooked through, 10 to 15 minutes. Sprinkle over queso fundido, into soups, or over huevos rancheros.

Italian-ate Sausage

MAKES 2 POUNDS

If you've ever been to Florence (South Carolina) or Milan (Ohio) or Rome (Georgia) or Venice (Florida), you've likely deduced that the official sausage of Italy is Italian sausage—*la salsiccia ufficiale,* if you will. It comes in two distinct Italian flavors: hot (*piccante*) or sweet (*dolce*).

If you have trouble finding real Italian sausage where you live, or just want something better than what your market offers, this recipe—inspired by the pork sausage from the *Zuni Café Cookbook*—is an *autentico* rendition of hot sausage Italiano. Oh, and there's no need to case it, if you're going to use it to make Sausage with Peppers and Onions (a specialty from the Italian region of New Jersey, a recipe for which you can find on page 211).

1 lb	boneless pork shoulder, cut into 1" cubes
½ lb	pork belly, cut into 1" cubes
1½ oz	pancetta, cut into large dice
1½ t	kosher salt
1 t	chili flakes
1 T	fennel seeds, lightly crushed, or a few fresh sage leaves, lightly pounded, then chopped
10	garlic cloves, coarsely chopped
¾ C	diced yellow onion
4 ft	hog casings or 12 ft lamb casings, soaked and cleaned (optional)

1 Combine the pork shoulder, pork belly, pancetta, salt, chili flakes, and fennel in a large bowl and toss well to distribute. Cover and refrigerate.

2 Assemble your grinder with the medium die (³⁄₁₆- to ¼-inch holes) and place in the refrigerator to chill.

3 Remove the meat from the refrigerator and fold in the garlic and onion, mixing to distribute. Grind the meat mixture.

4 Cook off a small patty to taste for seasoning and adjust accordingly.

5 Form the meat into patties. Cover and refrigerate for at least 8 hours. Uncooked loose sausage should keep for a few days in the refrigerator.

Variation: Chill the meat mixture well and then stuff into hog or lamb casings (see page 173). Cased sausage will hold in the fridge for a few days longer than loose sausage.

DETECTiVE SAUSAGE ON THE CASE

The act of casing your own sausage is the ideal mix of gratuitous, difficult, and fun—rewarding enough to be well worth your while and mysterious enough to be endlessly impressive to your friends and family.

Mortadella

Here's Marco Canora of Hearth restaurant on his mortadella recipe:

What's the difference between American bologna and Italian mortadella? At first glance, both are puréed, whipped, and poached pork forcemeats. Italians add pistachios, whole peppercorns, and diced fat to their mortadella. American bologna swaps out nuts and fat for a lot more processed shit. (Though don't kid yourself, Italians aren't above all that crap, either.) I started making my own mortadella back when we opened Craft nearly fifteen years ago. I consulted a couple of books that chefs have a cultish fascination with—*The Professional Charcuterie Series* by Marcel Cottenceau, Jean-François Deport, and Jean-Pierre Odeau—then set out to make my recipe. I puréed and poached pork over and over again. I found that most older published recipes call for too much spice—the results tasted like sucking on Christmas. It's not the recipes' fault—back in the day, overspicing meat was a tactic used to cover up the off flavors of meat gone bad.

I started backing down the spices and toying around with the recipes, but I could never figure out why my mortadella never quite tasted like the imported Italian stuff. Fast-forward a few years, to when George Kayden—the guy who really makes our restaurant work while I'm off opening wine bars and whatnot—took over the charcuterie program.

George did the research and found that it wasn't a spice we were missing, but a really surprising and random ingredient: almond extract. It was the missing link! Now we use a small blast of a superconcentrated extract marketed by Boyajian to season the forcemeat, then dashes of amaretto liqueur to adjust and tweak.

Homemade mortadella isn't as smooth as professional mortadella, which is made with industrial mechanisms that whip the pork into oblivion. We use a Robot Coupe food processor with ice packs strapped around it to keep the mixture cool. The resulting mortadella is best sliced a little thicker. We drizzle it with olive oil and serve it as part of a charcuterie plate, but you could fry it up for a sandwich if that's your thing.

1¾ lbs	fatback—1 lb cut into 1½" cubes, the rest cut into a ¼" dice	**2 t**	grated nutmeg
		1 t	almond extract
2	egg whites, lightly beaten	**½ C**	dried milk powder
1 C	pistachios	**2 C**	whole milk, frozen in an ice cube tray
5 lbs	boneless pork shoulder, cut into 1½" cubes	**+**	amaretto liqueur (optional)
2½ t	pink curing salt (Prague powder #1)	**4 T**	black peppercorns
5½ t	kosher salt, plus more as needed	**3 ft**	4-inch-wide collagen casing, 1 beef bung, or plastic wrap
2 T	paprika		

recipe continues

1 Put as many parts of your meat grinder and food processor as you can fit into your freezer. It's best to work with cold equipment and cold meat.

2 Blanch the ¼-inch-diced fatback in a saucepan of simmering water for 3 minutes, then chill in a bowl of ice water. Drain.

3 Toss the blanched fat in a bowl with the beaten egg whites and pistachios, then set aside. (The egg whites act as a glue that keeps the fat and nuts firmly anchored in the whipped pork, so you can slice the sausage without dislodging the tasty chunks.)

4 Combine the larger cubes of fatback and the pork shoulder in a large, chilled bowl. Sprinkle with the pink salt, kosher salt, paprika, nutmeg, almond extract, and milk powder. Give the seasoned meat a 5-minute time-out in the freezer, then put it through the meat grinder fitted with a fine die. Return the ground meat to the freezer while you set up your food processor.

5 Duct-tape a bag or two of crushed ice to the outside of the food pro-cessor bowl. (This move is optional but recommended for full DIY perversity.) Fill the food processor halfway with meat, leaving the rest of the meat in the freezer until its time has come. Crush the frozen milk in a plastic bag or in a blender, and divide it among the batches of to-be-puréed meat. Purée the meat until it's as smooth as your machine will make it.

6 Before proceeding to make another batch, test a lump of meat

from the first batch by poaching it for a couple minutes in a small pan of boiling water, then chilling it in an ice bath. (We register seasoning differently in hot meat than in cold meat, so this will be a truer test of the final product's flavor.) Add more salt if needed, which is very possible. George likes to add a dash of amaretto—about ½ cup for the whole batch—to each processorful of soon-to-be puréed meat. When you're satisfied with the seasoning, finish puréeing all of the meat.

7 Fold the whole peppercorns and the pistachio-fat-egg-white mixture into the finished purée. Pack the meat into gallon zip-top bags and squeeze out as much air as possible and seal. Let it cure in the refrigerator for 4 days.

8 Use a sausage stuffer or pastry bag with a wide nozzle to stuff the sausage into casings or the beef bung, twisting off every 10 inches. (Alterna-tively, you can wrap the meat in plastic wrap and torque the ends: Lay the meat in the center of a wide piece of plastic, pull the plastic around it, roll it into a cylinder, and twist the ends as tightly as you can without bursting the package open. Your mortadella might end up a little funny shaped, but it'll still be sausage.)

9 Bring a large pot of water to a sim-mer and submerge the sausage. Cook until an instant-read thermometer inserted into the deepest, most private regions of the pork reaches 155°F, about 1 hour. Plunge the cooked sausage into an ice bath and chill completely. Dry it off and put it in the fridge overnight.

Red Hot ("Texas Hot Gut")

MAKES 4 POUNDS (ABOUT 12 SAUSAGES)

These red devils are ideal for smoking, Texas BBQ-style. They're a real mix of animal parts—skin, tripe, sirloin, beef, pork—and come out of the smoker snappy and juicy. (They aren't great the next day, though, so eat them up quickly.) Ryan Farr of 4505 Meats in San Francisco, creator of this recipe, provides an excellent description of technique for the grinding and stuffing process that can be applied to various other sausages, so pay attention.

+	hog casings	**1½ t**	chili powder
1½ oz	tripe	**1 T**	sugar
3 oz	pork skin	**4 t**	mustard powder
1½ lbs	beef sirloin	**¾ t**	pink curing salt (Prague Powder #1)
1½ lbs	pork shoulder	**2 t**	black pepper
½ C	dried milk powder	**2½ t**	ground coriander
3 T	kosher salt	**½ C**	cold water
2 t	cayenne pepper	**2 t**	yellow mustard
⅓ C	paprika		

1 The night before: Soak the hog casings in a bowl of cold water in the fridge. Fill a large saucepan with water, and bring to a boil. Boil the tripe and pork skin until very soft, about 1 hour. Drain and refrigerate.

2 The next day, run cold water through the soaked casings to check for holes: Hold one end of each piece of casing up to the nozzle of the faucet and support it with your other hand while the water runs at a medium flow. If there are any holes in the casing, cut out the piece. Refrigerate or hold the casings in a bowl of ice water until stuffing time.

3 Cut all the beef, pork shoulder, cooked skin, and cooked tripe into 1-inch-square cubes, or a size slightly smaller than the opening of the

meat grinder. Lay in a single layer on a rimmed baking sheet, and place in the freezer for 30 to 60 minutes. Place your grinder in the refrigerator to chill.

4 Fit your grinder with the smallest die. Grind the beef, pork, cooked skin, and cooked tripe: Start the auger and, without using the supplied pusher, let the auger gently grab each cube of meat and bring it forward toward the blade and through the grinding plate. Continue grinding until all the meat has been processed. Place the meat in a clean, cold, nonreactive bowl or tub, and freeze for 30 minutes to 1 hour, until the surface is crunchy.

5 Combine the milk powder, salt, cayenne, paprika, chili powder, sugar, mustard powder, pink salt, black pepper, and ground coriander in a bowl. Whisk in the water and yellow mustard, until the dry ingredients dissolve.

6 Combine the cold meat and the seasoning slurry in a large, wide basin or bowl. Roll up your sleeves and, with perfectly clean hands, begin kneading and turning the mixture as you would with a large quantity of bread dough. Eventually, you will begin to notice that the mixture has acquired a somewhat creamy texture. This is caused by the warmth of your hands and is a sign that you have finished mixing. Pull off a few tablespoons of the mixture to use as a test portion, and return the remainder to the refrigerator.

7 Lightly fry the test portion of sausage mixture in a nonstick skillet over medium heat until cooked through but not caramelized (which would change the flavor profile). Taste for seasoning. Based on the result, you can adjust the salt in the remaining sausage mixture, if desired.

8 Prepare a chilled sausage stuffer and place the water-filled bowl of casings next to it. You will also need a landing surface of clean trays or parchment-lined baking sheets for your finished sausage.

9 Load the sausage mixture into the hopper of the sausage stuffer, compacting it very lightly with a spatula to be sure there are no air pockets.

10 Thread a length of casing all the way onto the stuffing horn and start cranking just enough to move a little sausage into the casing. As soon

as you can see the meat poking through the grinder, stop and crank backward slightly to halt the forward movement. Pinch the casing just where the meat begins, and tie into a knot. Now start cranking again with one hand while you support the emerging sausage with the other. Move the casing out slowly to allow it to fill fully but not too tightly, so that there will be some give in the sausage when it comes time to tie the links. When you get about 6 inches from the end of the casing, stop and leave that 6 inches unstuffed.

11 Measure 6 inches in from the end of the sausage-filled casing. Pinch gently to form your first link, and twist for about seven rotations. Move another 6 inches along the sausage, and this time, pinch firmly and twist the other way. Repeat this process every 6 inches, alternating forward and backward, until you reach the open end of the casing. Twist the open end to seal off the whole coil.

12 Hang the sausage links overnight in a refrigerator, or refrigerate the sausage on parchment-lined baking sheets covered with plastic wrap to allow the casing to form fully to the meat. This will also give you a snappier casing. (If you must, you can also cook the sausages right away.)

13 Heat your smoker to 175°F. (This is the point at which fat melts, so smoking at a higher temperature results in a less flavorful sausage.) Once the smoker is ready, hang the sausages in the smoker and smoke until the internal temperature reaches 155°F. Remove from the smoker and let rest for 30 minutes. Eat hot.

Breakfast Sausage

MAKES 3 POUNDS (ABOUT TWENTY-FOUR 3- TO 4-INCH LINKS)

Americans, have you ever noticed how breakfast tends to smell better than it tastes? Consider coffee: roasty and sweet, it's one of life's great olfactory pleasures. But no matter how "floral," "syrupy," "fruity," "masculine," "silky," or "like loquat" it's supposed to taste, it's still bitter, black bean juice. Bacon's also great. Sizzling in the pan (or on a rack in the oven, come on, do it right), it bathes the whole house in a perfume of smoke and pork. It tastes . . . good. But you know what tastes and smells incredible? Maple. Sage. Sausage. GOOD MORNING, AMERICA.

2 lbs	pork shoulder, cut into 1" cubes		**⅛ t**	grated nutmeg
½ lb	pork fatback, cut into 1" cubes		**⅛ t**	ground cinnamon
1 T	dried sage		**¼ C**	maple syrup
2 T	kosher salt		**2 T**	water
2 t	black pepper		**10 ft**	sheep casings, soaked and rinsed
1½ t	chili flakes, or more to taste			(see page 172)
½ t	dried thyme			

1 Toss together the pork shoulder, fatback, sage, salt, pepper, chili flakes, thyme, nutmeg, and cinnamon in a large bowl. Freeze for 30 minutes, or until the surface of the meat is hard.

2 Place the paddle and bowl of a stand mixer in the refrigerator to chill.

3 Grind the meat mixture first through the large die of your grinder, then again through the small die. Transfer the meat to the chilled mixer bowl, add the maple syrup, and whip the mixture on low until the syrup is incorporated, then drizzle in the water. Whip until creamy, sticky, and a little fluffy, 60 to 90 seconds.

4 Cook off a small patty to taste for seasoning, and adjust accordingly.

Cover and refrigerate the remaining raw sausage overnight.

5 Stuff the casings with the help of a sausage stuffer (see page 173). Twist the sausages every 3 to 4 inches—the links should be short. (If you don't want to work with 10 feet of intestines, you can make free-form patties, which, let's be honest, is definitely how it goes down at chez *Peach*.) If you're not casing the meat, form it into ½-inch-thick patties, about 4 inches in diameter. Refrigerate until ready to cook. Sausage, cased or pattied, can be wrapped in 1-pound packages and frozen for up to 2 months.

6 To cook the sausages, fry in a cast iron skillet over medium heat, flipping once, until they are browned and cooked through, about 10 minutes.

Lobster Sausage

MAKES ABOUT 2 POUNDS (ABOUT EIGHT 4-INCH LINKS)

Here's the thing about lobster: It comes in a hard red case with lots of sharp pointy parts that most of us who are not from coastal New England have a hard time negotiating. And, sure, we like to put on a bib and tear a sea bug or two apart from time to time, but you know what we like better than that: lobster meat that's ripe 'n' ready to eat. Lobster sausage is certainly in that category—all the work is on the front end, for the cook to do, so that at the table, there's nothing but flesh and flavor and time to enjoy it.

When making the farce for this sausage, you will want to have the sausage casings and equipment ready to go. It is essential that you make the sausages immediately after the forcemeat is prepared, because it sets very firmly and quickly, making it difficult to work with if allowed to sit.

5 ft	hog casings
1	small can pineapple juice
4	live chicken lobsters (1 lb each) or 4 lbs other live lobsters or 1 lb fully cooked lobster meat
½ lb	fresh or frozen peeled and deveined shrimp or fresh scallops
1	small carrot, finely diced
1	celery stalk, peeled and finely diced
½	small red bell pepper, finely diced
11 T	unsalted butter
1	large egg white
1	bunch chives, minced (about ¼ C)
6 T	breadcrumbs
+	kosher or sea salt
+	pinch of cayenne pepper
pinch	black pepper

1 Rinse the casings thoroughly in cold water and place them in a small bowl with enough pineapple juice just to cover. Let soak for at least 18 and up to 24 hours. (Don't leave them in for longer than that; if they become too tender, they will split open during cooking.) Rinse thoroughly in cold water and keep refrigerated until ready for use.

2 If using live lobster, steam or boil it. Let cool to room temperature. Use a cleaver or lobster cracker to crack and remove the meat from the claws, knuckles, and tails. Pick the meat from the carcass and remove all the meat from the walking legs. Remove the cartilage from the claws and the intestine from the tail of the cooked lobster meat.

Cut the lobster meat into ¼- to ½-inch chunks. Add the tomalley to the meat. If there is any roe, finely chop it and add it to the meat as well. Cover with plastic wrap and refrigerate.

3 If using shrimp, check to see that there are no fragments of shell and that they are cleanly deveined. If using scallops, pick them over, looking for pieces of shell as you remove the strap (the stringy little hard piece of flesh on the side of the scallop). Cover with plastic wrap and refrigerate.

4 Combine the carrot, celery, and bell pepper with 8 tablespoons of the butter in the smallest pot that you have. Place the pot over medium-low heat and simmer until the vegetables are cooked but still have a little crunch, 5 to 7 minutes. Remove from the heat and let cool to room temperature.

5 Purée the shrimp or scallops and egg white in a food processor until very smooth. Put the purée in a bowl and fold in the vegetable mixture. Add the chives, diced lobster, and bread-crumbs. Gently mix and season with 1½ teaspoons salt, cayenne, and black pepper. Refrigerate until ready to use.

6 Fit the soaked casings on the nozzle of your stuffer (see page 173). Fill the casings loosely, twisting off the sausages at 4-inch intervals. Lay them out on a baking sheet and refrigerate, uncovered, for at least 4 hours and up to 8 hours. If you do not plan to cook them within 8 hours, cover with plastic so the casings do not dry out.

7 When you're ready to cook the sausages, bring them to room temperature (because of their high moisture content, these sausages will explode if taken from the refrigerator and immediately exposed to high heat). To poach all the sausages at the same time, you will need a 12- or 14-inch skillet; or you can use a smaller pan and poach in batches. Fill the pan about two-thirds full with water and lightly salt it. Place the pan over low heat and wait until you see the first signs of vapor released at the surface. The temperature should be about 180°F. Cut the sausages into single links and gently lower them into the poaching water. Let them sit for about 8 minutes, never allowing the water to boil or simmer. At this point the sausages are almost fully cooked. Pour off the water and add the remaining 3 tablespoons butter to the pan. Increase the heat to medium and fry the sausages, gently turning so they become lightly brown on all sides. Serve at once.

Duck Crépinettes

MAKES 12 CRÉPINETTES

Crépinettes **bridge the gap** between cased and uncased sausage. Plus, they're an excellent way to use up all that caul fat you're always accumulating. What's that? You don't know what caul fat is? Caul fat is a thin web (of fat, duh) that surrounds the internal organs of your favorite edible farm mammals. Wrapped around a sausage patty, caul fat provides some structure but melts away once cooked, infusing its cargo with richness.

Suzanne Goin, empress of the Los Angeles restaurant scene, provides us with the how-to for these bundles of joy. The mix of ground duck and duck confit is both succulent and shreddable (like pulled pork), meaty and deeply satisfying.

2 lbs	duck leg meat, cut into 1" chunks
6 oz	pancetta, diced
2 oz	pork fatback, diced
3 T	white wine
1 T	kosher salt
2 t	black pepper
1 C	shredded duck confit
¼ lb	caul fat

1 Combine the duck, pancetta, fatback, white wine, salt, and pepper in a large bowl. Mix well, cover, and chill for at least 4 hours or overnight.

2 Grind the meat through a medium die. Gently fold in the duck confit.

3 Cook off a small patty to taste for seasoning, and adjust accordingly.

4 Divide the mixture into 12 portions. Shape each one into a ball and then flatten into a patty. Wrap each ball in enough caul fat so that it's covered in a web with the meat still visible. Refrigerate until ready to cook, or up to 24 hours (they also freeze really well).

5 Heat a cast iron pan over high heat. Sauté the crépinettes until the caul fat is well rendered and nicely browned on both sides and the duck is cooked to medium, about 15 minutes.

Boudin

Cajun cooking is American by way of French-Canada, with thanks to the British, who booted French colonists out of Acadia (in modern-day Maine and eastern Canada) in the eighteenth century. The displaced Acadians brought their frontier-French foodways to the South, where delicate French boudin became the kicked-up version you can find all over Louisiana today. Taste the diaspora!

This recipe in particular comes from Isaac Toups, a chef who's Cajun from his casing all the way through his filling, and the proprietor of the bluntly named Toups' Meatery in New Orleans. Toups says that if you don't feel like casing these sausages, you can make another Cajun specialty: boudin balls. Chill the meat mixture, then form it into 1.5-ounce balls. Roll them in breadcrumbs or panko and deep-fry until warm all the way through.

3 lbs	boneless pork shoulder, preferably with a fat cap
+	kosher salt
2 C	amber lager
12	scallions, chopped whites and greens kept separate
½ lb	chicken livers, rinsed
4 C	cooked Louisiana jasmine rice
1 T	cayenne pepper
¼ C	pimentón
2 T	black pepper
12 ft	hog casings, soaked and rinsed (see page 172)

1 Heat the oven to 425°F.

2 If your pork shoulder has a fat cap, use a sharp knife to cut shallow (about ⅛-inch-deep) diagonal slices every inch or so across the cap. Repeat on the other diagonal to create a cross-hatch pattern. Season with 1 tablespoon salt. Place it fat side up in a large Dutch oven and roast, uncovered, for 1 hour. Pour the beer and 1 cup water into the bottom of the pot and scatter in the scallion whites. Seal tightly with a lid or foil. Continue roasting for another 2 hours, until the pork falls apart when prodded. Remove from the oven and allow to rest.

3 When it's cool enough to handle, remove the pork from the pot and strain the braising liquid. Skim off the fat and reserve. Top off the braising liquid with water if needed to reach 2 cups.

4 Pour the braising liquid into a saucepan set over medium heat. Add the chicken livers and simmer gently until the livers are cooked through, about 6 minutes. Drain the livers, transfer to a food processor, and purée until smooth. Reserve the braising liquid.

5 Assemble your grinder. Break the pork into small chunks and grind through a meat grinder with a fine die, or pulse in a food processor until finely chopped.

6 Combine the ground pork, poached livers, skimmed pork fat, 1 cup of the braising liquid, the rice, scallion tops, cayenne, pimentón, and black pepper in a large bowl. Mix with your hands to combine. Taste for season- ing and add a bit more salt or cayenne if desired. The texture should be loose, a little saucy but not pourable (imagine 5-minute-old risotto). Add more braising liquid as needed.

7 Stuff the mixture into hog casings (see page 173), leaving the casings a bit loose—if you press into the sausage, the indentation should remain. The sausage may explode if it's stuffed too fully. Twist off at 6-inch intervals or coil the boudin into large rounds.

8 Bring a large, wide saucepan of water to 185°F. Poach the boudin in a single layer until warmed all the way through. Serve immediately or shock the sausage in ice water and keep chilled for up to 2 days. Reheat in the oven or in a pan before serving.

Pizza Sausage

MAKES 4 POUNDS (ABOUT TWELVE 7- TO 8-INCH LINKS)

Pizza sausage is the invention of Mike Sheerin, a meat whisperer and chef in the city of Chicago. We tasted it once—late at night, in the kitchen of wd~50, where Sheerin once cooked—and couldn't publish this book without the recipe. But from where did it come? "Pizza sausage started when my friend Nate called me up and said, *Hey I'm going to the Bears game,*" Sheerin says. "*Can you put pizza inside of sausage for me? I'm going to bring a pizza by. Just grind it into some sausage and put it in the casing for me.* And, honestly, that's kind of what we did."

PIZZA SPICE
1½ t	black peppercorns
1½ t	fennel seeds
1 T	coriander seeds
1½ t	chili flakes

SAUSAGE
3 lbs	ground pork
1 T	kosher salt
3 oz	parmesan, grated

8 oz	block cream cheese, frozen and grated
5½ T	tomato powder (available online)
1 t	garlic powder
4 T	cold water
½ C	basil leaves, chopped
2 T	oregano leaves, chopped
2 T	marjoram leaves, chopped
10 ft	hog casings, soaked and rinsed (see page 172)
+	unsalted butter

PIZZA SPICE

1 Toast the peppercorns, fennel seeds, and coriander seeds in a skillet over high heat until aromatic, about 1 minute. Pulverize in a spice grinder with the chili flakes.

SAUSAGE

2 In the bowl of a stand mixer fitted with the paddle attachment, beat together the pork and salt until combined, about 1 minute. Beat in the parmesan, cream cheese, pizza spice, tomato powder, and garlic powder and beat for 30 seconds. Add the water and fresh herbs and mix for 30 seconds until homogenous.

3 Stuff the farce into hog casings, twisting at 7- to 8-inch intervals to form 12 sausages.

4 To cook the sausages, heat the oven to 300°F. Arrange the sausages in a single layer in a baking dish. Pour enough water to come one-quarter of the way up the sausages. Bake until the sausages are firm and cooked through, 15 to 20 minutes. Sear a few links at a time in a blazing-hot cast iron pan, basting with butter, until the casings are crisp and browned, about 5 minutes.

Tingly Thanksgiving Sausage

MAKES 4½ POUNDS (ABOUT TWENTY 6-INCH LINKS)

Here's how Thanksgiving turkey gets treated in the Ying household: One breast becomes this sausage, which is basically a Chinesey *boudin blanc,* adapted from the incredibly excellent one in the *Chez Panisse Café Cookbook.* Breast two gets roasted (in the Torrisi style, which you can find online). Legs are confited in duck or pork fat. All the skin gets sandwiched in parchment and baked between two stacked sheet trays. The carcass becomes stock. In the end, you have a mixed platter of roasted breast, shredded confit, and crisp skin, but the sausage is always the star of the night.

2 lbs	skinless turkey breast, cut into 1" cubes	**2**	dried red chilies or ¼ t cayenne pepper
1 lb	boneless pork shoulder, cut into 1" cubes	**+**	pinch of grated nutmeg
¾ lb	pork fatback, cut into 1" pieces	**½ C**	fresh breadcrumbs
3 T	salt	**1½ C**	heavy cream
1 T	green Sichuan peppercorns (or 2½ t red Sichuan peppercorns + ½ t green peppercorns)	**2 T**	butter
		1	onion, sliced
		+	grated zest of ½ lemon
½ t	coriander seeds	**10 ft**	hog casings, soaked and rinsed (see page 172)
½	star anise		

1 Combine the turkey, pork, and fat in a bowl and season with the salt.

2 Toast the peppercorns, coriander, star anise, and chilies in a hot, dry skillet over medium heat for 1 minute. Pulverize in a spice grinder, then add the nutmeg. Mix the spice blend into the meat. Cover and refrigerate overnight.

3 The next day, stick the bowl of a stand mixer in the fridge. Soak the breadcrumbs in the cream.

4 Cook the onion in the butter over medium heat until softened, about 7 minutes. Let cool, then mix into the chilled meat mixture. In a meat grinder, grind the meat through a coarse die, then again with the finest die you have.

5 Transfer the meat to the chilled mixer bowl and combine with the breadcrumbs and lemon zest. Whip (slowly at first) with the paddle attachment until completely homogenous, slightly sticky, and almost paste-like.

6 Stuff the sausages (see page 173) in the casings, twisting off every 6 inches.

7 Prick the sausages with a skewer a few times. Poach them in a large pot until firm, about 10 minutes. Drain the sausages and brown them in a pan.

Merguez

MAKES 3 POUNDS (ABOUT TWENTY-FOUR 3- TO 4-INCH LINKS)

"You eat a sausage sandwich like this when you're either really broke or really drunk," says Mourad Lahlou of San Francisco's Aziza. "The night market in Marrakech stays open until four a.m., so if you're ever in either predicament, go find one of the guys standing behind a long brazier and strings of hanging merguez. Order four sausages on a roll, which he'll sprinkle with cumin, and serve with mint tea to wash it down."

On the other hand, if you're sober, have a little scratch, and aren't in Marrakech, then you can make your own merguez at home.

MERGUEZ

1½ T	kosher salt
3½ T	Harissa Powder (recipe follows)
1¼ t	ground cumin
1¼ t	black pepper
1¼ t	ground fennel
¼ t	ground allspice
¼ t	ground caraway seeds
½ t	citric acid (sometimes sold as "sour salt")
¾ C + 2 T	finely chopped shallots (about 5 small shallots)
¼ C	finely chopped garlic (about 1 head garlic)
¾ C	finely chopped flat-leaf parsley (about 1 medium bunch)

2½ lbs	boneless lamb shoulder, ground medium-coarse
1 lb	lamb fatback, ground medium-coarse, well chilled
10 ft	sheep casings, soaked and rinsed (see page 172)

HARISSA SAUCE

⅓ cup	Harissa Powder
1 cup	Kewpie mayo
+	sandwich rolls (like ciabatta)
+	watercress and as colorful a rainbow of pickles as you can manage

MERGUEZ

1 Mix the salt, harissa powder, cumin, black pepper, fennel, allspice, ground caraway, citric acid, shallots, garlic, and parsley in a bowl. Add the ground lamb and lamb fat and mix gently by hand to combine. Don't mix with a machine or let the fat melt, or you'll screw up the texture of the sausage.

2 Cook off a small patty to taste for seasoning, and adjust accordingly.

3 Fill the casings with the help of a sausage-stuffing machine, twist every 3 to 4 inches—the links should be short (see page 173). Refrigerate until ready to cook. (If you don't want to work with 10 feet of intestines, you can make skewers, which is actually how most Moroccans make merguez at home— sausage in casings are more street. You'll need sticks—metal or bamboo—and a little extra fat, maybe ¼ pound, to

recipe continues

help the merguez mixture bind and stay moist. After you've mixed it, form it around the skewers into vaguely sausage-looking kefta kebabs.)

4 When you're ready to cook, bring your merguez to room temperature and heat a grill to high heat. Once you put the merguez down on the grill, don't move them around too soon or too much; wait for a good sear. Cook the merguez until browned evenly on all sides, about 4 minutes.

HARISSA SAUCE

5 Combine the harissa powder and mayonnaise in a mixing bowl and stir to combine. The mayo must be Kewpie mayo! It has MSG, which balances the spices out.

6 Toast white bread rolls (like ciabatta) for a minute or so before you're ready to make sandwiches. Slather one side generously with harissa sauce (use even more if you made skewers, since they lose a lot of fat in the cooking), and transfer the kefta directly from the grill to the bread so the fat can soak into it. Optional but nice: garnish with watercress and pickles (I make cucumber, carrot, and pearl onion pickles). Gorge.

Harissa Powder

6 T	coarsely ground Aleppo pepper	1 t	kosher salt
1 t	granulated garlic	1 t	sweet paprika
1 t	citric acid	1 t	ground caraway seeds
1½ t	pimentón	pinch	cayenne pepper
1½ t	ground cumin		
1 t	roasted garlic powder (available online)		

Mix all the ingredients together in a small bowl.

Boudin Blanc

MAKES ABOUT 5½ POUNDS (ABOUT TWENTY 5- TO 6-INCH LINKS)

Boudin blanc is essentially the same thing as *boudin noir* but without the deep red pork blood that gives its sanguine sister her trademark hue. It pops up in various guises around Europe (as *Weißwurst* in Germany, and as white pudding in the U.K.), and you either love it for all its pasty whiteness and disquietingly smooth texture, or you really don't. This recipe, procured from Taylor Boetticher and Toponia Miller—owners of the Fatted Calf in Northern California—adds chestnuts for textural variety and brandy for a little zip.

2½ lbs	veal shoulder, cut into 1" cubes	**2 T + 1 t**	fine sea salt
1¾ lbs	pork shoulder, cut into 1" cubes	**1 C**	cooked, peeled chestnuts
¾ lb	pork fatback, cut into 1" squares	**1 C**	pork stock
2 t	white peppercorns	**1**	bay leaf
2 t	coriander seeds	**4 T**	brandy
1½ t	mustard seeds	**1½ C**	heavy cream
2	whole cloves	**½ C**	fresh breadcrumbs
¼ t	ground mace	**12 ft**	hog casings, soaked and rinsed
3	allspice berries		(see page 172)
1½ t	dried thyme	**+**	kosher salt
¼ t	grated nutmeg	**+**	neutral oil, as needed

1 Mix together the veal, pork, and fatback in a large bowl. Use a spice grinder to pulverize the peppercorns, coriander seeds, mustard seeds, cloves, mace, allspice, and thyme. Mix into the meat with the nutmeg and sea salt. Cover and refrigerate overnight.

2 Simmer the chestnuts, stock, bay leaf, and 2 tablespoons of the brandy in a saucepan until the chestnuts are tender, about 45 minutes. Remove from the heat, discard the bay leaf, and refrigerate.

3 Combine the cream, breadcrumbs, and remaining 2 tablespoons brandy in a bowl to make a panade.

4 Assemble your grinder. Grind the spiced meats twice through the finest die you have. Add the panade and mix well by hand for about 2 minutes, then fold in the braised chestnuts and their broth until incorporated, breaking the nuts into ½-inch pieces as you go.

5 Stuff the sausage into the hog casings, twisting it off into 18 to 20 evenly sized links (see page 173).

6 Poach the sausages until their internal temperature reaches 150°F. Shock in an ice water bath. To serve, sear in a skillet with a little oil or grill over low coals to char the casing.

Bratwurst

MAKES 3¾ POUNDS (ABOUT FIFTEEN 4- TO 5-INCH LINKS)

These brats—made by Sutter Meats in Northampton, Massachusetts—are reminiscent of a classic breakfast sausage, not spicy or sagey, but with traditional spices that Americans might think of as baking spices. Don't overcook them! (See Green Bay Brats, page 195.)

2¼ lbs	lean veal, cut into 1" pieces
1 lb	boneless pork shoulder, preferably with a fat cap, cut into 1" pieces
2 T	kosher salt
1 t	ground white pepper
¾ t	ground ginger
½ t	grated nutmeg
½ t	mustard powder
¾ C	heavy cream
8 ft	hog casings, soaked and rinsed (see page 172)

1 Combine the veal, pork, salt, white pepper, ginger, nutmeg, and mustard and toss together. Cover and chill overnight.

2 Chill grinder attachments and a baking sheet or roasting pan in the freezer.

3 Assemble the chilled grinder with a coarse die. Grind the meat once, then a second time onto the chilled baking sheet, arranging it in a loose, even layer. Place the pan with the meat into the freezer and chill until it is nearly frozen, somewhat crisp (indicating ice crystals) when touched, about 30 minutes. Keep the grinder chilled (either fill it with ice or clean it and return to the freezer).

4 Assemble the grinder with the fine die. Grind the meat twice, arranging it back into a loose, even layer on the pan. Refreeze until crisp, about 20 minutes. Meanwhile, chill the bowl of a stand mixer and the paddle attachment. Place the cream in the freezer.

5 Assemble the stand mixer with the paddle attachment and mix the chilled meat for 1 minute on low. Increase the speed to medium and drizzle in the cream in a slow, steady stream. Continue whipping the farce until emulsfied, 2 to 3 minutes longer.

6 Stuff the casings with the farce, twisting at 4- or 5-inch intervals to form about 15 bratwurst (see page 173). Hang the sausages in the refrigerator or arrange on a parchment-lined baking sheet. Chill until the casings are dry to the touch, about 12 hours.

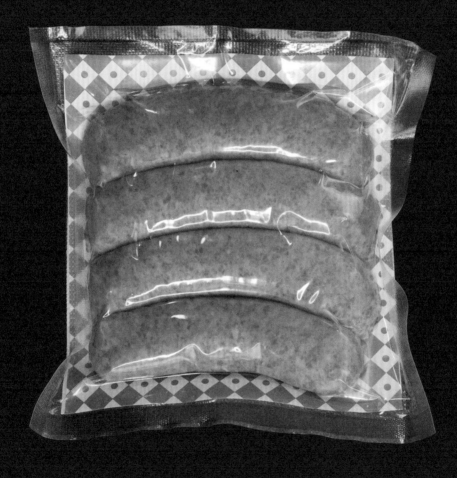

Käsekrainer

MAKES 3 POUNDS (ABOUT TWELVE 4-OUNCE, 5- TO 6-INCH LINKS)

My first slice into a Käsekrainer left me disappointed. I don't know what I'd expected exactly—cheese, I guess—but inside I found only tightly grained pork. Then suddenly, out of nowhere, molten Emmentaler came trickling out of some tiny pocket I hadn't noticed. I was mesmerized as each subsequent slice released a new fount of cheese whiz. Sausage magic.

"For this emulsified sausage, it is imperative that the ingredients hover around thirty-two degrees throughout the sausage-making process," explains Elias Cairo of Olympia Provisions in Portland, Oregon. "Monitor the temperature, and if it creeps up to thirty-five, pop the mixture back in the freezer to cool. When the sausage is properly emulsified, the cheese will be perfectly encased and little individual pockets of melted cheese will ooze as opposed to melt into the meat."

2 lbs	trimmed pork shoulder, cut into 2" pieces	**½ t**	paprika
¾ lb	pork fatback, cut into 2" pieces	**½ t**	pink curing salt (Prague Powder #1)
¾ C	beer or ice, frozen and crushed	**½ t**	sugar
¼ C	dried milk powder	**10 oz**	Emmentaler cheese, cut into ¼" cubes
5 t	kosher salt	**+**	hog casings, thoroughly soaked and rinsed (see page 172)
1 T	chopped garlic		
1½ t	black pepper	**+**	wood chips, soaked for an hour in warm water

1 Place the bowl of a stand mixer in the refrigerator to chill. Arrange the pork shoulder and fatback in a single layer on a rimmed baking sheet and freeze until the edges of the meat are hard, about 30 minutes.

2 Set up a bowl of ice water. Grind the pork, fat, and frozen beer through the ¼-inch die of a meat grinder into a bowl set in the ice bath. Fold in the milk powder, kosher salt, garlic, pepper, paprika, curing salt, and sugar, and put through the grinder again. Monitor the temperature of the farce, popping it back into the freezer as needed to keep the temperature of the mixture below 35°F.

3 Combine the farce and Emmentaler in the chilled bowl of the stand mixer. Whip with the paddle attachment until the mixture looks creamy and tacky against the sides of the bowl, 3 to 4 minutes.

4 Working quickly, stuff the farce into the hog casings and tie off at 5- to 6-inch intervals (see page 173). Hang or lay the sausages in open air in the refrigerator overnight to dry.

5 Heat a smoker to 70°F (or pile 8 briquettes of lit charcoal on one end of a charcoal grill). Smoke the sausages for 1 hour, maintaining the temperature between 70°F and 120°F. Insert a heat-resistant thermometer in the center of one sausage, and increase the heat to 180°F (add more hot briquettes to the pile one or two at a time to achieve this with a charcoal grill).

6 Smoke the sausages until the internal temperature hits 155°F. Eat immediately or chill the sausages quickly in an ice bath and refrigerate for up to 5 days. To reheat, warm the sausages in a bath of steaming water or beer, then sear or grill to firm up the casings.

Mum

MAKES THREE 1-POUND SAUSAGES

Are any of you going to make mum? Honestly, unless you're a chef from the northern regions of Thailand like Prin Polsuk of Bangkok's Nahm, I doubt it. *Then what's it doing in this book?* Well, it's here to commemorate that mum is, in fact, very delicious—crumbly, a little sour, not too offaly—despite the admittedly unsettling prospect of eating a purple-black ball that's been hanging outside for three days. It's also here to demonstrate the very spirit of sausage: taking a bunch of things that you don't really feel like eating and combining them into something you do. It's about innovation through necessity. In other words, if you find yourself in possession of some beef spleen and a spare gallbladder, not only can you make this, you *should*.

For the intrepid, here are notes on the ingredients. Thai garlic has small, spicy, aromatic cloves. You can find it in many Thai markets, particularly in summer, but if you can't find it, just use standard garlic cloves. Second, since this is a fermented, air-dried sausage, we recommend using pink salt, even if they don't in Thailand. And finally, if you're in the market for organ meats, check out White Oak Pasture's website.

2¼ lbs	lean beef	**4 ft**	beef casings or gallbladder, thoroughly soaked and rinsed (see page 172)
8 oz	beef liver		
3 oz	beef spleen		
3 oz	skin-on Thai garlic cloves, or peeled garlic cloves	**+**	oil, for grilling
5.5 oz	sticky rice (about ¾ C)	**+**	sliced bird's eye chilies, sliced fresh ginger, cilantro, and cabbage, for serving
1.75 oz	kosher salt (about 4 T)		
½ tsp	Prague Powder #1 (pink salt), optional		

1 In a food processor, mince together the beef, beef liver, spleen, and garlic.

2 Toast the rice in a dry skillet over medium heat, shaking and stirring until it's golden brown, about 12 minutes. Transfer to a mortar and grind it very fine with a pestle (or use a spice grinder).

3 Add the salts and rice to the meat and mix vigorously until homogenous and smooth, about 10 minutes.

4 Stuff the mixture into the casings or gallbladder (see page 173), twist into links, and hang in the open air (70° to 85°F) for 3 days, then store in the fridge for up to 3 days.

5 To cook, brush the skins with a little oil and grill over medium heat, turning often, until the internal temperature reaches 145°F, 12 to 15 minutes. Let stand for 5 minutes before slicing and serving with chilies, ginger, cilantro, and cabbage.

Thai Sour Sausage (Sai Krok Isan)

MAKES 3 POUNDS (ABOUT 40 LINKS)

Achieving the sourness that defines *sai krok isan* takes a bit of getting over our nervous Western ideas of food safety. "The authentic method, and the one that yields the best-tasting results, consists of hanging the sausages outdoors to ferment naturally," says Bangkok-based travel writer Joe Cummings. "This allows the links to lose water through evaporation, creating a denser, more flavorful sausage." After a few days, it also has the effect of basically rotting the meat and rice just enough so that they're perfectly pungent and somewhat acidic. Remember, you aren't a true member of the sausage faithful until you've fermented your own Thai sausages, and just as the Lord directs in Exodus, true believers should dangle a string of sai krok isan from their doors to avoid the vengeance of the sausage god.

2¼ lbs	pork shoulder, cut into 1" pieces
10 oz	pork fatback, cut into 1" pieces
1¼ C	cooked sticky rice
½ C	garlic cloves, peeled and left whole
1 T	kosher salt
½ t	fresh ground white pepper (optional)
8 ft	hog casings, thoroughly soaked and rinsed (see page 172)

1 Combine the pork shoulder, fatback, rice, garlic, salt, and pepper (if using) in a large bowl and mix with your hands. Grind the mixture through the coarse die of a meat grinder. Knead the mixture until it is tacky, about 3 minutes.

2 Stuff the farce into the hog casings and twist at 1½-inch intervals (see page 173). Hang the attached links from hooks in an area with clean, open air that is between 68 and 86°F (a screen porch is perfect). Set a drip pan below the hooks to catch any fat that may fall. Let the sausages dry and ferment for 1 to 6 days, depending on the weather and the desired flavor (letting them go longer will yield a more sour, deeper flavor). If the weather is extremely dry, place pans of water below the hanging sausage so that the meat and skins don't dry out too much. If the weather is in the 70s, breezy, and not too dry, the sausages will take about 4 days to cure.

3 When you've reached your desired level of fermentation, refrigerate the sausages for up to 3 days. To cook: grill the sausages over medium heat until browned and cooked through.

PLAY WiTH YOUR WiENER

Mustard-only purists would do well to skip this section. Herein we present a fashion show of our best-dressed dogs, from a corndog stained black by huitlacoche to an avocado-and-mayo-smeared Chilean specialty.

Green Bay Brats

The manner in which one makes brats in Wisconsin is less of a recipe and more of a way of life. See, there is a sport called American football and a team called the Green Bay Packers and if you think the people of Rome, with their marble palaces and grand halls of worship were devoted, you should visit America's Dairyland during the last quarter of the year, when the blue tint of television illuminates every living room, and, statewide, there are bratwursts bathing in beer, waiting to be called out of the hot tub and into someone's belly, either to help elevate the joy of coming victory or soften the blow of an impending loss. The bath of beer sits perched on the turned-down or otherwise dampened grill, keeping the brats warmish throughout the course of the game's ups and downs. Accompany with ice-cold cans/bottles/kegs of Milwaukee-brewed pilsner. An oversize novelty foam wedge of cheese is acceptable—even encouraged—headgear while eating said brats.

2	large onions, halved and peeled
4–6 C	lager beer
8	bratwursts
+	buns and mustard, for serving

---

1 Slice three onion halves and place in a large disposable aluminum roasting pan. Dice the remaining onion half and set aside for garnish.

2 Heat a grill to medium heat. Place the roasting pan with the sliced onions in one corner and add the beer. Once the foam subsides and the beer begins to simmer, lay the brats directly on the grill grates and cook, turning often so that they don't split, until they are nicely browned, about 5 minutes. As they are done browning, drop them into the roasting pan of gently simmering beer and onions. Poach the brats in the beer for at least 15 minutes. Reduce the heat to the bare minimum and they can hang out there for the length of a football game. One can then fish a brat out of the beer whenever one needs it. Serve on buns with diced onion and mustard.

Hot Dog Chili

MAKES 4 TO 6 SERVINGS

For the first ten years of my life, my parents owned an ice cream store in California. They used to set me up in the back office with a couple chili-cheese dogs from the nearby Wienerschnitzel franchise, and I'd exist happily for most of the day, only poking my head out to score the occasional taste of pralines 'n' cream. Most of my opinions about food were formed during this time, so, for me, hot dog chili will forever be a bean-free zone. (For a lengthier justification, see "No Beans in the Chili" on page 107.) Kevin Pemoulie of Thirty Acres recalls this type of chili "as a 99-cent add-on to deep-fried hot dogs all over New Jersey." This recipe is his—it's ideal for spooning over hot dogs and covering in cheese and onions—and although it comes from clear across the country, I feel a deep kinship to it.

2 T	olive oil
½	large onion, finely chopped (about 1 C)
+	kosher salt and black pepper
1 lb	ground beef
¼ C	ketchup
2 T	Dijon mustard
¼ C	Tapatío hot sauce
½ t	Worcestershire sauce
1 T	pimentón, plus more as needed
½ C	water

1 Heat the oil in a skillet over high heat. After a minute, add the onion and a pinch of salt, and cook until the onion has begun to color and wilt, 5 to 10 minutes. Add the beef, jabbing it with a wooden spoon to break it into small pieces. Cook the beef through, but don't worry too much about browning it— about 10 minutes will do.

2 Fold in the ketchup. Cook until the ketchup is lightly caramelized and dried out, 2 to 3 minutes. Stir in the mustard, hot sauce, Worcestershire sauce, pimentón, and water, and bring to a simmer. Cook, uncovered, for 10 minutes—this isn't a Bolognese braise that needs to ride out for hours.

3 Season to taste with salt and black pepper, adding more pimentón for smokiness as desired. Hold warm on the back of the stove for a few hours, or store in the fridge for a few days.

Completo

I'm sure if you asked them, Chileans would find any number of our American dining creations to be curious and off-putting. But would any of them be so strange at first blush as the *completo*?

The complete—as served in Santiago or Stateside at San Antonio Bakery in Queens—is a hot dog on a roll, with sauerkraut, diced tomatoes, avocado, and a thick squiggle of mayo. It should not work. It should not be legal. But something about the temperature contrast of the hot, salty dog and cold, bracing sauerkraut, and the thick layers of intermingling fat in the form of avocado and mayo, just clicks. That's more than you can say for plenty of American inventions (think Tex-Mex egg rolls . . .).

2	avocados, chilled
+	kosher salt
4	foot-long hot dogs
4	large sub/hoagie rolls, sliced open but not split apart
1 C	sauerkraut, rinsed and warmed
1 C	chopped plum tomatoes, chilled
½ C	mayonnaise

1 Mash the avocados in a bowl with a fork until smooth. There should be about 2 cups. Season lightly with salt, and chill.

2 Place the hot dogs in a medium pot of cold water and set over medium heat. Bring to a simmer, cover, and remove from the heat.

3 Lightly toast the rolls and keep warm.

4 Place a hot dog in a bun and top with sauerkraut and tomatoes. Fill the bun with ½ cup mashed avocado and smooth the top even with the bun. Squirt or swipe with 2 tablespoons of mayonnaise and serve immediately. Repeat to make 4 completos.

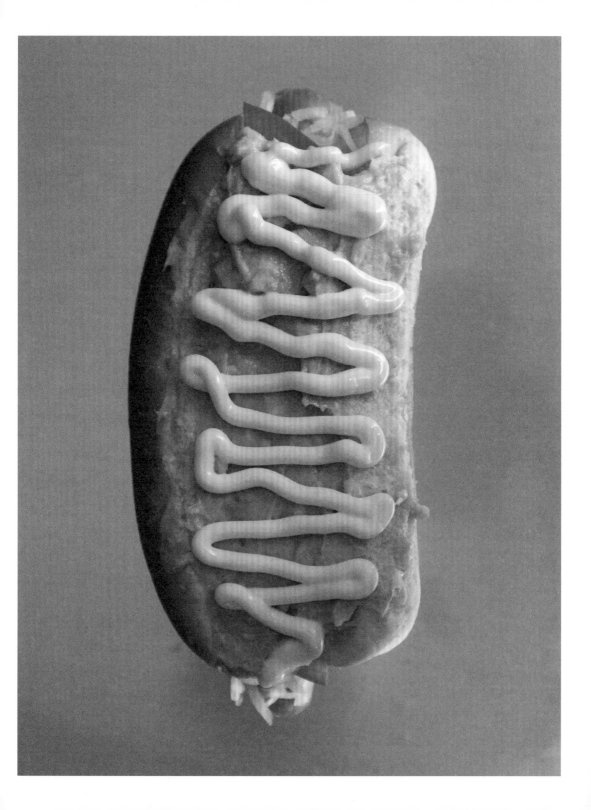

Danger Dog

It is known by several names. The Tijuana Bacon Dog. The Bacon-Wrapped. The Street Dog. The Sonoran Hot Dog (with beans, onion, tomato, mayo, salsa, jalapeño, mustard, and a grilled chili on the side). Whatever you call it, it is ever thus: a hot dog swaddled in a slice of bacon and griddled until crispy. On the streets of San Francisco and Los Angeles, vendors anoint Danger Dogs with charred onions and peppers. It is not meant for sober consumption. It is meant for emergencies only, when you are already in danger of making other bad decisions and the prudence of eating mystery meat from a converted shopping cart is the least of your concerns. Making it for yourself at home removes much of the danger. But not all of it.

4	hot dogs
8	slices bacon
+	toothpicks
+	vegetable oil
1	onion, thinly sliced
1	bell pepper, sliced
4	hot dog buns
+	kosher salt

1 Wrap each hot dog with 2 slices of bacon in a spiral fashion, securing the bacon to the hot dog with toothpicks.

2 Heat a griddle or large cast iron pan over medium-low heat. Add a thin film of oil, then add the hot dogs, congregating them to one side of the pan and encouraging the rendering bacon fat to pool opposite the dogs.

3 After a minute or two, add the onion and pepper to the pool of rendered fat and cook them, stirring every few minutes while simultaneously turning the hot dogs a quarter turn every couple of minutes so they render evenly. Do this until everything is a similar dirty golden color, the bacon is crisp, and the onion and pepper are wilted, 12 to 15 minutes.

4 Insert the dogs into the buns. Sprinkle the onion-pepper mix with a pinch of salt, toss, and divide among the dogs.

Huitlacoche Corndog

MAKES 8 CORNDOGS

PDT, Jim Meehan's cocktail bar in Manhattan, is attached to a deep-fried, Jersey-style hot dog shop called Crif Dogs. Ever since the earliest days of the bar, they've played up this advantage by serving a menu of hot dogs with toppings devised and supplied by their chef friends. During the years when Sam Mason's restaurant in New York, Tailor, was twisting up people's minds about the lines between sweet and savory in a meal, he submitted this corndog to the offerings at PDT. The dog's distinctive dark color comes from huitlacoche, the mushroom-like fungus that grows on corn and appears in quesadillas and tacos in Mexico.

1 C	fine yellow cornmeal		1 C	milk
½ C	all-purpose flour		+	water
1 t	kosher salt		+	neutral oil, for frying
⅛ t	cayenne pepper		8 pairs	disposable chopsticks (or thick wooden skewers)
¼ t	baking powder			
⅛ t	baking soda		8	all-beef franks
½ C	puréed huitlacoche (thawed if frozen; straight out of the can is okay)			

1 Combine the cornmeal, flour, salt, cayenne, baking powder, and baking soda in a large bowl and stir with a fork until the mixture is homogenous. Add the huitlacoche and, stirring, pour in the milk. Add water as needed to thin the batter—it should be like just-poured concrete. Scrape the batter into a tall, narrow container, like a quart container from the deli or a widemouthed canning jar, something that is at least as deep as the franks are long. This will make for clean and easy battering.

2 Add oil to a deep pot, enough to submerge the battered dog with the stick sticking out of the oil but there should be a couple inches of clearance in case the oil bubbles up when you add the corndogs.

3 Heat the oil over medium-high heat to 375°F.

4 Skewer the dogs with the chopsticks and dip them one at a time in the batter. Holding the stick, let excess batter drip off, then drag the tip in the oil for a couple of seconds before gently releasing it. This will allow the end of the batter to set, acting as a life jacket and keeping the corndog afloat as it fries. Fry for 7 to 8 minutes—the batter should be on the road to turning black. If you can't get the dogs submerged most of the way, use a long-handled spoon to "baste" the unsubmerged batter with boiling fryer oil. Be careful. Remove them to a plate lined with paper towels and let them rest for a few minutes before serving—they'll stay hot for a while.

Waffle Hot Dogs

MAKES 10 WAFFLE DOGS

Here's L.A.-based chef Kris Yenbamroong of Night+Market, on this Thai street staple:
How ubiquitous are these things in Thailand? They are so prevalent that companies manufacture single-purpose cast iron presses to make them. (Even here in the Home of the Brave, just Google for "waffle dog maker," and you can have a nonstick electric waffle-dog press delivered to your doorstep!)

2	eggs	2¼ T	sugar
1½ C	whole milk	1 t	salt
3½ T	margarine, melted and cooled (plus a bit more to grease the machine surface)	20	bamboo skewers (7")
		10	hot dogs, halved crosswise to cocktail-wiener size
2½ C	all-purpose flour	+	waffle dog maker
1½ t	baking powder	+	Kewpie mayonnaise and/or ketchup

1 Whisk together the eggs, milk, and melted margarine in a large bowl. Whisk in the flour, baking powder, sugar, and salt until thoroughly combined.

2 Skewer the halved hot dogs through the cut side until the point of the skewer almost pokes through the other end. Try to maintain as straight a line as possible when you skewer.

3 Grease the surface of the waffle dog maker with a bit of margarine. Spoon enough batter into each mold to fill it three-fourths of the way up.

4 Place a skewered hot dog into the center of each mold with the skewer hanging over the edge. (The waffle dog maker only holds 6.) Gently twirl each skewer so that the hot dog gets coated in batter. Spoon just enough extra batter over each hot dog to completely coat it.

5 Press the lid of the machine down on the hot dogs and secure the latch, if there is one. Wait 7 to 8 minutes, depending on the model of waffle dog maker you're using.

6 Gently lift the lid, as some of the batter may be stuck to it. Use an extra skewer to unhinge the waffle dog from the machine. The 6 dogs will be joined by excess waffle edges. Cut these off with a pair of scissors or break them off with your hands. Repeat with the remaining batter and skewered hot dogs.

7 Serve the waffle dogs topped with a zigzag of mayonnaise and/or ketchup.

Wiener Blossoms

MAKES 3 TO 4 BAGFULS

And now, Kris Yenbamroong on how to make hot dogs look like flowers:

Wiener blossoms can be made with any type of hot dog, but the recipe really works best with crappy pork-and-chicken or pork-and-turkey-blend wieners. You want to taste the sodium and nitrates. Beefy dogs don't taste as good in this context. Neither do "natural"-type dogs. The texture and consistency should evoke chicken-liver mousse, not country pâté. That is to say, you want it smooth.

The "sauce prik" in this recipe is a generic term for any sauce that's kind of spicy, bottled, and sold next to ketchup in a Thai supermarket. It will range from something like sweet sriracha to what you might think is watered-down orange marmalade with chopped garlic and chilies. That's the kind you want for this recipe. Some stores will sell it under the description "BBQ chicken sauce."

¼ C	"sauce prik" or other hot sauce	+	canola oil, for frying
¼ C	ketchup	+	sturdy plastic sandwich bags
2 t	distilled white vinegar	+	rubber bands
8	hot dogs	+	bamboo skewers

1 Whisk together the hot sauce, ketchup, and vinegar in a bowl.

2 Prepare the wieners for blossoming: Cut the hot dogs crosswise in half to cocktail-wiener size. Next, make a cut into the flat, cut end of the halved dog, cutting through the center, toward the round end, but stopping just a tad more than halfway. Rotate the wiener 90 degrees and make a similar slice again, again ending halfway toward the round end. The idea is that you are scoring the wiener with a deep X, two perpendicular lines that intersect in the center of the wiener, creating four petals.

3 Pour enough canola oil into a Dutch oven, wok, or heavy-bottomed pot to submerge the dogs opulently. Heat the oil to 360°F.

4 Fry the wieners in batches. Remove with a wire strainer once the petals bloom outward (about 30 seconds).

5 Cinch little handles onto your plastic bags by pinching one of the top corners and slipping it through a rubber band, then looping the rubber band repeatedly around the corner to secure it. On the last loop, secure the rubber band by knotting it. In the end, you will have a little ring to hang the bag from your finger. (You can omit this step and just hold on to a corner of the bag, but that is infinitely less deluxe.)

6 Put a handful of wiener blossoms into the bag, then top with a generous helping of sauce. To eat, use a bamboo skewer to spear the blossoms.

Grilled Carrot Hot Dogs with Lamb-Neck Mole

MAKES 5 DOGS

Vegetarians who accidentally purchased this book thinking it was, I don't know, about peach cookery, may have felt some relief upon seeing the words *grilled carrot hot dog,* but they will have been deflated by the end of the dish name. Avowed carnivores likely rode the same emotional roller coaster in reverse. Rest assured, there's something here for everyone.

Trevor Kunk of PRESS restaurant in Napa braises carrots with loads of sausagey aromatics that render them tender and meaty. (Trimming the carrots to sausage shape adds to the masquerade.) Vegetarians can stop here. Otherwise, Kunk tops the carrot-sausage with a rich, meaty mole. This is a strange and tasty chili dog.

MOLE

4 oz	dried guajillo chilies or a mix of other smoky dried chilies, stemmed and seeded
4 C	chicken stock
2 T	neutral oil
3	garlic cloves, minced
2	celery stalks, finely chopped
2	red onions, finely chopped
1	carrot, finely chopped
1 t	kosher salt
1 t	black pepper
1 t	ground chili powder
1 t	pimentón
½ t	ground cinnamon
12 oz	hoppy, bitter beer, suchlike Lagunitas Little Sumpin'
2 C	cooked and minced lamb neck (or lamb shoulder, pork belly, or pig head)
0.5 oz	semisweet chocolate

CARROT HOT DOGS

5	large carrots (at least 1" wide at the stem end; about 1 lb), peeled, tops and bottoms cut off
1 t	kosher salt
2 t	crushed peppercorns
1 t	ground cloves
1 t	coriander seeds
1 t	fennel seeds
3	whole star anise
3	juniper berries
3	allspice berries
1 T	sugar
3 T	honey
3	rosemary sprigs
3	fresh sage leaves
3	oregano sprigs
3	thyme sprigs
3	parsley sprigs

SERVING

+	neutral oil
½ C	minced shallots
1	lime, juiced
5	hot dog buns
+	fried shallots (store-bought is fine)

recipe continues

MOLE

1 Place the chilies in a small saucepan, cover with water, and bring to a boil over medium-high heat, then cover and turn off the heat. Steep the chilies for 10 minutes, then drain. Place the softened chilies in a blender with the chicken stock and blend until smooth. Set the chili broth aside.

2 Heat a Dutch oven or large saucepan over medium-high heat, then coat with the oil. Add the garlic, celery, onions, and chopped carrot and sweat until soft, about 10 minutes. Stir in the salt, black pepper, chili powder, pimentón, and cinnamon. Add the beer, bring to a simmer, and reduce until the pan looks dry. Add the chili broth, bring to a simmer, and reduce by about half, about 10 minutes. Add the diced meat, return to a simmer, and reduce gently until it reaches a thick stew/chili viscosity. Remove from the heat and stir in the chocolate until melted. Keep warm.

CARROT HOT DOGS

3 Heat the oven to 350°F.

4 Combine the carrots, salt, peppercorns, spices, sugar, honey, and fresh herbs in a deep roasting pan and add enough water to submerge the carrots by 1 inch. Cover tightly with foil and braise the carrots in the oven until they are tender and aromatic but not falling apart, about 1 hour. The cooking time will depend a bit on how large and old your carrots are.

5 Remove from the oven and carefully extract the carrots from the liquid. Brush off any spices that are stuck to the carrots. Store them in a single layer in the fridge until you're ready to serve them. The carrots will keep, refrigerated, for 3 days.

SERVING

6 Heat a grill or cast iron skillet to medium heat. Rub the carrots with a little oil and grill or sear them until they are charred on all sides and heated through, about 4 minutes.

7 Heat 2 cups of the mole to a simmer in a saucepan, then remove from the heat and stir in the shallots and lime juice.

8 Slot the carrots into buns, top with the mole, and a generous sprinkle of fried shallots.

INTER-NATIONAL SAUSAGE CAFE

Imagine the newest theme hotel on the Vegas strip. An eighty-store cylindrical tower, arcing into the sky. The observation deck at the peak looks like a twisted knot of sausage casing wrought from steel and glass. It's called Wiener Palace, and it draws guests from around the world. This section is the all-you-can-eat buffet menu.

Sausage with Peppers and Onions

As I'm sure it is with many Americans, a big bowl of sausage and peppers is a frequent presence on the Ying dinner table (it's one of two or three things that my wife knows how to cook), and this supremely simple version from Frankies Spuntino in Brooklyn is our go-to. Serve the sausage and peppers hot, over polenta or pasta, or with thick slices of toasted bread.

2	red bell peppers	+	fine sea salt
2	yellow bell peppers	2 lbs	sweet Italian pork sausage, casings
1	large yellow onion, peeled		removed
1 T	grapeseed oil	1	can (28 oz) San Marzano tomatoes

1 Roast the peppers: If you have a gas stove, turn the burners on high and lay a whole pepper over each. Roast, using tongs to turn the peppers every couple of minutes, until the skins of the peppers are thoroughly blackened and blistered, about 7 minutes. (If you don't have a gas range, you can roast the peppers over a hot fire on a grill outdoors or lightly coat them with oil and roast them under the broiler, turning frequently, for about 15 minutes.) Once the peppers are roasted, put them in a small bowl and cover it with plastic wrap. When the peppers are cool enough to handle, stem, core, and scrape away as much of the blackened skin as possible. Slice the roasted pepper flesh into ½-inch-wide strips and set aside.

2 Halve the onion through its root end, then cut the onion halves into ¼-inch-wide strips lengthwise, with the grain. (Onions cut across the grain will melt in the sauce; onions cut with the grain will keep their shape in the sauce.)

3 Heat the oil in a wide skillet over medium-high heat. Add the onion and a pinch of salt and cook, stirring occasionally, until the strips soften and start to take on a golden color, about 15 minutes. Remove them from the pan and set aside.

4 Without wiping out the pan or turning down the heat, add the sausage. Sauté the sausage, jabbing it with a wooden spoon to break it into small pieces, until well browned but not dried out, 10 to 12 minutes. Add the canned tomatoes, crushing them in your hands as you add them to the pan. Bring to a simmer, scraping the bottom of the pan to loosen any browned bits. Stir in the peppers and onion and continue simmering until warmed through, about 10 minutes.

International Sausage Café

Brown Jambalaya

As with lighter fluid, when you cook with andouille, everything tastes like it. Unlike lighter fluid, andouille is delicious. Melissa Martin of the Mosquito Supper Club in New Orleans makes this jambalaya with 1 pound of andouille. It's a brown jambalaya, she clarifies, because it has caramelized onions and no tomato. She also offers reassurance for nervous cooks: "Don't worry if there are bits of kinda burned stuff on the bottom. We call that the 'graton,' and for some people it's their favorite part."

2 lbs	medium shrimp, peeled and deveined, shells reserved	**2**	celery stalks, finely diced
7 C	water	**4 C**	Louisiana long-grain rice
¼ C + 2 T	neutral oil	**+**	kosher salt
4	big yellow onions, finely diced (about 8 C)	**+**	black pepper
		1	bay leaf
1 lb	diced andouille sausage	**5 dashes**	Louisiana hot sauce
3	garlic cloves, minced	**pinch**	cayenne pepper
1	green bell pepper, finely diced	**4**	scallions, sliced
		1 T	chopped parsley

1 Simmer the shrimp shells and water in a saucepan over medium heat for 10 minutes, then remove from the heat and steep for 20 minutes. Strain the stock and discard the shells. If the stock has reduced, add enough water to measure 6½ cups.

2 Heat a Dutch oven over medium-high heat, then coat with ¼ cup of the oil. Add the onions and cook, stirring often and adjusting the heat to keep the onions from scorching, until deeply caramelized, 35 to 40 minutes.

3 Meanwhile, heat a large skillet over medium-high heat and coat with the remaining 2 tablespoons oil. Brown the sausage, flipping once, until golden and lightly rendered, about 5 minutes. Set aside.

4 Stir the garlic, bell peppers, and celery into the Dutch oven. Season, cover, and cook until softened, about 5 minutes. Add the sausage and smother in the veg. Cook for 5 minutes. Fold in the rice. Pour in the shrimp stock and bring to a boil. Cover, reduce the heat to low, and cook until the rice is just tender, about 15 minutes.

5 Meanwhile, toss the shrimp with 1 tablespoon salt, 1 teaspoon pepper, the bay leaf, hot sauce, and cayenne.

6 Fold in the shrimp, cover, and continue cooking over low heat for 10 minutes. (Add a splash of water if things look too dry.) Remove from the heat, add the scallions and parsley, and fluff the jambalaya. Cover and let stand for 10 minutes before serving.

Pigs in a Blanket

MAKES 4 SERVINGS

Humans are predictable. You give them something starchy next to something meaty, and they'll want to wrap the former around the latter. It's in our nature. Once in a while, this yields vital discoveries, like pigs in a blanket.

In the vacation resort of my imagination, I'm presented poolside with a cigar box full of salty breakfast sausages rolled up like robustos in golden-brown pancakes, along with a footed tureen of warm maple syrup. The pancakes in this recipe are the ones from that dream—fluffy and light and tender. For maximum airiness, whisk the ingredients together within a couple minutes of cooking—the baking powder will be most active during this period.

1 C	all-purpose flour	**1**	egg
1 T	light brown sugar	**1 t**	vanilla extract
2 t	baking powder	**4 T**	butter
½ t	salt	**8 links**	breakfast sausage
1 C	whole milk	**+**	maple syrup, for serving

1 Whisk together the flour, brown sugar, baking powder, and salt in a medium bowl. Whisk together the milk, egg, and vanilla in a small bowl. Set both bowls aside.

2 Heat 1 tablespoon of the butter in a large, heavy skillet over medium-low heat. Pan-fry the sausages until they are nicely browned and cooked through, 7 to 8 minutes. Place the sausages on a plate and wipe out the skillet.

3 Melt 2 tablespoons of the butter in the skillet over low heat. Pour the melted butter into the milk-egg mixture, whisking vigorously. Pour the wet ingredients into the flour mixture and whisk just to combine. It's okay if there are some small lumps in the mixture.

4 Melt the remaining 1 tablespoon butter in the same skillet over medium heat. Working quickly, pour in ¼ cup batter, coaxing it into a round shape with the back of a spoon. Repeat for as many ¼ cupfuls as will fit comfortably in the pan. Cook, moderating the heat so that they don't burn, until the bubbles that form around the edges of the pancakes pop, about 4 minutes. Flip and cook until the pancakes are slightly puffed in the center and golden brown on the bottom, 2 to 3 minutes longer. Transfer to a plate and repeat for the remaining batter.

5 To serve, wrap the sausages in the pancakes, and serve with maple syrup.

Bacon-Wrapped Kielbasa

MAKES 6 TO 8 APPETIZER SERVINGS

My wife is half-Polish. The day before our wedding, the guys from Mission Chinese Food put on an outrageous crawfish boil in a field overlooking the Russian River. Newspaper-lined tables spilled over with heaps of mudbugs, shrimp, sausage, corn, potatoes, and chunks of crusty bread. On an unoccupied corner of one of the tables, a modest slow cooker sat alone and unmolested. *Lucky Peach* editor and discerning eater, Dave Chang, found his way over to the cooker and peered in. He lifted the lid and extracted a toothpick-skewered round of kielbasa, dripping shimmering pork fat back into the pot. He ate it and then another. "What *are* these?" he said aloud to no one in particular. "These are the best things I've eaten this year."

These hors d'oeuvres—made by my sister-in-law at every remotely special occasion—are about as Polish as tacos, but I still love them deeply. Just like my wife. Love you, honey!

1 lb	bacon slices, halved crosswise
1½ lbs	kielbasa, cut into 1" lengths
+	toothpicks
1½ C	light brown sugar
+	slow cooker (optional)

1 Wrap slices of bacon around the diameter of each piece of kielbasa and secure them with toothpicks. Place the wrapped, skewered sausages in a large bowl and cover with the brown sugar. Toss gently. Cover and refrigerate for at least 2 hours but preferably overnight, stirring occasionally to redistribute the sugar.

2 Turn on your broiler and move a rack to the upper tier of the oven—close but not so close that the kielbasa will bump up against the heat source.

3 Spread the kielbasa onto a foil-lined baking sheet and slide under the broiler. Broil until the bacon has crisped and browned, about 4 minutes, checking now and then to make sure nothing's burning. Use tongs to flip the sausages over and then return to the oven for further browning.

4 Let cool for a few minutes before serving. Or, if you've got company coming, you can slide the whole batch (and any juices) into a slow cooker on low heat.

Little Smokies with Grape Jelly and Chili Sauce

MAKES 4 TO 6 SERVINGS

Have you ever spent days conceiving, prepping, and cooking something to dazzle and impress friends at a potluck, only to see your savory ratatouille cheesecake left half-eaten on the buffet table? Meanwhile, not a morsel remains of the garbage semihomemade concoction brought by your talentless coworker, who's basking in the praise of the party guests, who are your friends, not hers—you just brought her because she was sniffing around about your weekend plans and it would have been awkward not to invite her.

Well, this is a recipe for the latter dish. It's morally repugnant, easy like Sunday morning, and appeals to our basest instincts. The original ingredients will be indecipherable once merged. There is not a hint of Concord-grape flavor, nor can you pick out the horseradish notes from the chili sauce. Teenie Weenie Alchemie.

After eating several of these, your mouth will be chafed and you will want to drink several glasses of water, which won't help remove the slick of corn syrup and the tang of history. Then you'll go back for just one more dog.

For a slightly more up market approach, you could stir in 1 tablespoon horseradish, 1 to 2 teaspoons sriracha, or a squeeze of fresh lemon juice at the end to perk things up.

1 lb	smoked cocktail weenies
1	bottle (12 oz) Heinz chili sauce
1 C	Welch's grape jelly

Combine the weenies, chili sauce, and jelly in a saucepan and bring to a simmer over medium heat, stirring to dissolve the jelly. Reduce the heat, partially cover, and simmer gently until the weenies are plump and the sauce is thick, about 20 minutes. Serve with toothpicks.

Toad in the Hole

Bubble and squeak. Bangers 'n' mash. Welsh rarebit. Spotted dick. Fitless cock. Hare on the glen. Lord and gentry. Barmy burrito. Willy buttoons. Neville longbottom. The queen's buns. Squish baileywick. Binnymore peeps. Spitted quackadoods.

British food names tend to be blunt and to the point. But there's one item in the British catalog that I've just never been able to decipher. Unlike the above (half-real) dishes, it's impossible to figure out what it is from the name alone: toad in the hole.

"It's pretty straightforward—Yorkshire pudding batter and sausages," explains Lee Tiernan of Black Axe Mangal in London. "Toad in the hole is one of my favorite things to do. Great family meal. Heinz baked beans are the best accompaniment—beans and a healthy helping of HP Sauce." (HP Sauce, I assume, is shorthand for Harry Potter sauce.)

3 T	lard or butter	**⅓ C**	whole milk
6 links	Cumberland sausage or bratwurst	**⅓ C**	beer
	(about 1½ lbs)	**2**	large eggs
1 C	all-purpose flour	**+**	Heinz baked beans, mashed
½ t	kosher salt		potatoes, and HP Sauce, for serving

1 Heat the oven to 450°F. Place an 11 × 7-inch ovenproof ceramic dish (or three smaller gratin dishes) in the oven to heat.

2 Meanwhile, heat the fat in a large skillet over medium heat. Add the sausages and sear them, turning often to brown evenly, about 15 minutes. Reserve the sausages and drippings separately.

3 Place the flour and salt in a bowl and make a well in the center. Add the milk one-third at a time, whisking between additions. Repeat with the beer to form a smooth batter.

4 Place the eggs in another bowl and whip them by hand until they are thick and frothy, about 2 minutes. Fold the airy eggs into the batter.

5 Remove the roasting dish(es) from the oven and pour in the drippings, then the batter (or divide among the three dishes). Top with sausages. It should all spit and splutter nicely. Close the oven door and bake (without opening the door again) for 10 minutes. Reduce the heat to 400°F, and bake until the batter is puffed and golden and the sausages are cooked through, about 10 minutes longer.

6 Serve with Heinz baked beans, mashed potatoes, and plenty of HP Sauce.

Franks and Beans

MAKES 8 SERVINGS

You know you're from New England when your mawm made franks and beans every Satuhday night. A huge paht of growing up is pizzar on Friday, franks on Satuhday, and THE PATS on Sundays. But if you move fah away from the Bahston areya—maybe to staht a new jawb as a cawp or a bahtenda or a paht-time aht depahtment lecturah, you smahtie pants—you might have a wicked hahd time finding franks and beans like you had in Southie. (No self-respecting New Englandah would dayah buy theiya franks and beans from thah can.) Nawt to feayah, no mattah where you ah, with this recipe, you can always have a hawt bowl of beans to go with your cold beeyah. Just wartch out for thah fahts!

1 lb	dried navy beans
½ t	baking soda
½ lb	salt pork, sliced
1	onion, peeled but left whole
½ C	molasses
1 t	salt
1 T	mustard powder
8	hot dogs, cut into ½" coins

1 Check the navy beans for rocks and other alien particles, then dump into a container along with the baking soda. Add water to cover by at least 4 inches. Soak the beans until they have tripled in size, about 12 hours. Drain and rinse.

2 Place the beans in a large saucepan or soup pot and cover with cold water by 2 inches. Bring to a boil and let simmer until the skins look loose and beans are almost tender, about 45 minutes. Drain.

3 Heat the oven to 325°F.

4 Line the bottom of a bean pot or medium Dutch oven with two-thirds of the salt pork slices. Add the whole onion and the beans. Whisk together the molasses, salt, mustard powder, and 3 cups water in a large bowl. Pour the mixture over the beans (they should be almost submerged in liquid), top with the remaining slices of salt pork, and cover with the lid. Bake until the beans are completely soft, the liquid has reduced by a third, and the pulp of the beans and the braising liquid are a homogenous tan color, about 3 hours.

5 Remove the pot from the oven and fold in the sliced hot dogs. Bake for another 10 minutes, then let rest, covered, for 20 minutes.

Choucroute Garnie

MAKES 6 TO 8 SERVINGS

This is the apex of Alsatian cooking—an ideal blend of the German affection for sausage with too much sauerkraut, and French sensibility. On our sausage jaunt from Frankfurt to Vienna (see page 45), we detoured to Strasbourg specifically for choucroute garnie and were not in the least bit disappointed by what we found at a little rustic tavern called Au Coin des Pucelles. We made off with the recipe and share it with you now.

The key is to splurge on good duck fat and wine. The rest is adaptable. Use any flavorful stock in lieu of duck stock. Use whatever mix of bone-in and boneless cured/smoked pork you like (hocks, bacon, ham, or loin will do). And don't fret about the pork liver or finding the exact sausages. Use some nice hot dogs or brats and some coarse smoked sausage if you aren't within reaching distance of knacks and Lorraine sausages. All is forgiven in the pot, where the wine and fat and smoke and salt meld into a glossy, brothy, slightly acidic, wintry casserole.

8 C	raw Alsatian sauerkraut, or other fresh sauerkraut	1 lb	salted pork collar (neck)
½ C	duck fat	1 lb	smoked pork collar/neck
1	whole onion, peeled and halved	1 lb	smoked country bacon
2	garlic cloves, peeled but whole	1 lb	salted bacon (unsmoked)
8	juniper berries	10	black peppercorns
4	whole cloves	+	Guérande salt (gray sea salt)
2	bay leaves	4	Strasbourg knackwursts
1	large thyme sprig	4	small Lorraine sausages (or from Montbéliard)
2 C	dry Alsatian white wine, like Edelzwicker or Riesling	4	quenelles pork liver (optional)
+	kosher salt	4	potatoes, baked until tender, then peeled
4 C	duck, pork, or chicken stock		

1 Place the sauerkraut in a large strainer and rinse it with hot water until the water runs clear.

2 Melt the duck fat in a very large, flameproof Dutch oven or casserole over medium-low heat. Add the onion halves, garlic, juniper berries, cloves, bay leaves, and thyme. Cover and let the onion and garlic steam and sizzle until translucent around the edges, 3 to 4 minutes.

3 Stir in the sauerkraut and white wine. Taste and season with a pinch of salt if needed.

4 Add enough duck stock to cover everything in the pan, cover the pan with a lid, and simmer for 30 minutes—the cabbage should retain a little crunch. Remove the sauerkraut with a slotted spoon and set aside.

5 Add the pork and bacon to the broth in the pan along with the peppercorns, and enough water to cover everything. Bring to a simmer and season with Guérande salt. Cook until the meats are bouncy-tender when pierced with a skewer, 1 hour 15 minutes to 1 hour 30 minutes.

6 Just before serving, warm the sausages, pork liver quenelles (if using), and baked potatoes in a saucepan of barely simmering water until everything is heated through. The water should not reach a boil.

7 On a large plate, spread the sauerkraut in an even layer. (You can rewarm the sauerkraut in a separate saucepan with a ladle of the braising liquid, too, if you like.) Place the meats and potatoes on top.

Parmentier de Boudin Noir aux Pommes

MAKES 8 SERVINGS

You want to be a cool foodie, but you just don't like blood sausage. We get it. Blood sausage is difficult. It looks exactly like it sounds, and you just can't get past the fact that it's so . . . *bloody.*

Think of this dish from Au Coin des Pucelles in Strasbourg as cheat-code blood sausage. We're talking unlimited lives, full armor, walk-through-walls, level-warp whistle, Up, up, down, down, left, right, left, right, B, A start. It's blood sausage, yes, but it's covered with creamy mashed potatoes and applesauce. Babies would love this dish. You will love it. If you don't love blood sausage but want to, try this recipe.

MASHED POTATOES

1¾ lbs	potatoes
+	kosher salt
6 T	butter
5 T	olive oil
⅓ C	heavy cream
+	black pepper
+	grated nutmeg

APPLESAUCE

2	medium apples
5 T	butter

1	onion, thinly sliced
1 t	gray sea salt or kosher salt
1 t	black pepper
1 t	ground cinnamon
1 T	light brown sugar
¼ C	dry Alsatian white wine

PARMENTIER

+	butter
8	boudins noirs (about 1½ lbs total)
3 oz	Gruyère cheese, finely grated (about 1 C)

MASHED POTATOES

1 Peel and cut the potatoes into small cubes. Place the cubes in a saucepan, cover with water, and add a pinch of salt. Bring to a simmer over medium-high heat and cook until tender, about 25 minutes.

2 When the potatoes are cooked, drain them in a colander. Position a food mill over a large bowl and pass the potatoes through the food mill into the bowl. Mix in the butter, olive oil, cream, a few grinds of black pepper, and a small pinch of grated nutmeg until smooth. Correct the seasoning with salt, pepper, and nutmeg if necessary.

APPLESAUCE

3 Peel the apples and cut into small cubes. Place the cubes in a saucepan with the butter, onion, salt, pepper, cinnamon, brown sugar, and white wine. Cover, bring to a simmer over medium heat, and cook until the apples and onion are very tender, about 20 minutes.

PARMENTIER

4 Heat the oven to 425°F. Grease a large baking dish with butter. Spread a thin layer of mashed potatoes on the bottom of the dish.

5 Cut the sausages down the middle lengthwise and remove their casings. Arrange them on top of the mashed potatoes. Pour the applesauce over the sausages and top with the rest of the mashed potatoes—you want the sausages to be completely covered. Top with the Gruyère.

6 Bake until the top is light brown and the mixture is heated through, about 30 minutes.

Nem Nuong

MAKES TWELVE 3.5-OUNCE, 4-INCH SAUSAGES

Do you follow Dan Hong on Instagram? He's an Australian chef, who posts a maddening number of pictures of his sneakers. It's almost enough to make me unfollow him, except that he also posts photos from the Monday-night dinners his Vietnamese mom makes (#mondayhongdinners). Looking at them makes me want to be related to the Hongs, or adopted by them, or kidnapped by them. Dan's a terrific chef, but for this recipe, there was only one Hong we turned to: his mom, Angie.

Nem nuong, she wrote to us, is "Vietnamese skinless sausage, to eat with 'pork liver sauce,' green banana, star fruits, garlic chives, sorrel, mint, perilla, Vietnamese coriander, cucumber, lettuce, and rice paper." Grill these skewers of pork over charcoal, then present them family-style, along with all the fixings for people to make their own rice paper roll-ups.

NEM NUONG

2 lbs	ground pork shoulder
½ lb	ground pork fatback
2 T	toasted rice powder (store-bought; or refer to the Mum recipe, page 192)
1 T	baking powder
1 T	fish sauce
1 T	fried garlic
1 T	honey
1 T	kosher salt
12	lemongrass stalks (8" long)

LIVER SAUCE

6 oz	small shallots
½ C	raw peanuts, soaked in water overnight
1 lb	pork liver, cut into 1" pieces
2 T	neutral oil
1 t	kosher salt
1 T	sugar
+	rice flour (optional)
2 T	crushed roasted peanuts
1 T	toasted sesame seeds
½ t	minced Thai chili, or more to taste

SERVING

+	rice paper wrappers (and a dish of hot water to dip them in to soften)
+	lettuce, herbs (cilantro, mint, perilla, rau ram, sorrel, and/or garlic chives)

NEM NUONG

1 Combine the pork shoulder, fatback, rice powder, baking powder, fish sauce, garlic, honey, and salt in a large bowl and knead together until combined. Working in batches, pulse the meat mixture in a food processor until smooth and tacky, about 20 pulses.

2 Divide the farce into 12 balls, about 3.5 ounces each. One at

recipe continues

a time, lengthen and flatten the balls into a 4-inch-long rectangle and wrap it around a lemongrass stalk. Repeat with remaining meat and lemongrass. Refrigerate until ready to cook.

LIVER SAUCE

3 Peel the shallots and grate them into a fine-mesh strainer set over a bowl. Press gently on the solids to release a bit of the shallot juice and discard the juice. Reserve the squeezed shallots.

4 Drain the peanuts (there will be about ¾ to 1 cup soaked peanuts) and grind in a food processor until smooth, adding splashes of water as needed to form a paste. Scrape the peanut paste into a bowl. Then process the liver until finely chopped and set aside.

5 Heat the oil in a seasoned wok or nonstick skillet over medium-high heat. Fry the shallots until they are golden and sweet smelling, 3 to 4 minutes. Add the peanut paste and cook, stirring, until the mixture takes on a toasty aroma, about 5 minutes. Dump in the liver and season with the salt and sugar. Fold the mixture over itself until combined, then stir in ¾ cup water. Reduce the heat to medium-low and continue cooking and stirring the mixture, adding a splash of water if it thickens before cooking through, until there are no longer pink spots, about 5 minutes. Sprinkle over a pinch of rice flour to thicken the sauce, if desired. Stir in the roasted peanuts, sesame seeds, and chili. Keep warm for serving.

SERVING

6 Build a medium-hot fire in a charcoal grill. Rub the grates with oil. Grill the *nem nuong*, turning frequently to char evenly, until they are cooked through, about 8 minutes.

7 Transfer to a platter and serve with softened rice paper wrappers, lettuce, herbs, and liver sauce, for dipping.

Pork and Fennel Sausage Rolls

MAKES 4 ROLLS

It's bonkers that sausage rolls aren't available in every coffee shop and bakery in America. What's not to love about a thick log of pork sausage wrapped in puff pastry bark? It's the ur-Hot Pocket. The Brits and their Commonwealth cousins—including Bourke Street Bakery in Sydney—are having a laugh at us Yanks for not catching on yet. Let's teach them a lesson, just like we did back in 1776.

1 T	extra virgin olive oil		1 lb	lean ground pork
1 T	finely chopped garlic		¼ C	dried breadcrumbs
2 T	fennel seeds		2 T	milk
2 t	dried thyme		1 T	kosher salt
¾ C	finely chopped onion		¼ t	ground white pepper
½ C	finely chopped celery		1	14-oz package all-butter puff pastry
½ C	finely chopped carrots		1	egg, beaten

1 Heat the oil in a saucepan over medium heat. Add the garlic and cook for 30 seconds. Add the fennel seeds and thyme and stir for 1 minute. Add the onion and celery and cook until the onion has softened, about 5 minutes. Add the carrots and cook, stirring often, until the vegetables are mushy, about 20 minutes. Set aside to cool.

2 Place the pork in a large bowl and add the cooled vegetables, breadcrumbs, milk, salt, and white pepper. Mix forcefully by hand for 3 minutes to thoroughly combine. Roll up a little ball of the meat mixture and cook it in a hot skillet to check the flavor. If you find it too salty at first, note that the pastry will balance out some saltiness.

3 Heat the oven to 400°F. Line a baking sheet with parchment paper.

4 Roll out the puff pastry into a 12-inch square and cut it in half lengthwise to yield two 12 × 6-inch rectangles.

5 Divide the filling mixture in half. On a clean work surface, roll each portion of meat into a 1-inch-wide log. Place each log lengthwise in the center of a pastry rectangle and brush one long edge of the pastry with egg wash. Fold the dough over, overlapping and pressing to enclose the log tightly, leaving the ends open.

6 Halve each roll and place on the lined baking sheet, seam side down. Brush the top of each roll with egg wash. Reduce the oven temperature to 375°F and bake until they are golden brown logs of steaming, oozing goodness, 35 to 40 minutes.

Sausage Gravy

MAKES 5 CUPS (ABOUT 10 SERVINGS)

This homemade facial treatment, adapted from Blackberry Farm in Tennessee, is good for all skin types.

---

1 T	vegetable oil
1 lb	mild or spicy pork sausage, casings removed
¼ C	all-purpose flour
4 C	heavy cream
½	small onion, minced (about ½ C)
1 t	kosher salt
1 t	black pepper
+	hot biscuits, for serving

---

1 Heat the oil in a large cast iron skillet over high heat. Brown the sausage, jabbing it with a wooden spoon to break it into small pieces, until browned, about 8 minutes.

2 Reduce the heat to medium and stir in the flour, coating the sausage pieces and scraping the bottom of the skillet to incorporate the flour into the rendered fat. Cook, allowing the flour to sizzle without darkening, for 3 to 5 minutes, reducing the heat as necessary.

3 Stir in the cream, minced onion, salt, and pepper and bring to a simmer, stirring the whole time. When the gravy is thick enough to coat the back of the spoon, reduce the heat to low. Simmer very gently until the gravy is silky, about 15 minutes, adding splashes of milk or cream if the gravy is too thick. Serve hot, with biscuits.

Wurst Practices

GRILLING SAUSAGE

The disrespectful immolation of sausages over a hot grill is so commonplace as to be unremarkable. And, because sausage is delicious and forgiving, it usually tastes great even when cooked carelessly—but the innards are often drier than they should be, all because the cook is in thrall to the idea that browned sausage is all that matters. If you want to elevate your sausages with flame rather than relying on their hardiness to persevere through a heavy torching, then you will want to do this:

- Make a fire. Light a chimney full of charcoal and wait for the coals at the top to ash over and flames to subside. Dump the coals into the grill and arrange them for two-zone cooking, one side with about double the depth of coals as the other. Keep one area free of coals, so you have a place to drag the sausages should there be a flare-up.

- Set the grate over the coals, rub the grate with an oily rag, and let the coals burn down until you have medium (450°F) and low (300°F) heat zones. Place sausages over the medium zone and sear them, turning every 20 to 30 seconds, until they are marked on all sides and the casings have dried and begun to brown. Transfer to the cooler side of the grill for slower indirect cooking. Continue turning sausages until they are evenly brown and puffed. Slowly getting to browness is the surest way of knowing your sausage will be in good shape all the way through. When you see liquid bubbling within the casing or clear liquid simmering out of the ends, they're ready to meet their maker; remove them from the heat and let them rest for a few minutes before eating.

- Many cooks think it wise to check the temperature of an in-process sausage with a digital thermometer, but we don't like to go and stab up our whole fleet. If you must be a nerd who knows the temperature of their sausage on the grill, do this: Before cooking, choose one lucky sausage and insert a roasting thermometer (the kind with an ovenproof wire connected to a digital box outside of the oven) through one end of the sausage into the middle of the meat. Set the alarm to beep at the desired cooking temp (145°F for beef, 150°F for pork, 160°F for poultry), and fuggedaboutit.

BRAISING SAUSAGE

In many dishes there is tandem deliciousness: there is the meat and the vegetable (or condiment or starch), and they are both good but they are separate. Braising sausage with its accompaniments is like making an ouroboros of flavor: Deliciousness knows no end or beginning, textures are rapturously harmonized, ingredients are sublimated into a higher form. Our recommended process is this:

- Sear the sausages to firm up their casings and develop a little brown flavor, then remove them from the pan. In the same pan, sauté aromatics in the sausage fat. You will want onions, definitely onions, more onions than you might immediately suspect you should use. Maybe some peppers or fennel or carrots and celery. You'll probably also want additional fat (see Jonathan Gold's red beans and rice rant, page 126, for inspiration on that front). Cook until they begin to brown but hold their shape, about 5 minutes over medium-high heat. Do not season them with more than a pinch of salt at this time—you can correct the seasoning at the end.

- Tuck the sausages into the wilting aromatics. This would be the time to add a smothering-type ingredient—rinsed sauerkraut, chopped or canned tomatoes, chopped apples, kimchi, etc. Add enough stock or water to submerge everything by ½ inch. If you forgo kraut or tomatoes or another acidic addition, you'll want to introduce a little acid in the mix. Use cider, beer, or wine for half of the stock, or a little splash of vinegar. This will help tenderize the sausage and balance the fat in the resulting dish. Cover and braise in a 300°F oven for 2 to 3 hours, until the sausages are very tender. (Or set-it-and-forget-it in a slow cooker!)

- Taste and see the goodness of the braise before serving: It probably wants a little bit of salt and maybe a fresh dose of acid—lemon juice or cider vinegar or the like—before it goes to the table. A shower of appropriate fresh herbs (your soft-leaf family, like tarragon, parsley, or cilantro) will also do what our moms would probably refer to as "jazzing up" the finished dish, adding freshness to the molten meaty truth of your triumphant braise. Serve with the stewed vegetation and maybe some additional greens and beans.

SMOKING SAUSAGES

For this, we turn to Jonathan Hooper, a friend and sausage-smoking savant:

I'm always looking to smoke some meat, but the usual suspects—pork butt, ribs, and beef brisket—take a while to prepare and cook. When dinner is in a few hours and I haven't done any prep, I'll buy a few packages of fresh Italian links—hot for adults and sweet for the kids—and throw them on the smoker. There's nothing fancy about these sausages, but when they're done right, they're transformed into something great: You get the essence of smoke, the sizzle of fat, and the snap of the skin.

I use a Weber Smokey Mountain Boy (a gift from my wife and probably the best birthday present I've ever received), which gets to temperature fast, holds strong for the first 3 to 4 hours, and controls the intensity and flavor of the smoke really well. Here's how I do it:

- Place a chimney directly in the smoker, fill with charcoal briquettes, and light it up, then take a couple of chunks of cherrywood and place them on top of the chimney so they get a head start. Surround the chimney with a few unlit coals and a few more chunks of wood.

- When the charcoal in the chimney is white, dump it into the base of the smoker.

- Fill the basin with hot water and wait 10 to 15 minutes for the smoker to stabilize at 250°F.

- The smoke should be a bit translucent (never white and billowy) and have the faint smell of fruitwood. (I like to start off pretty strong, and then let it fall back naturally as the sausages cook.)

- Put the sausages in the smoker, ideally all on the top rack, because it's hotter and smokier up there.

- At this point you can walk away, but keep an eye out for consistent smoke. If there isn't enough smoke after about 20 minutes, give the charcoals and wood a stir.

- After 35 to 40 minutes, turn the sausages so they're uniformly colored.

- After another 15 minutes, feel the sausages to see if there is some action going on under the skin. If the fat is bubbling, they're done. If not, give them some more time, but not so much that they start to shrivel.

- Once the sausages are done, remove them from the smoker and serve. These are best dipped in mustard while they are still piping hot. You can also put them on a hot dog bun and add a bunch of greens and pickles to make a super sausage, which is all any-one really needs for a complete meal. And if you have any leftovers, they're as good refried the next day as they are eaten cold, summer-sausage-style.

STUFFING EQUIPMENT

For those of you in the market for a DIY sausage setup, here are some tips from our in-house sausage expert, Mary-Frances Heck.

The two main types of mechanical sausage stuffers are (1) dedicated piston stuffers and (2) attachments that can be added to a meat grinder (or electric mixer). We prefer the piston stuffer.

Grinder attachments are great for pushing chunks of meat through a blade and dye, but because they use a rotating screw mechanism to push the meat into the casing, they generate more friction and heat that can wind up breaking the sausage farce. Piston stuffers use vertical pressure, which creates less friction. By design, they also eliminate air pockets that can cause the casings to burst. For serious sausage stuffing, a piston stuffer is easiest and best.

For the recipes in this book, we employed an LEM Products 5 Pound Stainless Steel stuffer (available online). It's large enough to handle a full recipe in one go, but small enough to store in a kitchen cabinet. It's also a snap to clean.

As far as stuffing procedure goes, here are the basics:

- Run water through the casings then soak in cool water for an hour or overnight. Some people soak the cas-ings in pineapple juice to tenderize them. This is nice for fine-textured sausages, but does make the casings more inclined to burst.

- Assemble your stuffer with the appro-priate nozzle for the casing you're using. Slide/bunch the casing onto the nozzle, leaving an inch or two hang-ing off the end. Have a bowl of water handy to keep things lubricated.

- Push the farce through the nozzle, guiding the sausage away from the stuffer and into a coil as you go.

- Find a rhythm where you're stuffing and coiling without falling behind. Use a toothpick to prick any stray air pockets that may have made it into the sausage.

Acknowledgments

I acknowledge that this book is a real pot of stone soup. A great multitude of people brought a little fat, a little salt, a little sugar, and a lot of sausage to our communal broth. I can't possibly list every writer and chef who received an email from me with the subject line URGENT SAUSAGE QUESTION—NOT A JOKE and took the time to reply, but your deep familiarity with the making and consuming of tube meat made this book possible. Thank you.

I acknowledge that getting the quality and breadth of contributors we managed to wrangle for this book is downright crazy. I'm constantly baffled and proud that serious, honest-to-god writers and artists consider *Lucky Peach* to be a legitimate place to publish.

I acknowledge that this book is not comprehensive and that inevitably there will be disgruntled readers who are upset about the particulars of their local sausage being omitted or misrepresented. But through the tireless efforts of our squadron of research soldiers—Ashley Goldsmith, Taylor Lee, Anna Lipin, and especially CB Owens and Michael Light—and their commanding officer, Aralyn Beaumont, I feel confident about the authenticity and accuracy of what we've put out there.

I acknowledge the limitless talent and creativity of Gabriele Stabile, Hannah Clark, and Mark Ibold, who generated most of the photography in this book and did so with unflinching patience and great humor. I acknowledge that I can be a pain to work with.

I acknowledge Rica Allannic, Marysarah Quinn, Christine Tanigawa, Derek Gullino, Doris Cooper, and Aaron Wehner—our team at Clarkson Potter—who also have intimate awareness of what a pain I can be. Kim Witherspoon knows, too. Thanks, guys, for your understanding and support.

I acknowledge that I'll never be as good a cook as any of the recipe authors in this book, especially Mary-Frances Heck, who always seems game to hang guts in her garage.

I acknowledge the delight I feel every time I see Tim Lahan's art, and that it was a real coup to get him to dedicate so much time to drawing wieners for us.

I acknowledge some degree of jealousy of Walter Green's inimitable style and ability as a designer. Honestly, it's unfair how good he is.

I acknowledge that this book, like everything we make at *Lucky Peach,* is a child reared in a *Full House* household, with multiple father and mother figures and siblings and cousins. Peter Meehan and Joanna Sciarrino were especially nurturing. Rachel Khong, Brette Warshaw, Ryan Healey, Devin Washburn, and Priya Krishna all changed diapers and did feedings, too. And let's not forget our group's legal guardian, Dave Chang.

And I acknowledge that I would be nowhere at all without Jami, my family, and my dog, Huck.

Contributors

Lisa Abend is a journalist based in Copenhagen, where she covers the Nordic region, writing about Swedish gender neutrality and Danish giraffes.

Rick Bayless is the chef of Chicago's Frontera Grill, Topolobampbo, and Xoco, writer of eight cookbooks, and star of Emmy-nominated *Mexico: One Plate at a Time.*

Marco Canora is the chef and owner of New York's Hearth restaurant and Terroir wine bars, creator of Brodo Broth Company, and author of *Salt to Taste* and *A Good Food Day.*

Joe Cummings has authored more than forty books, has twice been honored with the Lowell Thomas Travel Journalism Gold Award, and is a recipient of Mexico's Pluma de Plata (Silver Quill) for outstanding foreign journalism on Mexico.

Serena Maria Daniels is the dining editor of Detroit's *Metro Times.* She has a particular passion for politics, social justice, and urban renewal.

Fuchsia Dunlop is a cook and writer based in London. She is the author of four books about Chinese food and has won four James Beard Awards.

Jamie Feldmar is a New York–based writer, editor, and strategist, and a cofounder and partner at Mona Creative, a boutique creative agency that works with food and lifestyle brands.

Jonathan Gold is the restaurant critic for the *Los Angeles Times.*

Adam Leith Gollner is the author of *The Fruit Hunters* and *The Book of Immortality.*

Amelia Gray is the author of four books: *AM/PM, Museum of the Weird, THREATS,* and *Gutshot.* Her fiction and essays have appeared in *The New Yorker,* the *New York Times, Wall Street Journal, Tin House,* and *VICE.*

Jonathan Hooper was raised in eastern North Carolina where he learned to love chopped barbecue and fresh-picked seafood. On weekends, he is honorary pit master at Spring Lake Cabins, where he loves to barbecue with friends.

Todd Kliman is *Washingtonian*'s food and wine editor and restaurant critic. He was previously the food columnist for *Washington City Paper,* where he won a James Beard Award in 2005 for the country's best newspaper column.

Tim Lahan is an artist and illustrator living and working in New York. He is the author of *The Nosyhood* and *Whatever Man.*

Harry Leeds lives in Tatarstan and talks about America for a Russian audience in a fiction book, and about Russia for an American audience at New York University's Jordan Center.

Gideon Lewis-Kraus is the author of the digressive travel memoir *A Sense of Direction* as well as the Kindle Single *No Exit.* He is a contributing writer at the *New York Times Magazine,* a contributing editor at *Harper's* magazine, and a contributing writer at *WIRED.*

Scarlett Lindeman is a New York City–based food writer, perpetual line cook, and sociology PhD candidate.

Tris Marlis is a freelance writer based in Singapore.

Swedish-born **Magnus Nilsson** is head chef at the restaurant Fäviken in Sweden.

Pat Nourse is a Sydney-based writer. He is the deputy editor and chief restaurant critic for *Gourmet Traveller.*

Ivan Orkin is a native New Yorker. He spent a total of thirteen years in Japan but now calls Dobbs Ferry, New York, home.

Kevin Pang has spent the last decade writing about food for the *Chicago Tribune.*

Lucas Peterson lives in Los Angeles but is from the great state of Illinois. He hosts *Dining on a Dime* on Eater and is a two-time *Jeopardy!* champion.

David Prior is a contributing editor at *Vogue Living* and contributes to *T: The New York Times Style Magazine, NOWNESS,* and *Monocle.*

René Redzepi is the chef and co-owner of Noma in Copenhagen, Denmark, which opened in 2003. He is the author of *Noma* and *A Work in Progress.*

Myffy Rigby is the Fairfax *Good Food Guides* editor and creative director of Food and Drink events.

Robert Sietsema is a food journalist based in New York City. He is currently a featured writer for Eater New York.

Gabriele Stabile is an Italian photographer based in New York and Rome. His photographs have been shown in solo and collective exhibitions and have appeared in many fine publications.

Vincent Vichit Vadakan worked for twenty years as a literary agent in Paris and London. He now spends his time traveling and cooking for friends.

Index

Page numbers in **boldface** refer to recipes.